The
Vanishing
Land

ROBERT WEST HOWARD

The Vanishing Land

VILLARD BOOKS   NEW YORK   1985

LIBRARY OF CONGRESS CATALOGING IN PUBLICATION DATA
Howard, Robert West, 1908–
  The vanishing land.
  Bibliography: p.
  Includes index.
  1. Agriculture—United States—History. 2. Farms, Small—United States—History. 3. Food industry and trade—United States—History. I. Title.
S441.H725 1985   630'.973   84-40171
ISBN 0-394-53948-6

Manufactured in the United States of America
9 8 7 6 5 4 3 2
First Edition
Grateful acknowledgment is made to the following for permission to reprint previously unpublished material: Christopher Hall; Dr. Paul C. Manglesdorf; Paul Bailey; Delores Langren Neill; Dr. Paula Diane Relf; John H. Davis.

Grateful acknowledgment is made for permission to reprint excerpts from previously published material:

The Antioch Review: Excerpt from "World Food Resources for a Hungry Planet" by Marv Lamborg. Copyright © 1980 by *The Antioch Review,* Inc. First appeared in *The Antioch Review,* Fall 1980. Reprinted by permission of the Editors.

Dr. Nicholas Georgescu-Roegen: Excerpt from a lecture delivered to the University of Alabama on December 3, 1970. Copyright © 1970 by Dr. Nicholas Georgescu-Roegen. Published by Pergamon Press, Inc., in 1976 as *Energy and Economic Myths.*

For Herself

Instead of looking only to someone else to solve society's problems;
instead of clamoring only for corporate social responsibility, or for
government action on every crisis, we should ask ourselves:
What have I done to help, even a little bit,
on any of the problems I am fussing about?
How much have I put back into the soil of America
that has yielded so much to me?
How good has my stewardship been?
When I am through, will I leave my part of this
world in as good condition as when I entered it?

—Louis B. Lundborg,
former board chairman,
Bank of America,
in *Future Without Shock*

CONTENTS

The Earth Song

The illusion of huddling in a cellar during a tornado dominated the 747's takeoff. The engines, each spewing a whirlwind of vapor, thundered gravity into submission. The tiled walls and pink church towers of Lisbon dropped away. The Tagus River shrank to a turquoise thread curling across the squares and crescents of a green and tan quilt. We snarled into the gloom of a cloud. The land and its scarabs of civilization vanished. Symbolism during a 747 takeoff? Fears about vanishing land had been the decisive factor of our decision to return home for the final decades of our earthspan.

My wife and I were happy during our years in Europe and Africa. We thrilled at the Greeks' devotion to the tawny cliffs, flowered plains, terraced vineyards, and purple seascapes of their *patria mou*, the Bavarians' *Freude* in hiking litter-free trails through prim forests and farmlands, Sudanese graciousness to travelers who dared the desert trek from Khartoum to ancient Meroë, the Iberians' delight in garlanding railroad stations, airports, and tiled balconies with gardens. All of these had strengthened our belief that the homeland instills an earth song in every human being, just as it inseminates it into salmon, eel, bird, and most species of wild animal. The need to go back home and hear bobwhite whistling from a raspberry patch and to smell a batch of apple butter gurgling in a backyard kettle was as important to us as the urge to spawn in the ancestral creek is to a salmon.

But reports from back home had become more and more ominous. What was happening to America the Beautiful? Were technology and indifference transforming our swath of North America into a wasteland? Were machines, junk foods, chain stores, bureaucracy and dollar-madness destroying our most essential resource: the land?

The interdependence between man and the land was, is, and must always be the foundation of civilization. The land provides breathable air, palatable water, and the joys of earth song, as well as our all-essential foods and fibers.

No cities were possible until the rudiments of diversified agriculture were invented about fifteen thousand years ago. Only then was there assurance of a constancy of food and fiber for families huddled behind a city's dirt and stone ramparts. Roads and overland trade routes could not develop until agriculturists learned how to domesticate the ox, the donkey, the camel, and—only fifty centuries ago—the horse.

Logically, these inventors of civilization worshiped the sun and the land and its botanic and zoologic wealth. They peopled their worldview with gods, gnomes, leprechauns, and sprites. Zeus, Poseidon, Athena, Demeter were all agricultural deities with specific botanic and zoologic chores. Ancient festivals were fashioned around the spring and fall equinox and the midwinter solstice. Santa Claus is an adaptation of the ritual fire dance performed by dwarfs in scarlet cloaks during the Scandinavians' pre-Christmas festival of the winter solstice; *klaas* then meant "fire." The name Saint Nicholas was an early Christian interpretation. Holly, mistletoe, and pine trees attest to the rich agricultural heritage of Christmas, just as floral bouquets, lamb and ham roasts, and the prolific rabbit come from earth song associations of Easter.

The 747 began to detour around thunderheads piled in dioramas of pearl gray and black. One mass had eddied into a profile of a horseman. Another resembled a covered wagon. A third, gushing golden stabs of lightning, was certainly a tractor.

More symbolism! In America's art, as well as in our folklore and poetry, the horseman, the wagonman, the pioneer woman assumed the same stature the ancients accorded to their earth gods. From James Fenimore Cooper to John Steinbeck, our native literature depicts phases of four centuries of land conquest, flagrant waste, and stoic persistence. The spirituals, the blues, jazz, cowboy songs, square dance tunes, symphonies, and drama—all gloried from the tragedies, triumphs, and hope of the American earth song. Dvořák, Gershwin and Copland used the themes in the *New World Symphony, Rhapsody in Blue,* and *Appalachian Spring.*

Most important of all, our concepts of democracy and individual freedom were inspired by agricultural crops. The right to "life, liberty and the pursuit of happiness" grew from our daring practice of ownership of land "in fee simple."

The wealth wrested from our topsoil, coupled with the freedom of initiative that the rural economy stressed, enabled awesome developments in science and technology after 1810. Then cities grew with mushroom speed. Concrete and macadam ribbons of highways and runways crisscrossed our three thousand counties. The self-sufficient regime of horse power and ox power was obliterated by speedier, but far costlier, machine power.

As the wild west vanished, the young focused their dreams of adventure and independence on the stars. The star war movies, the space programs, the moon walks are a reversion to the sky worship of the ancient Babylonians, Greeks, and Egyptians. But spaceship explorations testified that no other known planet has the soil, water, gravity, atmosphere, and sun power that makes the Earth habitable by humans and by the familiar life forms of botany and zoology.

Obviously, then, although we dream of a new civilization "up there somewhere," our future depends—as it always has—on "down" under our feet. Earth is a whirling sphere with a molten core. We live on the rind of this sphere and derive food, fiber, and breathable air from plants and animals nourished by topsoil that is rarely more than two feet thick.

Faith in technology has blinded governments, industries, educators, and workers to the catastrophes that can explode from neglect of the land. During our years in Greece we watched the rapid deterioration of Athena's superb temple, the Parthenon, atop Athens' massive rock Acropolis. Between the end of World War II and 1982, archaeologists told us, automobile fumes and acrid smoke from mills and refineries did more damage to the Parthenon than the previous two thousand years of earthquakes, bombardments, winds, and rain had caused.

During the same third of a century, American technology took more than sixty-five million acres of cropland out of production, reduced the number of farms by 500,000, allowed hundreds of billions of tons of topsoil to erode into the oceans, lowered our national water reserves to near-drought level, poisoned our waterways and atmosphere, and quadrupled the retail price of food.

The letters, magazines, and technical reports we read and studied during our years abroad indicated that, by 1982, the machinery, fuel, and maintenance costs of our 2.4 million farms and ranches had risen so frighteningly that they totaled $10 billion more a year than the income earned from crop and livestock sales. But profits of the food processing industries rose steadily and so did retail prices. Blind dependence on technology was bringing the American land to the brink of disaster!

In medieval banquet halls, a flourish of drums announced the youths carrying the meal's entree—a garlanded boar's head, Sir Loin, or roast mutton. On American-operated 747s, luncheon is heralded by a chrome booze-cart. The trays that finally reached us contained a mixture of processed wheat, steer flesh, carrots, spinach, dried leaves from a tea plantation, roasted beans from a coffee ranch, pasteurized milk, cellophane sacks of sugar, cardboard tubes of iodized salt, a slice of defrosted cake topped with imitation whipped cream—plus the ten to twenty chemical additives deemed essential for shelf storage.

The vegetables probably came from the Pacific coast; more than 50 percent of all our fruits and vegetables are now grown there. The steer came from a trans-Mississippi feedlot where it had been crammed with the surplus corn and wheat that cause excessive fat. The milk originated on a dairy farm threatened by bankruptcy because of high operating costs and government quibbling. The processing of the food took place in two or three of the twenty-two thousand factories that now cook, grind, freeze, and can more than 55 percent of all the foods Americans eat. The 8,267 additives mixed in had names like thiamine mononitrate, sodium erythorbate, dextrose, and diglycerides.

A fast-food restaurant would charge three dollars for the contents of the tray. A restaurant with linen tablecloths and haughty waiters would present a bill, face down, for $9.82, plus a minimum 15 percent tip. The farmers and ranchers who produced the tray's ingredients received no more than fifty cents for their share in the repast.

Meanwhile, our jet engines contributed to the techno-perils of our land's future. The carbon monoxide and sulphur the 747 was vomiting into the sub-stratosphere added to those technologic fumes threatening Earth's protective envelope of ozone, the most chemically active form of oxygen. The ozone layer— i.e., ozonosphere—floats approximately thirty miles above the Earth and prevents excessive ultraviolet and other high-energy radiation produced by the sun from reaching the earth's surface. Without ozone's protection, life as we know it could exist only in ocean depths.

The nitric acids, sulphuric acids, lead, and other technology wastes spewed into our atmosphere since 1958 have caused an 8 percent increase in atmospheric carbon dioxide. The increase has triggered chemical reactions that produce rainstorms with a high acid content. Soils are being poisoned. Trees are dying. Fish and aquatic organisms choke to death. Iron and toxic aluminum in drinking water have increased. Biochemists contend that acid rains cause far-reaching, probably irreversible, changes in soils from Canada's Hudson Bay to Florida's west coast and are intensifying on our Pacific coast. But Washington politicians remain blandly indifferent and claim that there isn't enough evidence to take action.

Nevertheless, the existence of acid rain, coupled with the known ability of scientists to cause rainstorms by "seeding" clouds with chemicals, raises the prospect that international warfare could one day achieve technologic control over the weather. Satellites and low-frequency power transmitters could penetrate the ozonosphere to alter weather in any pre-selected area on earth or could change weather patterns in such a way as to abort crop production by diverting the swift air currents (called "jet streams") that continually swirl seven to eight miles above the earth and activate our weather conditions. Weather control would be cheaper than atomic warfare and, unlike mushroom-cloud devastation, could be turned off.

Pollution from below. Devastation from above. Was this the American earth song after only four centuries?

Those gray specks down there on the blue and white swirl of mid-Atlantic were tramp steamers or container ships. Most of them were filled with wheat, corn, soybeans for the USSR and the nations of the Near East and Third World. They travel eastward because of the skill, dedication, and courage of our agriculturists who annually produce the earth's most lavish cuisine for 220 million of their urbanized neighbors, plus $40 billion worth of crops for export, yet earn incomes that average only 66 percent of the wages earned by a worker in a manufacturing industry.

Washington's decision to use grains and legumes to offset our deficits in overseas trade did not solve crop surplus and low income problems even when exports exceeded $40 billion a year. But it did, unfortunately, convert millions of Africans and Asians from dependence on native grains and legumes to a craving for white bread and white man's food. According to the Food and Agriculture Organization (FAO) of the United Nations, only 10 percent of our overseas grain and legume shipments go to drought-stricken regions and to the truly needy of the Third World. The rest go into livestock pens and to white-bread converts at dictatorship prices.

The Atlantic was not iridescent with oil slicks, or noxious with garbage, atomic wastes, and acid rain, during the first decades of the seventeenth century when ships no larger than fishing schooners—and not nearly as seaworthy—sailed westward toward the New World. Dutch, Swedish, French, English, Iberian—their passengers had a common goal. They all sought freedom of land. "The people who first farmed American land," Christopher Hall, editor of the British periodical, *The Countryman*, told me, "had escaped in some sense or another from oppression—political, religious, or economic. The holding of land was a symbol of freedom. The land holder could do as he wished with his land, in contrast to the situation in which he and his ancestors had lived in Europe."

Aboard the first ships to cross the ocean to the New World, the women's petticoat hems and apron pockets sagged with pouches made of dried pig bladders, sheep intestines and snips of parchment—all filled with vegetable and fruit and grain seeds. Below decks cows, sheep, pigs, chickens, a few horses, and bundles of tools rocked and bumped. The motivating force? Ownership of land and individual initiative, the most awesome promise of liberty offered to mankind in 4,500 years of peasantry, serfdom, and subservience. No more bootlicking to dukes, counts, or knights. The vision of life, liberty, and the pursuit of happiness rose like a midsummer sunrise a century and a half before the Declaration of Independence.

A 747 doesn't clatter into a station like a train. It seems to stand still for a quarter of an hour while the clouds grow larger and the white lace on the ocean becomes waves cresting against the continental shelf. A white and green blob, shaped like a fishhook, rode over the horizon, then slowly grew to the beaches, moors, Hidden Forest, and church steeples of Nantucket. The blink-on of the "Fasten Seat Belts—No Smoking" signs synchronized with the materialization of Cape Cod and the rooftops of Plymouth. We roared down through another cloud layer toward factories spewing gray and yellow smoke and over the dress-parade precision of identical houses on identical lawns facing identical streets.

The Puritans founded Boston as a seashore farming and fishing community. The famed Common began as pastureland for their livestock. Bunker Hill was summertime grazing land, too steep for iron-tipped plows and ox teams to furrow into cropland. Concord and Lexington became farm villages along the pack-pony trails to the White Mountains and the Connecticut valley's wheatlands. Yankee harangues against taxation without representation sparked the American Revolution and made Boston famous as the "Cradle of Liberty."

Boston's brick walls, black streets, tarpaper roofs, and tan skyscrapers emerged beyond the smog pall. A maze of 637,000 people dominates the metropolitan area of 92 cities and towns with a total population of 2.9 million. Back Bay, Beacon Hill, and Louisburg Square are still national symbols of conservative elitism. The codfish weathervane still shimmers above the State House. But a report published by the Brookings Institution in August, 1982, found that high unemployment, pervasive crime, poverty, deteriorating housing, and racial hatred have turned Boston into "one of the nine most seriously declining American cities."

Is this what the farmer Minute Men fought for at Concord, Lexington, and Bunker Hill? How did the 1621 Thanksgiving become the 1982 techno-jungle? What happened to America's earth song?

Boston is not unique. The United States has spawned 170 cities with populations of more than 100,000; *city* and *sophistication* are American synonyms. All our cities grew at some form of crossroads. The contours of the land determined their location. Because of the crossroads' bustle, they attracted universities, museums, zoos, theaters, symphony orchestras, sports arenas, and stores as big as a king's palace. Initially, each city lured in the best "vittles" of its regional cuisine and served them up with a dazzle of silver, bone china, potted palms and waiters who spoke textbook French. Cities were marvelous! and each one had its own uniqueness.

Then technology muscled in. Each city had to have skyscrapers, shopping centers, fast-food drive-ins, and prefab houses built

on lots forty feet wide. Cloverleaf bedlams, pot-holed macadam, a festering encirclement of tenements around midtown,
muggers, dope peddlers, and shrouds of poisonous smog inevitably followed. Cities lost their distinction: Chicago looked like
Cleveland and Cleveland looked like Columbus—or Syracuse or
Minneapolis or Oklahoma City or Houston. Despite their dependence on topsoil and clean air and adequate water and sunlight for supplies of food and fiber, most city dwellers developed
a smug indifference toward the health of the land.

Our urbanites speak one language; our agriculturists speak
another. The sixteen million employees of federal, state, and
local governments use their own jargon. The scientist holds to
Latinized cadence; the educator chants in polysyllabic abstrusity.
We live in a Tower of Babel. No group listens or understands
or really gives-a-damn about the needs of the other groups. But
all are as dependent on the land and its bounties as Thebes and
Athens and Tyre and Babylon were in 2000 B.C.

The 747's wheels clanked out of their cocoon. Pigeons and
sparrows fluttered in for sacrifice as the slime of bayshore lifted
toward us. Logan Airport, too, was now a maze of concrete and
glass shoeboxes; there wasn't a flowerbed in sight. A boarding
ramp, shaped like a gargantuan plastic phallus, was thrust against
the plane.

The quarter mile of tunnels leading to Customs was plastered
with posters of bikinied blondes proffering granola bars, presidential jellybeans, salted peanuts, or mammoth burgers. The
message seemed to be that the blondes created all the delights
advertised. No agriculturists. No land. No topsoil erosion or
pesticides or acid rain or drought or mortgages or tornadoes. No
nature. No earth song. Just a wallow of junk food miraculously
appearing in the hands of half-naked blondes.

The wheels of our luggage cart squealed. I growled back at
them.

"What are you muttering about?" Herself asked.

"Isn't the Customs inspector going to ask us, 'What do you
have to declare?' "

"He always has."

"This time I'm going to tell him. I'll declare my love for the American land. You and I will wander back roads and front roads and libraries and laboratories and stores and offices. I can't believe that Reagan or Nixon or Ike or Roosevelt was responsible for this mess."

Herself nodded, then smiled. "We'd better start in a supermarket. That's where too many people think it all comes from."

The
Vanishing
Land

CHAPTER ONE

The Plastic Curtain

In a way, this book is yet another diet book. The root of the word *diet* comes from a Greek phrase meaning "a way of living." Thus our daily diet includes the air we breathe and the water we drink as well as the food we eat. Air and food are themselves products of various types of dirt that have been influenced by sunlight, water, and microorganisms. By 1983, America's dirt was rapidly vanishing, the water that had not vanished was being poisoned by toxic wastes, the air was polluted, thousands of chemicals were being mixed into processed foods, and 72 percent of the cost of food went to processors and storekeepers. This book is about how the American diet has bumbled toward catastrophe since 1600 A.D. and explains what we can do to ensure ample food supplies, palatable water, healthful air, and a modicum of bucolic escape for our tomorrows.

The stockade gate, the Common, Courthouse Square, the shopping center—each has been vitally important in the evolution of the American diet. Each in turn has served as the marketplace where the harvest became the groceries and the agriculturist adapted to the whims of the cook.

Through three of these centuries—the seventeenth with its stockade gate, the eighteenth with the Common, and the nineteenth with Courthouse Square—producer and consumer were in direct, often shrill, communication. But after the shopping center materialized in the 1930s, a plastic curtain emblazoned with trade names and machine symbols segregated producer from consumer.

Subsequently, the retail prices of foods rose 300, 500, and then 1,000 percent; groceries that cost $29 in 1930 cost $290 in 1982. Both the quality and the variety of fresh fruits and vegetables deteriorated. Aggressive advertising campaigns lured a majority of homemakers from traditional regional cuisines to factory-processed fast foods. The corporate profits of food processors and chain stores tripled; the producers' incomes dropped to 28 percent of the retail dollar. Paunchiness, high blood pressure, and nervous tension became national maladies. Frequent snacking was everybody's bad habit.

The modern American shopping center is a slab of concrete and tar built on appropriated farmland on the outskirts of a residential area. The one- and two-story shops surrounding this bleak parking lot usually include a pizza parlor, an instant-hamburger chalet, a chain drugstore, a photo shop, a Mexican taco factory, a dry cleaning establishment, a row of video game machines, a branch bank offering a free set of ovenware for a $1,000 deposit, a gas station, and a supermarket as long as a football field.

More than 100,000 supermarkets now retail more than two-thirds of our groceries. A space-age imitation of the department store idea that New York and Chicago merchants copied from the French during the 1860s, the supermarket is a conglomerate of grocery store, butcher shop, delicatessen, bakery, fruit and vegetable stand, fish market, ice cream parlor, hardware store, stationery and bookstore, boutique, and, in most states, wine cellar. All of its twelve thousand products are displayed on enameled shelves or in refrigerated bins along wide aisles spotlit by fluorescent light. Each product—including the 50-foot vista of dog, cat, and bird feed, the 123 brands of cigarettes, the 50 to

100 varieties of cheese, the 200 feet of "meats"—is machine-sealed in plastic.

A strong metal fence, hip-high, encloses the entrance platform of most supermarkets. Its dozen or so openings are barely wide enough for a plump shopper to squeeze through. The fence imprisons the store's most important psychological sales weapon: the shopping cart.

Surveys show that three out of every four shoppers make at least one impulse purchase during a supermarket visit. The size and convenience of the shopping cart encourages this sort of buying. A shopping cart is a yard-long basket of heavy chromed wire mounted on four small wheels and guided by a waist-high pushbar. The basket tilts up for storage near the store entrance. A second basket, comfortably large enough for a baby or even a smallish three-year-old, unfolds inside the cart's top. A wedge of foil-wrapped cheese, a bagged cauliflower, a plastic-sealed mound of hamburger, a lone container of cottage cheese or a six-pack of granola bars looks forlorn in the cart's cavernous depths. Status anxiety plus the lures of the twelve thousand multicolored displays continuously nag the shopper into impulse purchases.

The shopping cart was invented in Oklahoma by Sylvan N. Goldman, who was born in Ardmore, Indian Territory, on November 15, 1898. His father owned a one-room general store, and Sylvan was weaned to the rigors of placating waspy customers, inspecting the flour bin for weevils, and passing out chunks of bologna and lollipops when monthly bills were paid. He became a shipping clerk for a wholesale grocer when he was fifteen and by 1937 was president of the Standard–Humpty Dumpty chain of grocery stores in the Oklahoma City area.

The supermarket was still a novelty, and one of its peskier problems, Goldman realized, was lack of shopper mobility. Most shopping was done by housewives during school hours. Babies and pre-kindergartners had to be brought along. The only grocery carriers available were wire or wicker baskets that could be held in one hand while the other arm carried, or shepherded, little Melinda and Jimmy.

Brooding over this crippler of convenience (and sales) one

evening, Goldman found himself staring at a folding chair. If the folding chair principle could be used for a basket on wheels, he reasoned, greater shopping mobility should lead to more sales. Months of trial and error with a carpenter named Fred Young resulted in the first shopping carts. The vehicles were advertised in Oklahoma City newspapers during June, 1937, with circus poster headlines that proclamed, "Basket Juggling is a Lost Art at your Standard Food Stores!"

The vehicle worked the transformation Goldman had envisioned. He became a multimillionaire and received honorary degrees for his generous gifts to universities and museums. Today every supermarket maintains a fleet of one hundred to five hundred of his ingenious invention. In 1983, each cart cost $190—which explains the necessity for squeeze-through fences around the doorways and loading platforms of supermarkets.

Cart mobility encouraged supermart expansion to the present spectacle of some twelve thousand products in a block-long fluorescent maze. "Degrading exhibitionism," sociologists contend, "and a basic cause of waste." According to studies by the U.S. Department of Agriculture, "one third of the food hauled home is eventually thrown out" either as refrigerator spoilage or as leftovers from "heaping too much on plates" at mealtimes.

"Some of our units carry as many as 13,000 different items," Safeway Stores, Inc., claimed in a recent annual report. "These range from a full line of traditional grocery products to new or expanded categories such as automotive supplies, toys, greeting cards, nursery items and small appliances."

Incorporated in California in 1926, Safeway grew to 2,500 supermarkets in the United States, Canada, Europe, and Australia. It established produce prepacking plants, bakeries, ice cream plants, milk plants, egg-candling plants, coffee roasting plants, fruit and vegetable canneries, frozen food factories, jam and jelly and candy and shortening and cereal and soup, soap, gelatin, and soft drink factories, a score of central meat cutting and aging plants, cracker and cookie factories, plus scores of distribution warehouse centers.

Like other large supermart chains, Safeway contracts for crops from huge tracts of cropland and orchard. Most of the fruits and vegetables grown on contract for chain stores and processors come from seeds and grafts that have been hybridized by university and independent botanists to yield products that will have better "shipping qualities." Hence the juiceless pale-pink tomato; the massive, but insipid, strawberry; the blueberry as big as a marble but flavorless; cabbage-like lettuce; rock-hard nectarines and avocados; thick-skinned oranges; lemons that yield less than a tablespoonful of juice; mealy apples. This same obeisance to the perils of long truck rides and warehouse storage has caused the banishment from supermart counters of such American delights as russet, pound sweet and Northern Spy apples, garden-fresh strawberries and asparagus, aromatic peaches, snap beans that actually snap, tree-ripened citrus and beets with edible greens.

There are more than 135,000 Safeway employees. Its distribution fleet of trucks and trailers averages five thousand vehicles. Between 1967 and 1977, Safeway's gross profit almost tripled from $719,441,000 to $2,067,356,000.

The complex and costly system of operation for Safeway and its competitors in retailing the 1,043 pounds of meat, poultry, and fish; the 1,752 pounds of vegetables and fruit; the 1,136 pounds of diary products; the 550 pounds of flour and cereal products; the 320 pounds of sugar; and 60 pounds of salt annually consumed by the typical American family not only includes high rentals, high wages, and high taxes, but more than a billion dollars a year for advertising—plus contributions to professional lobbyists and legal consultants in Washington and in every state capital.

Between 1975 and 1979, chain store and processor expenditures for promotional advertising rose from $745 million to $1,090 million annually; more than half of this amount was spent on television commercials.

Most of the 1.3 million clerks, butchers, warehouse workers, truckers, chefs, analysts, and other workers employed by supermarkets are unionized. In 1983, base pay averaged $10 an hour for clerks and scaled to $25 an hour for "specialists." During the winter of 1981–82, basic pay for the 27,000 members of Local 400 of United Fruit and Vegetable Workers, AFL–CIO, in the Washington, D.C., area became $10.10 per hour, or $404 for a 40-hour week, plus $2–4 an hour for fringe benefits. The new contract terms also specified that working on a holiday boosted the base rate to $27.88 per hour, or $223.04 for an 8-hour day.

The national food bill in 1982 totaled $298 billion, and $214 billion of it went to the processors, distributors, and retailers. The growers received only twenty-eight cents of the consumer dollar. Producer-to-consumer labor costs totaled thirty-two cents of that consumer dollar. Packaging, advertising, and transportation took another forty cents.

The market journey of peanuts from Georgia to Virginia illustrates why most agricultural producers have remained impoverished while retail prices have been soaring.

Farms on the sandy plains of south Georgia produce an average of four to six thousand pounds of peanuts per acre each September—if bugs and weather have been moderately compassionate. During the fall of 1982, warehouses in that part of Georgia were paying growers thirty cents a pound for raw peanuts. (Any "goober" devotee who wanted a sackful could buy them washed and graded from the warehouse for forty-five cents a pound.)

Four hours up the throughway in Atlanta, raw peanuts retailed for sixty-five cents a pound at the Farmers' Market. North another hour or two, roadside stands charged $1.75 for one-pound plastic bags of roasted peanuts. In Washington, D.C., supermarkets charged $2.19 for a 12-ounce bag of roasted peanuts, $2.50 for a 12-ounce jar of shucked and salted peanuts, and $3.25 for a 12-ounce jar of peanut butter that contained between 3 and 4 ounces of sugar and had the vitamin-rich seed germs of the nuts removed. (That fall, the Christmas catalogue of Pepperidge Farm, a subsidiary of Campbell Soup Company, offered a 1½-pound tin of salted peanuts for $9.95, plus a $1.50 shipping charge.)

A forty-five-cent pound of south Georgia's raw peanuts roasts to succulent crunchiness when placed in a two-hundred-degree oven for five hours. If you have a garden you can share the fuel cost—not more than a quarter—by drying your pre-frost picking of thyme, basil, tarragon, parsley, and chives in the oven at the same time. Shucking and skinning the roasted nuts, while munching, takes a relaxing half hour. Dump the skinned kernels in a blender, add safflower or sunflower oil—they don't have any cholesterol—in a ratio of three tablespoons of oil to a cupful of peanuts; add a sprinkle of sodium-free salt substitute. Turn on the blender for two minutes. The result is a rich, nutritious peanut butter a cardiologist can approve of. The overall cost is seventy cents, plus a little finger exercise.

Much of the $2.55 difference between homemade peanut butter and the sugary, low-vitamin product available at groceries could be saved by community groups through the cooperative practice of group buying. Peanuts could be ordered in bulk from southern warehouses and delivered via truck, U.P.S. or parcel post.

But what the shopping cart, the assembly-line efficiencies, the massive production of house brands, the dazzle of twelve thousand products, and advertising budgets of more than a billion dollars a year have produced, the majority of shoppers will not put asunder.

Wander the labyrinth of a supermarket. Here are plastic-swathed mounds of bacon by Smithfield, cold cuts by Oscar Mayer, hams by Gwaltney, English muffins by Thomas, buttered peas by Green Giant, cheese by Kraft, corn chips by Frito-Lay, oleo by Promise, oats by Quaker, oranges by Sunkist, frosted shredded wheat by Nabisco, peanuts by Planters. The greatest food show on earth! Can anything be missing?

The land is missing! Agriculture is missing! Those few inches of all-important topsoil are missing! The sunlight, water, fertilizer, and the agriculturists who produced all this are missing!

Here and there a carton of eggs or milk contends, in small type, that it is "farm fresh." But at some time or other, most of the twelve thousand items in these aisles were farm fresh, including the cotton towels, the bags made from jackpine pulp, and the lanolin enriched beauty aids. (Lanolin is the chemist's term for sheep tallow.) Items on the health food aisles proclaim that they contain "natural" ingredients, yet many of them, like the popular granola bars, are 25 to 35 percent sugar and dangerously rich in fat. All-natural yogurt contains dried skim milk, sugar syrup, modified food starch, and annatto extract. Natural beer uses tannic acid as a preservative.

A few years ago, a Humane Association in Massachusetts established a model farm to demonstrate the most effective methods of humane treatment for livestock and household pets. But neither farm nor animals impressed many of the young visitors. "The most frequent comment we had from city youngsters gawking through the barns," an official reported, "was 'Whadda we need all this stuff for, anyway? You can get everything you need at the supermarket!' " Social studies in schools have also been antisocial in their failure to emphasize America's dependence on topsoil, water, compatible atmosphere, and photosynthesis. This insularity is the most effective, and potentially the most dangerous, form of segregation confronting the United States.

Some American consumers, fortunately, are viewing supermarkets with more thoughtful perspectives. The calculated efficiencies of the supermarts and processors, the razzle-dazzle monotony of their television commercials, the rivalry that causes retail prices to bounce up and down with trampoline abandon, the "circus bodoni" clutter of their huge ads in the newspaper have created a backlash that has contributed to the survival of thousands of convenience and mom-'n-pop independent stores, as well as to a burgeoning return of the farmers' market.

The average supermart is an assembly-line operation. Managers and assistants usually sit in elevated cages, transmit their orders via loudspeakers, and seem to feel obligated to be brusque with customers who dare stand on tiptoe to ask them questions. Check-out clerks, wearing the chain's uniform, are so involved with electronic gadgetry and stuffing purchases into moisture-prone paper sacks that they have little time for more than a farewell mutter of "haveagoodday." Butchers are sealed in glass cubicles—hence can be queried only by pushing a wall button that may, or may not, clang a gong. When asked about the disappearance of kidneys, sweetbreads, scrapple, tripe, hocks, Rocky Mountain oysters, Lebanon bologna, headcheese, and veal chops from the array of meats, the butcher can only shrug and say, "I dunno. Funny, huh?"

The bonhomie that endeared the butcher, baker, and green-grocer to customers a half century ago never made it to the supermarket, and most managements seem adamant against attempting a renewal. During 1981–82, Barbara Salsbury wrote a book on the subject of cutting your grocery bills in half, then began giving lecture seminars at Utah's Brigham Young University. "My intention," she explained, "is not and never has been to undermine supermarkets. I want to teach consumers to use these stores to their best advantage." But the Utah Retail Grocers Association promptly complained to university officials and offered to provide an industry-approved teacher to take Salsbury's place.

The owners of successful independent and convenience stores insist that openness about the flavor and quality of the produce, knowing the names and problems of customers, taking the time for casual pleasantries, and willingness to fulfill special requests are their lifeline to profit. The independent owner, however, cannot place the massive orders that supermarts can, and for this reason some wholesalers will refuse to service the independent's shop. Supermarket chains own processing plants, egg and broiler factories, canneries, livestock feedyards, or laboratories. Consequently, an independent food store must pay higher prices for products. But the smaller operation can stress quality, maximum value for the dollar, and a willingness to fulfill special orders. The independent owner can treat customers as human beings rather than as computer digits, and he or she can make a comfortable living doing it.

Another road to success for the independent grocer is via astute purchasing of fruits and vegetables through contracts with local growers. The four stores operated by Magruder's in the Washington, D.C., area are excellent examples of this technique. During the first week of October, 1982, chain stores in the Washington area sold eggplant for 59 cents a pound, mushrooms for $1.37 a pound, cauliflower for $1.10 a head. In the same week, Magruder's sold local eggplant at 19 cents a pound, local mushrooms at 70 cents a pound, and local cauliflower at 59 cents a jumbo head. Astute purchasing of fruits and vegetables grown in Virginia, Maryland, and Pennsylvania enabled this underpricing of competitors who bulk-order "fresh" produce from California, Idaho, Florida, or Texas, and are burdened by transportation, wholesaler, and warehouse costs.

Over on the processed and canned food aisles, however, Magruder's, the chain stores, health stores, convenience and corner groceries must all bitterly compete for small profits from the cornucopia of easy-to-fix foods trucked in from processors. More than 55 percent of all the food Americans eat comes from 22,000 food processing establishments. They are the creators of frozen dinners, frozen pastries, vegetable mixes, canned soups, potato and corn chips, breakfast cereals, pizzas, tacos, and thousands of other edibles that lure buyers by means of blatant packaging. Often, the package costs two and three times as much as the contents. Potato chip packages, for instance, cost 214 percent more than the chips. Breakfast cereal packages cost an average of 164 percent more than the ingredients. Containers of frozen dinners and ready-for-the-oven side dishes and desserts cost 141 percent more than the edibles inside. The average can of fruit or vegetables costs 101 percent more than its contents.

Processor packaging now uses 50 percent of our annual production of paper, 40 percent of all the aluminum we smelt, 75 percent of all the glass we make, and 33 percent of all our plastic bottles, tubs, bags, and wrappings. Consequently, every American must somehow dispose of four hundred pounds of glass, aluminum, tinned steel, foil, plastic, Styrofoam, and paper containers per year for edible products purchased. The annual cost of this convenience is estimated to be $34 billion, or $154 per person, plus billions more for garbage processing and disposal.

Corporate profits of the food manufacturing industry, before taxes, increased from $4.8 billion in 1970 to $13 billion in 1982. Economists fear that development of conglomerates in food processing will be so rapid that by 2000 A.D. all our food processing will be controlled by four or five giants. Campbell Soup Company, Ralston Purina, and General Mills currently control products that range from pet foods, cake mixes, coffees, and soups to chocolates that retail at $25 a pound. The annual sales of these three conglomerates for 1981, as reported to Dun & Bradstreet, totalled $13 billion, with net earnings of $400 million and "retained earnings" of $3 billion.

Polysyllabic explanations of the changes that occur in the processing journey from cropland to store shelf can be found in the "contents" label on processed foods. The list of ingredients on a box of corn meal—the most ancient all-American food—reports that it now contains traces of niacin, reduced iron, thiamine mononitrate, and riboflavin. The bouillon cube, according to the label on a plastic jarful, is currently composed of hydrolized vegetable protein, corn syrup solids, monosodium glutamate, disodium gaunylate, disodium-inosinate, a sprinkle of garlic powder, and some beef fat. Cottage cheese is now fortified with carrageenan and locust bean gum. The frankfurter label admits to dabs of sodium erythorbate, sodium nitrate and corn syrup. Consumer insistence on white flour enables millers to sell 65 percent of the wheat kernel back to livestock growers as feed, keep the vitamin-rich germ for separate retailing, and then "enrich" the bleached endosperm that remains with niacin, iron, thiamine mononitrate, riboflavin, and salt. The two-dollar coffee ring on the baked goods aisle contains thiamine mononitrate, riboflavin, mono- and di-glycerides, guar gum, sodium acid pyrophosphate, monocalcium phosphate, calcium sulfate, annatto extract, white flour, dried apples, and natural flavors.

Few of the chemical names mean anything to the consumer. And for good reason—little has been done to see if these chemicals are fit to be eaten. In fact, a survey released by the National Research Council of the National Academy of Sciences during February, 1984, indicated that sufficient information to determine the health hazards of the 8,267 additives to the U.S.A.'s processed foods had been obtained to date on only approximately 1,600 of them.

The Chemical Manufacturers Association and the Food and Drug Administration have cooperated in my preparation of "A Food Labels Dictionary" that provides definitions of the chemicals most commonly used to fortify, sweeten, color, or salt our processed foods. (The dictionary appears as an appendix to this book.)

Loopholes in our Pure Food and Drug laws enable processors to use a variety of terms in listing the increasing quantities of sugar and salt used in canned goods, bakery products, and fast foods. Sugar is listed on labels as corn syrup, corn sweetener, dextrose, fructose, invert sugar, glucose, maltose, cane syrup, maple syrup, molasses, honey, brown sugar, or turbinado. Salt is listed as sodium chloride, sodium nitrate, sodium phosphate, sodium ascorbate, sodium saccharin, or monosodium glutamate (MSG).

Labels cite the chemical contents of a product in descending order by dry weight. Efforts to pass legislation that would order processors to list the percentages of sugar, salt, and other questionable chemicals on package labels have been repeatedly thwarted by lobbyists. A flurry of publicity during the summer of 1982 about the health hazards of too much salt in the American diet circumvented legislative apathy by influencing some processors to offer salt-free products. In its fall, 1982, catalogue, California's House of Almonds featured pages of salt-free and sugar-free nuts and sweets. Chicken of the Sea soon launched a series of television commercials promoting its "water-pack tuna with half the salt removed." Stores began to feature salt-free potato chips and crackers. Campbell ballyhooed sodium-free soup. Fleischmann's introduced a low-fat, low-salt, low-sugar margarine. Morton and other processors launched advertising campaigns for a salt substitute having less than 10 mg. of sodium per 100 g.

Centralized production of processed foods has, of course, multiplied the transportation problems that beset the chain stores' dependence on not-so-fresh fruits and vegetables from Florida and the Pacific coast. Tandem trucks, piggyback trains, and air freight add $15 billion annually to the retail prices of fresh and fast foods. Many states have become as dependent as a drought-ridden African or Asian dictatorship on imports from the West and South. Without the daily bedlam of trucks, trailers, jets, trains, and delivery vans, they would be on rationing within four or five days.

A study conducted in 1981 by *Organic Gardening* indicated that Pennsylvania—the very birthplace of the family farm—imports 70 percent of its foods, thus necessitating 6,500 truckloads per week; transportation costs were adding $400 million a year to Pennsylvania's food bills. Subsequent surveys in Massachusetts, New York, and Illinois stressed similar dependency on the trucker, railroader, and pilot.

Fears of atomic war have traumatized Americans since 1945, but the comparable disasters that can develop because of our vanishing land have not been deemed worthy of editorials or political debates or even two-minute overviews by television commentators. Similarly, our dependence on chain stores, frozen dinners, junk-food chalets, TV chefs, repetitive food editors, discount coupons and lotteries, and restaurant cuisines that stuff us with calories from Oysters Rockefeller and Peking Duck to Cherries Jubilee and four-layer tortes has enabled the curtain of plastic wrap and conglomerate labels to conceal the precariousness of our current system of food supply.

During the winter and early spring of 1982–83, the jet stream of the upper atmosphere that literally steers our seasonal weather mysteriously changed course. Violent storms swept from west to east across the continent. Pacific coast crops drowned out. Fields could not be plowed or planted West and South. Because of dependence on California and Florida vegetable and fruit crops, supermarket prices promptly soared. Asparagus rose to $1.80 a pound and stayed there, even after it was being harvested in

Carolina, Virginia, and Maryland truck gardens. The price of leaf lettuce zoomed from 90 cents to $1.50 a pound. Citrus and strawberry prices also rocketed; the Chinese gooseberry—redubbed "kiwi fruit" by California wholesalers—retailed at fifty and sixty cents apiece.

The storms generated by the jet stream's change in course sounded a warning about our dependence for national provisioning on one or two small areas of production. But neither Washington nor the processors nor the wholesale distributors seemed to be listening. If the jet stream does not return to the pattern we have long considered normal, the result could be a drastic decrease in food production, sequeled by inflation, bread lines, and even slow starvation.

We are confronted by a vanishing food supply because of public neglect of the importance of our land to the life, liberty, and pursuit of happiness we brag about. The erosion of topsoil has become so excessive that our most productive agricultural states, including Iowa, have lost more than half of the thin rind of earth that produces their spectacular harvests. Our water reserves have been pumped so avidly that huge sections of the West may become semi-desert before 2025 A.D. Increased use of chemical fertilizers by producers struggling to break even adds to the release of nitrous oxide in the atmosphere, forming another threat to deterioration of the troposphere's vital ozone layer. Bugs have developed such strong immunities to chemical pesticides that, genetic engineers warn, new banks of botanic plasma must be established, intensive searches made for the still wild relatives of major crops, and methods devised for starting all over again with major grain and fiber crops.

Machinery and production costs so exceed crop prices paid to farmers and ranchers that multi-thousands of our most skilled producers of crops are being forced into bankruptcy each year. The sprawl of suburbias, factory sites, new airports, and highway extensions continues annually to remove 3 million acres of tillable land from potential productivity; to date, we have lost 50 million acres this way. Political appointees to important government positions demonstrate a determination to open our national parks and forests to technologic plunder. Lobbyists dissuade the federal government from researching marketing techniques for the vast sources of fuel and protein known to be available from tobacco, corn, and other major crops.

Today the "farm problem" is no longer a remote project for Congress to fuss with. The welfare of our land is as much of a live or perish obligation to residents of New York City and Los Angeles as it is to the owners of farms, ranches, orchards, dairies, vineyards, and poultry farms. Better communication and more cooperation between that 97.6 percent who are dependent consumers and the 2.4 percent who are producer-providers is the best hope for all of our tomorrows.

Land is our most precious heritage. It is vanishing. The American future is not up among the stars; it is down here with our topsoils, our waterways, our forests and nature trails, and those unprobed mysteries of potential energy, heat and moisture from the earth's depths.

Cooperative effort among farmers, ranchers, our 40 million dedicated gardeners, consumer groups, scientists, and the schoolteachers of our three thousand counties can assure perpetuation of our highest living standard on earth. But the task will be far more challenging than punching a few socio-economic holes in the plastic curtain, or piling new laws on top of the mountains of old ones. Radical changes must be made in government policy. The "old hick" image of the farmer must be modernized to the astute scientist he has become. Consumers must learn why "dirt" and "soil" are *not* merely synonyms for "filth."

But a mechanic does not attempt to repair an engine without knowing what he or she is looking at. The same rule applies to the task of repairing our agriculture, its domineering distribution system, and our vanishing land. All the perils of our food production and distribution systems are by-products of two facets of our history—the ruthless treatment of virgin land and forest by our early settlers, and the indifference toward land welfare by the urban majority of our population since 1865.

History is like the surveyor's benchmark. It tells where we

came from and how we got here. History enables us to realize what we are looking at and, by assessing the triumphs and errors of our forebears, can help guide us toward a future of life, liberty, and the pursuit of happiness. As we peer ahead into the twenty-first century, the prospects are grave. But they are not hopeless! And we'll be better prepared to meet those prospects if we can comprehend the good and evil of the American land's saga, the saga initiated between 1600 and 1620 when the first New Mexicans, the first Virginians, and the first Yankees encountered a vast array of new food crops that had been domesticated by benighted savages.

CHAPTER TWO

The Sharing of the Green

Ever since the techniques of agriculture were painstakingly developed millenniums ago, ownership of land has signified achievement of independence. Before agriculture, mankind did not enjoy individual freedom or democracy or assurance of a next meal. Nor were cities and highways possible until sources of power were discovered that could plow and harvest large fields and haul out the crops.

The donkey and camel were the first beasts of burden to be domesticated. Wild cattle were so nimble and belligerent that the bull became a symbol of supernatural power and was worshiped as a deity throughout the Mediterranean basin and Near East.

Then, about 3500 B.C., tribes living near the Caspian Sea began domesticating *Equus Caballus,* one of the families of horse that had evolved from a rabbit-sized browser American paleontologists call eohippus, but the British insist on calling *Hyracotherium.* These tribesmen eventually discovered that their speedy new power tool could be controlled—more or less—by a rawhide gadget that snugged two handstraps over the animal's nose and upper jaw, hence could be painfully twisted or jerked.

The saddle and stirrup were far in the future. Riding bareback, with reins in one fist and spear in the other, horsemen conquered most of the Mediterranean basin and Near East. The Greeks called the conquerors Centaurs, considered them deities, and depicted them as creatures with horse bodies and hairy human torsos.

Next, the horsemen, with rowdy folkways remarkably like those our novelists and moviemakers ascribe to the cowboy, invented a two-wheeled chariot drawn by a two-horse span. The vehicle could go up to thirty-five miles an hour on battle charges and would turn on a dime.

Horse and chariot conquests flourished from Greece to China's Yellow River valley. Vast cultural changes followed: a horseman with a lance and rope could deftly subdue a wild bull; bull worship lost most of its followers; and cattle domestication rapidly progressed. The ox joined the donkey and the camel as an agricultural power tool. Cities and highways evolved.

The horse became an object of veneration and a dominant symbol of power. The national religion imposed on Greece by the Centaurs and their charioteer successors, the Mycenaeans, was based on horse worship. Zeus used the horse Pegasus to fly the firmaments up to his home on Mount Olympus. Zeus's brother, Poseidon, was god of horses as well as of the oceans. Zeus's arrogant daughter, Athena, became the goddess of horsemen because she had revealed the bridle and its values to mortals. The huge wooden horse hiding Odysseus and a company of swordsmen was trundled inside Troy's walls, the blind poet Homer reported, because the Trojans assumed it to be a placation to Athena.

About the same time, rulers of city states in distant China so valued their horse teams that the animals, their grooms, and drivers were killed and buried with them.

While horse domestication drastically changed the course of civilization between 3000 and 1000 B.C. by providing new power sources, it instituted a class structure that would prevail in Europe until migrations to the New World began in 1500 A.D. The rigid rule was: *Only warriors can own or ride horses; consequently, only warriors can own land.* Kingdoms, dukedoms, city states, and the feudal system were built on this foundation of horseman superiority. Horse stealing was punished by death on the gallows. Eating horseflesh was a criminal offense; the taboo still persists in Great Britain and the United States. The Bible reports that Jesus rode a donkey for his "triumphal entry" into Jerusalem. The implication is that if He had ridden a horse, He could have been arrested and crucified for it and His followers would certainly have abandoned Him as a status-seeking elitist. Horse classism gave rise to the use of ass, donkey, mulish, dumb ox, cowlike as derogatory terms.

The 1493 news raced across Europe that Columbus's western Indies were sparsely occupied by swarthy tribes who had no horse power or wheeled vehicles or guns. Never, in all remembered time, had freedom of land been offered to the commoner; the definition of "farmer" was an operator of leased land. But now a youngster could ship out as a sailor or soldier or as an indentured servant to a nobleman who had been granted a huge tract of wilderness. Once in the New World, it would be fairly simple to pioneer a parcel of land as his very own. No obeisance to perform. No horsemen raping your womenfolk, butchering your livestock, guzzling your beer and mead, then riding off with your winter's supply of turnips, cabbage, and grain. A man's home could finally, after 4,500 years of horse slavery, become his castle. Praise God, you could even have your own horses!

The term "benighted savage" would become a clergyman's slur imposed on the New World's natives by European immigrants. But the benighted savage had perfected great agricultural skills. His experiments with wild grasses, vines, shrubs, and trees yielded so many varieties of grain, vegetables, fruits, and herbs that 57 percent of all harvests in the United States still derive from redman agriculture. Corn, squash, tomatoes, beans, peanuts, potatoes, plums, maple sugar, tobacco, chewing gum, turkeys, rubber—all are redman gifts. (In 1930, Congress passed a law enabling botanists to patent new varieties of plants and to collect royalties on the sales. If Indians had patents on their botanic and zoologic contributions to the United States, they would be receiving royalties on harvests averaging more than $100 billion a year!)

Since most of our history texts have been written by easterners, the pioneering of the Pilgrims and Puritans and Virginians has been stressed. But the Spanish preceded the Anglos by a century. In 1521, Juan Ponce de León landed two hundred settlers with bags of seed, farming tools, and a herd of pigs at Charlotte Harbor on Florida's Gulf coast. Indians ambushed the settlement before stockades could be built and wounded de León so severely that he died during the retreat to Puerto Rico. The pigs are the most significant aspect of this first American settlement: pork, in its multitudinous forms, became our "poor man's meat" for the next four centuries. The landing place of the pig is as worthy of a memorial as the landing places of the Pilgrims and the F.F.V.'s.

Eighteen years later Hernando De Soto, an adventurer out of Spain's Extremadura, landed on Tampa Bay with a company of soldiers, bags of seeds, another herd of pigs, and a royal patent to colonize Florida. Instead, with all of the bullying curiosity of Balboa, the Pizarros, and other Extremaduran farm kids, he headed west. Presumably the toothsomeness of de León's pigs had become legendary. De Soto's company, time after time, suffered Indian attacks with the obvious goal of getting his group's pigs on barbecue spits. The pigs died. So did De Soto. Finally, in 1565, a party of six hundred Spaniards succeeded in establishing St. Augustine as the first American city.

The destiny of the American West was changed by a caravan of two-wheeled carts and guardian horsemen that toiled up a bank of the Rio Grande in 1598, nine years before the London Company's ships reached Virginia. Days behind them padded herds of cattle, flocks of sheep, bands of horses, and families of pigs, each guarded by soldiers. Their leader was Juan de Oñate.

Horses, sheep, goats, and cattle are fairly easy to herd, but pigs are something else. The oldest pig-drive trick, perhaps another Greek contribution, is to blindfold or blind the boar; then he can be led. Sows and young pigs will follow him. (The trick was tucked into the American language in another form during Prohibition when "speakeasy" and "blind pig" became synonyms.)

After battles and treaties with the local Pueblo tribes and studies of their skills with corn, bean, and squash crops and domesticated turkey flocks, de Oñate's New Mexicans founded Santa Fé, Isleta, and other fortress centers, then sprawled out on land grants where black and Indian slaves did the field labor and cared for the livestock. They called each land holding a *rancho*, meaning "a place where livestock is raised." Their favorite building material was adobe, made from mud and straw, then whitewashed. They introduced vineyards, garlic, peppers, figs, and other Spanish favorites to their fields. Two feudal taboos were also transplanted from Spain: only whites could own guns; any Indian or black found riding a horse could be executed without trial.

A century before the Spaniards arrived, the Pueblo tribes had experienced other, and even more brutal, invasions by the Athabascans from the far north who had been trekking out of Canada and across the high plains since approximately 1200 A.D. They reached the Sangre de Cristo Mountains of the Rio Grande's headwaters about 1400 A.D. and built villages of grass and reed huts shaped like the Eskimo's igloo. The Zuñi called them the *Apachu*, meaning "brutal enemy." Quick and stealthy as mountain lions, the Apachu lived on wild game, nuts, and fruit. Each fall they would stalk into the pueblo plazas to trade furs, pine nuts, and herbs for blankets and grain, beans, and sun-dried squash. When their trail led past a white man's rancho, they would stand for hours glaring at the horses grazing in the pastures.

Horses responded as zestfully to New Mexico's climate as their eohippus ancestors had millions of years before. By 1680, historians estimate, there were between five and seven thousand of them on the Rio Grande pastures. The colony as a whole prospered. Each of the one thousand white families had black and Indian slaves. Irrigation ditches assured enough water for prime crops. An annual "conducta" carried crop surpluses, handicrafts, and furs down to Chapultepec, then creaked back with tools and luxuries from Mexico City and the Manila galleon.

But the medicine man of the San Juan Indian tribe hated the whites. He was called Popé and was reputed to be the greatest orator in all of the Native American pueblos of the upper Rio Grande valley. "God and Mary are dead," he exhorted to elders and warriors assembled in the village kivas. "The white man must be driven from our homeland." Folklore has it that Popé's strategist was a gigantic black who had fled slavery on a Santa Fé rancho, had somehow won the respect of the Apachu and "lived majestically in a vast cave in the Sangre de Cristo Mountains." By promising the Apachu "many horses and guns," the black won them as allies in a valleywide assassination plot. He is also reputed to have devised a signal system based on the number and position of knots in pieces of yarn delivered to each pueblo by "traders."

As the first rays of sunrise gilded the peaks of the mountains on August 9, 1680, Indian and black house servants and yardmen methodically knifed and strangled the rancho whites in their beds. Then columns of Pueblo and Apachu warriors, chanting "God and Mary are dead," charged the walls of Santa Fé, Isleta, and other forts.

The forts surrendered. White survivors were permitted to march south, but without provisions. So many died during the trek across the White Sands desert to the site of El Paso, Texas, that the trail is still called *Jornada del Muerto*, the Journey of Death.

More than five thousand horses became Apachu booty. "By 1686," George E. Hyde reported in *Indians of the High Plains,* "the Caddoans of the eastern border of the southern plains had some horses and metal weapons and were striking back against the Apache. LaSalle's men (exploring down the Mississippi) . . . found these Indians imitating the Spanish cavaliers, some of the men even wearing boots and spurs. They fought mounted with long lances, both men and horses protected by rawhide armor." "For once, the redman was lucky," Colonel Edward N. Wentworth, author of *Horses and Men*, once mused. "Those horses were the seed stock of the redman herds that transformed the way of life west of the Mississippi. The New Mexico horses were third or fourth generation get out of Andalusia and Extremadura. Thanks to the Moors, they had some Arab and Barb blood. They were wiry and could adapt to violent temperature changes. An Indian horse would gnaw bark from a willow tree and put on weight from the stuff. Just suppose that, instead of the Spanish horses, the Apache and their Navajo cousins had stolen a lot of those huge holdovers from knighthood, such as the Shire horses and Flemish cart horses. Those animals wouldn't have survived the first blizzard. There wouldn't have been any red horsemen or Indian wars."

Between 1700 and 1800, Sioux and Cheyenne, too, adapted from brush-hut scavengers in the Minnesota forests to the most fearless horsemen the earth had known since the Mongol invasions. The *coureurs de bois* out of Canada and the "bush runners" of Virginia and the Carolinas soon learned that it was more profitable to trade horses for furs with the prairie tribes than to haul in saddlebags full of beads and junk jewelry.

Popé's Revolt rarely appears in our history books, but for the 1,500 miles of high plain and mountain between the Missouri River and the Pacific's coastal plain it was as significant as the Concord and Lexington battles were to the American Revolution of 1775–83. Native Americans and their travois finally won access to the plains and vast herds of bison and game animals. Indian horsemen established the routes that became our wagon trails during the 1830–90 migrations to the Southwest, California, and Oregon Territory. The pinto, Appaloosa, and storied mustang were products of the Indian's open range and interbreeding. The great quarter horse that became the cattle rancher's favorite mount inherited some of its speed from the Indian's interbred mounts. Comanche raiders, the Apache wars, the Custer massacre, the

shame of Wounded Knee were all in the horseman heritage of
the Popé Revolt.

Meanwhile, back East, the sharing of the green sired three of
our folkways traditions: the habit of smoking tobacco, the corn
cuisine, and the cowboy. Coincidentally, the geographic boundaries of the farm and the plantation were permanently established.

In 1584 Sir Walter Raleigh financed England's first North
American colony on Roanoke Island. Queen Elizabeth approved
the name Virginia for the region. The Roanoke colonists mysteriously vanished within two years. In 1606, the founders of the
London Company decided that since the Spanish had looted so
much gold and silver out of Central and South America, there
must be lodes of it in Virginia, too. They sent out a party of 120
males, with three shiploads of supplies, to locate gold or silver
mines in Virginia and to exchange trinkets for furs with the natives.

The ships' pilots missed Roanoke, bumbled into Chesapeake
Bay and up the murky James River. So Jamestown was founded.
Malaria, ambushes, and a starving time killed most of the 120
miners and traders. The London Company decided that agricultural development was the best hope of recovering their investment. Livestock, women, seeds, and tools were shipped in.
A haphazard agriculture began.

Sir Walter Raleigh became a devotee of smoking the Native
American's tobacco in a long-stemmed clay pipe. The Spanish
in Mexico and the West Indies were already exporting the plant's
sun-cured leaves, and got extravagant prices for them in London.
John Rolfe migrated to Virginia in 1610, secured some tobacco
plants in the West Indies, and began experimenting with them
on swampy bottomlands. In 1614 he courted and married Pocahontas, daughter of the powerful war chief, Powhatan. Rolfe
took Pocahontas and prime samples of his golden Virginia tobacco
to England. His wife was received at Court; Rolfe passed out

small sacks of tobacco, bragging that it was "as sweete and pure as any growne in ye Indies."

The first shipment of "golden Virginia" drifted down the James in 1617. The prices paid for it in London were so remunerative that the new colony adapted to a one-crop economy. In 1619, a shipload of marriageable girls was sent to Jamestown and they were auctioned to tobacco growers for an average of 120 pounds of tobacco each. That August, a Portuguese or Dutch ship loaded with blacks from a Portuguese slave compound on the West African coast sailed in; two and a half centuries of black slavery began.

By 1621, ship captains were being offered grants of "fifty acres of prime tobacco land" for every settler they landed in Virginia. The offer inspired British deportation of prostitutes, convicts, occupants of debtor prisons, prisoners of war, and the younger sons of landed gentry. Each settler was promised a plot of land when his or her years of indentured servitude ended. By 1622, Golden Virginia sold for a fabulous sixpence a pound. Growers began to call themselves planters and their holdings plantations. King James I declared Virginia a crown colony and gave it the monopoly on all of Great Britain's tobacco imports.

Inevitably, as it would throughout the saga of the American land, production exceeded demand; the price of tobacco dropped to a pence a pound. The government failed to solve the problems of surplus crops withering in the fields as well as the poverty that followed. Posses of hooded night raiders recruited by the more aggressive planters burned the curing barns and fields when growers refused to cut back on tobacco plantings. (Government subsidies for crop control were still three centuries away.)

In imitation of Britain's gentry, successful planters built drafty stone or wood mansions with pillared verandas and flagstone patios, encircled by herb gardens, lawns, and fruit trees. Because of the hazard of flash fires from fat drippings, kitchens were built as separate units, connected to the main house by a stone or brick walk. The slave who carried the meal from kitchen to dining room was compelled to whistle throughout the two-minute journey. This attested that he or she was not "nibblin' vittles" en-route. From Virginia south, the kitchen-to-dining room route became known as the Whistling Walk.

Use of the term "dogtrot" for the yard space crossed by the Whistling Walk came from the same social urge that built the mansions. By 1675, fox hunts and horse races were stylish throughout the tobacco lowlands. The horses were Irish ponies crossed with Spanish or French Barbs from the West Indies and a few Bretons from Nova Scotia. Most of the hounds were mongrel crosses of beagles and British bloodhounds.

When the odors of a roast or fish fry began to waft from the kitchen, the hounds assembled on the Whistling Walk, uttering moans and howls. A cook who deserves a memorial mixed corn meal with egg, fried it in thumb-big pellets, then tossed platefuls out to the hounds with the command, "Hush, you puppies!" Both the dogtrot and the hushpuppy became Old South traditions.

Hammered up behind the gardens and hedges of azalea, boxwood, and hibiscus was the row of one-room cabins provided as homes for the cook, maids, carpenters, grooms, field hands, and other black slaves. Virginia's slaves quickly revealed their abilities as craftsmen. (Prehistoric carvings, jewelry, handicraft found along the West African coast from Senegal to Gabon testify to ancient native skills.) Their womenfolk became superlative chefs and are responsible for most of the creations that became known as southern cuisine. The "Mammy" not only cooked but was often the beloved magistrate of the white man's nurseries and children's quarters. The blacks' talents for gardening introduced such delectables as okra, kale, and "greens." And, certainly, the blacks of the South were responsible for the introduction and perpetuation of the peanut.

The peanut is a native of South America. The Portuguese introduced it to West Africa during the 1500s, where Bantu tribesmen called it *nguba*, meaning "nut of the ground." Raw peanuts proved the most durable and nourishing food for the slave ships' grim journeys across the South Atlantic. Some slaves managed to smuggle peanuts ashore and plant them. The nuts grew lavishly on Virginia bottomland and would yield several bushels to the acre. The planters approved the crop as a cheap, durable slave food, but mispronounced *nguba* as "goober." Two and a half centuries later an ex-slave named George Washington Carver would discover and popularize hundreds of new uses for the peanut.

Circumstantial evidence also suggests that slaves from Ghana introduced their ancient method of washing dirt for flakes and nuggets of gold. Initially a wooden bowl was used. But iron- and tin-coated pans were better. After gold "strikes" in North Carolina and Georgia between 1785 and 1830, the technique of "panning for gold" traveled west to trans-Rockies destiny.

Horses, cattle, and pigs became so plentiful that Virginians built few shelters for them. "All the care they take of horses at the end of a journey," a French visitor to Virginia reported in 1686, "is to unsaddle, feed a little Indian corn and so, all covered with sweat, drive them out into the woods, where they eat what they can find, even though it is freezing." Cattle and pigs were similarly mistreated. A few acres of salt hay or marsh grass were enclosed with rail fencing. Plantation cattle would be pastured there through the winters. "If fed at all," reported Philip A. Bruce in his *Economic History of Virginia in the Seventeenth Century,* "they received only husks of the maize and a few grains."

This slothfulness encouraged the livestock to become feral. The smells and flavors of wilderness grasses and brush had the same mystic appeal that they held for Spanish horses two thousand miles west. Moreover, many of the Virginia animals were from Irish stock whose ancestors have revelled in open range for a thousand years. In 1670, planters around Williamsburg complained about the crop damage caused by "bandes of wild horses." Between 1694 and 1712, the legislature of adjoining Maryland enacted a series of laws "to prevent the great multitude of horses in this province."

Horses, cattle, sheep, and pigs established feral range areas in the Blue Ridge and Great Smokies of the Appalachians, Virginia to Georgia. They were joined by Spanish horses and cattle that had "followed the green" north from the fort towns of Florida. Free breeding produced a long-maned, nimble horse that stood thirteen and a half hands high and weighed about 700 pounds; lanky and aggressive pigs; and horned cattle as rambunctious as Europe's storied aurochs.

Ignorance and poverty caused Virginians to follow the feral livestock westward. The intricate chemistry of topsoil had not yet been analyzed. Most planters sneered at the fertilization techniques used by the blacks for their gardens. So fields were replanted to tobacco year after year without fertilizers or fallowing or composts. Within seven years, tobacco plants consumed most of the topsoil's nitrogen and other beneficial elements. The eighth year produced a runt crop hardly worth harvesting. Consequently, virgin land had to be prepared for cropping every seven years. This pattern of land-rape would become commonplace throughout the United States and hasten the perils of desert, drought, and diminishing food supplies that confront us today.

Owners of small plantations could not survive tobacco's "seven-year curse." Some became tenants or overseers. Others moved west of the river fall-lines to become hunters of feral livestock, Indian traders, trappers, or subsistence farmers. Thus were instituted the enmities between planters and "uplanders."

Between 1614 and 1700, Virginia pioneered the plantation system that would spread across the South and West to the Mississippi. Rice, indigo, and eventually cotton followed the Virginia model of one major crop, lavish and elegant plantation homes, abject dependence on the skills and labor of black slaves, and a feudal aristocracy.

Virginia established the plantation. Far across the mountains and prairie, the New Mexicans had set up the ranch. On granite inlets a two weeks' sail up the seaboard, the Yankees were developing communal rudiments of the farm.

The *Mayflower* was a sluggish ship of 160 tons that had for a long time freighted casks of wine across the English Channel. In 1620 it was commanded by Christopher Jones, who, unfortunately, lived more than three centuries before Alcoholics Anonymous was founded. His besotted navigation brought the ship and its 101 refugees from Church of England discipline to the tip of Cape Cod on a blustery November morning. Jones insisted that they had reached Virginia, so, after a month of exploration for a village site, landed his passengers on a rocky beach at the foot of the cape. Several of the passengers had been tenant farmers. Their luggage included farm tools and packets of seeds. Thus the Pilgrims, as historians would name them, introduced the terms "farm" and "farmer" to the future United States of America.

Caves dug above the high-tide mark, ample supplies of driftwood for fires, an abundance of deer and turkeys and fish enabled most of the colony to survive the winter. When spring finally howled in and maple trees began to cascade scarlet bud cases, the men whacked out communal garden space, then forked in mounds of nitrogen-rich seaweed. The seeds the women planted included such herb essentials as dandelion, thyme, savory, mustard, and sage. Adjoining rows were for turnips, carrots, beets, flax, and lettuce. But the most auspicious hour of planting time came when an Indian who called himself Squanto showed up lugging a basketful of dead fish and a pouchful of strange seeds.

Squanto spoke English fairly well, explaining that he had been kidnapped five years before by a British sea captain, then lived in England for four years and returned home only the year before. The best of all crops known to Native Americans, he went on, grew from the oblong red, blue, orange, and yellow seeds in his pouch. The two other kinds of seeds he had brought grew best in teamship with the multicolored seeds. All of these needed dead fish to get a healthy start.

Each of the brightly colored seeds, he explained, grew a thick stalk as tall as a man. A cluster of thin branches at the top of the stalk would send out puffs of yellow dust when you shook it. Halfway down the stalk would appear growths that contained hundreds of seeds like the ones he held in his hand. When the growths began to turn yellow and the silky strands coming out of the ends were a deep brown, the seeds were ready to harvest. Then the seeds could be pounded into a powder that made excellent bread or could be used to thicken stews.

His listeners realized that this was a strange, new kind of grain. The English had a common name for all types of grain; they called it "corn." This, then, was a New World corn. But what about those other kinds of seeds and those smelly fish?

The fat white seeds, Squanto patiently explained, grew vines that crawled up the stalks of the corn. In midsummer, these vines would produce long pods. Each pod contained eight or ten seeds. Dried, the seeds would keep for years but anytime could be boiled slowly with some fat meat and herbs to produce either a thick soup or a delicious paste that could be eaten with the fingers. Also, the seeds could be cooked with kernels of corn to make a delicious dish called *misickquitash*.

Beans, of course! The Pilgrims knew about beans, but this, like the corn, was a new variety.

The third kind of seed, the flattest one, grew a vine that sprawled for yards beneath its canopy of big leaves. It would grow yellow blossoms that could be fried or used in a stew. However, let some of the blossoms grow, because they would turn into great orange spheres, sometimes too big for one man to lift. All of this orange sphere was edible, even the hundreds of seeds inside its inch-thick flesh. A tasty bread could be made from its thick rind, after it was boiled and mixed with corn meal.

A puzzler! But the seeds grew such gigantic and multi-useful spheres that the plant was given the name of "pumpkin," an ancient term meaning "a kind of melon."

The dead fish? Oh! Fish does something to the dirt, Squanto explained. It makes it richer, richer even than seaweed. You got better crops when you placed a dead fish in the same hillock with the three kinds of seeds.

Thus, during the spring of 1621, the American crop trinity of corn-beans-pumpkin was revealed to the Pilgrims. Corn grew so lavishly and was so much simpler to harvest and mill than wheat that it became the favored grain in all of the Thirteen Colonies. Wheat continued to be essential for some types of bread, cakes, pastries, and puddings, but colonial milling methods could not separate the outer coating of bran from the white endosperm of the kernels. Until the 1870s, practically all of our wheat flour was the speckled tan "whole wheat." Corn bread, grits, hush-puppies, corn puddings, corn starch, corn syrup were easier to make; livestock flourished on the kernels, stalks, and silage.

The American devotion to corn persisted. By the 1980s, our corn crop used seventy million acres of land annually, with an average yield of more than 8 billion bushels.

The pole bean and the pumpkin also became staples of the American diet. Baked beans, brown bread, and Indian pudding remain a New England Saturday supper ritual; pumpkin pie is as essential to a Thanksgiving dinner as the roast turkey.

Some time later in 1621 Squanto wandered back with another gift of corn, but the seeds were smaller, rounder, and a deep scarlet. He brushed ashes away from the embers in a cabin fire-place, dropped on a few of the seeds and stood back. After a moment, the seeds exploded and popped against the andirons as fluffy white balls the size of marbles. He picked up the popped corn and offered it for tasting. Not only good to eat hot, he reported, but it could be pounded into a powder called *nookick*. A pouchful of nookick assured a traveler of food during a journey, because it could be mixed into a porridge with water or snow. The Pilgrims called the exploded kernels "parched corn" and used them as a breakfast food with cream or milk.

Throughout the centuries, Americans have maintained a love affair with popcorn. Dyed red or green, the exploded kernels were strung on thread as cheap but magnificent decoration for Christmas trees. Mixed with syrup and a few nutmeats and pressed into spheres the size of baseballs, it was and is a gooey childhood favorite. After 1910, when every village had a movie house, the popcorn vendor in the lobby was as important as the Pearl White or Charlie Chaplin feature. Still in 1983, with movie tickets sell-ing for five or six dollars, the popcorn machine earned a theater more profit than a showing of *E.T.* or *Gandhi*. National popcorn production zooms along at five to six million pounds a year.

Perhaps Squanto did not know that a third type of corn had been developed. But four hundred miles west, the Seneca and Cayuga Indians knew it. They grew white kernels on a blood-red cob that was much sweeter and juicier than the field corn grown on the Massachusetts shore. They kept the secret from the white man for 158 years.

The Pilgrims settled in, imported some livestock, and, by and large, minded their manners as pious farmers and fishermen. But the nine hundred Puritans who landed on the north shore of Massachusetts Bay in 1629 and founded Salem were more belligerent. Most of them came from Yorkshire and the Midlands and were sharp tradesmen as well as agriculturists. The necessities they brought ashore included 110 cattle, 13 horses, a few pigs, and some apple seeds.

The apple seeds probably came from Somerset which, for five hundred years, had been famous as producer of England's best "country draught," cider. The Normans introduced the apple and the process of crushing out and fermenting its juice soon after their 1066 conquest. Somerset's hilly countryside proved to be England's best for growing Pippin, Pearmain, Harvey, and other varieties considered prime for cidermaking. Coffee, tea, and lemonade were unknown. Beer and ale were too expensive for most laborers. Apple cider, in varying stages of fermentation, became the workman's favorite thirst quencher. "Years ago in many country districts," Patrick King wrote in 1734, "a laborer was judged by the amount of cider he could drink. In the belief, I suppose, that the harder you worked the greater your thirst. The two-gallon-a-day man was reckoned to be at the zenith of his profession."

Apple orchards became essential in Boston, Saugus, Gloucester, Springfield, and other villages the Puritans founded along their trails to the Connecticut valley and the White and Green Mountains. For 150 years cider was New England's standard dinner and fieldside drink, although a fragrant beer could be made from young needles of the spruce tree. For a lustier potion beside fireplaces on frigid winter evenings, hard cider was mulled with cinnamon, clove, and a chunk of sugar, then blended with a jigger of rum and topped with butter. For sheer debauchery, a keg of hard cider left in the woodshed over a sub-zero night would freeze most of the liquid but leave a core of colorless, sweet "lightning" that averaged 150 proof.

The apple's versatility ranged from cider keg to kitchen and root cellar. During Thanksgiving week, wives and children made scores of apple pies, then stored them in chests in a back room where they froze and stayed in redolent splendor until the springtime thaw. Apple butter was a cherished spread. Apples cooked with other fruits or berries provided the pectin to assure a firm jell. Apples boiled and mashed made the best "sass." Apples stored in the root cellar held their crispness all winter, so became favorite bedtime snacks. The brown liquid produced by boiling apple-tree bark dyed woolens and linen a pleasing yellow that held through years of washings.

Meager harvests from Boston's first apple trees caused the villagers to recall that hives of bees were always carted out to Somerset's orchards at blossomtime. Nobody quite understood what happened, but after those bees had zoomed around awhile, the blossoms developed a lot more apples. Appeals for hives of honeybees went to London. Bees arrived in 1635. Thereafter, the orchards had bumper crops. In 1646, Massachusetts' legislators declared that robbing an apple orchard was a criminal offense, punishable by a public whipping or confinement to the stocks.

West and south, apple trees followed the frontier. The appetite for the many forms and varieties of the fruit became all-American. By the 1980s, our total commercial production exceeded 8 billion pounds and at least another 2 billion pounds came from backyard and wild, back pasture trees.

The horse, also an eager connoisseur of crisp apples, fared better in New England than in Virginia and the South. Fear of Indian and Canadian-French attacks, as well as a few exchanges of gunfire with the Dutch colonists to the south, caused the Puritans to enclose their villages in timbered stockades. Inside these walls, homes and shops faced a central meadow called a Common. The Common was both a drill ground and an overnight pasture for livestock. There were few barns, but corrals were built in the shelter of the massive elm and oak trees near the villages. During the six or seven months of winter, stacks of hay and corn supplemented the animals' diet of moss and tree bark. The mares and stallions responded so lustily that, by 1668, nimble colts were as plentiful as oxen.

Between 1650 and 1700, British traditions of roast beef and horsemanship caused New England to become the birthplace of one of the U.S.A.'s most legendary figures: the cowboy.

Horse and cattle raising had long excited the Irish. The minstrels who composed the *Triads* before 900 A.D. chanted ballads from Cork to Belfast about "the cooboys." The "hobby horse" of the merry-go-round and children's playrooms takes its name from a breed of Irish pacers reputed to "have a gait as serene as a rockin' chair on th' hob." By 1350, hobby horses were popular as the gentleman's mount throughout England. Most of the horses imported by the Puritans were of Irish stock.

Nineteen years after Salem was founded, Oliver Cromwell bullied Parliament into ordering the execution of King Charles I. A few weeks later, Cromwell led an invasion of Ireland. His plunder included hundreds of Irish herdsmen, some of whom were shipped to New England as "indentures." The livestock herds needed them. An Irish "cooboy" could sundance a stallion into submission, round up cattle with whoops and the rifle-crack of a blacksnake whip, bundle-tie calves, castrate young bulls into steers, and brand each calf's rump with the farmer's insignia. The trail drive and roundup became a Yankee tradition. It is possible, after a study of early eighteenth-century maps, to still follow the livestock trails from the mountain valleys down to the seaports. Fleets of "jockey ships" ferried horses off to the cotton and sugar plantations of the West Indies, to return with ballast cargoes of sugar, rum, and cotton bales. These, in turn, persuaded New England merchants to enter the ghastly slave trade between West Africa and the South. Yankee meat packers provisioned West Indian and Southern slave plantations with corned beef, "jerky," and the tallow essential for greasing wagon wheels and machines; one packer was penalized for selling provisions to the infamous pirate, Captain Kidd.

By the time New England burgeoned into Massachusetts, Rhode Island, Maine, Connecticut, New Hampshire, and Vermont, this region had already made lavish contributions to an all-American cuisine. The versatilities of the corn plant, the apple tree, the pumpkin, and bean vines were complemented by the gustatory joys of cranberries, blueberries, bayberries, beach plums, maple sap, butternuts, grapes, turkey, fish and clam chowders, and a score of herb varieties. This sharing of the green between the Native American's and the European's agricultural skills would migrate west and south during the next two centuries.

But two of the American Indian's achievements would be banned by most whites and blacks. Folklore kept the tomato and the potato out of their diets until the middle of the nineteenth century.

Like the peanut, the tomato and potato were native to Central and South America. Cortés, the Pizarro brothers, and other conquistadores shipped potatoes and tomato seeds back to Spain and Portugal before 1550. The initial imports of tomato seed produced a shiny yellow fruit that was accepted by cooks in Lisbon, Barcelona, and Cadiz and given the name of "golden apple." But later introduction of a scarlet tomato evoked dread from French, Italian, and British housewives. They nicknamed it "the love apple," pronounced it a deadly poison, and would grow it only as a garden ornamental. Their fear migrated to New England. Tomato was not permitted in baked beans or clam chowder or in the marinade daubed on a barbecue. The bits of tomato flecking a Manhattan clam chowder, still viewed as heresy north of New Haven, testify to mid-nineteenth-century invention of that dish.

Experimental plantings in monastery gardens and cautious

tastings of the boiled tubers proved the potato to be edible as well as adaptable to the Iberian climate. In 1565, a sackful of potatoes was shipped to the new settlement of St. Augustine, Florida, for test planting. As audacious in agricultural experiments as he was in geologic research, colonization, and efforts to deflower Queen Elizabeth, Sir Walter Raleigh pirated some Spanish potatoes and sent them to the tenants of his estate in Ireland. The plants flourished; so did the Irish appetite for "taties."

But throughout most of northern Europe, the potato was nicknamed "devil's apple" and considered poisonous. (It still is, if eaten when the skin is green!) In 1718, Irish immigrants to New Hampshire brought along sacks of "taties" and grew successful crops in their granite-littered soil. But New England neighbors retained a distrust of the "devil's apple" for another century.

Almost constant warfare between the New Englanders and the Canadian French, who slowly encircled them with settlements and forts from the St. Lawrence valley to New Orleans, influenced New England's communal form of agriculture. Stockaded settlements, cropfields nearby, livestock on the Common, armed guards on the cattle and horse drives to the seaports—all were prompted by fear of raids by the French and their Indian allies. This dread did not end until 1763, when British and colonial forces captured Niagara, Quebec, and Montreal, and France formally surrendered Canada to Great Britain.

Finally there was opportunity to achieve the dream of self-sufficiency on a farm in Yankeedom. The Common could be abandoned as an emergency livestock pasture and beautified into a park. The system of using and re-using the same strip of cropland close to the village stockade could be exchanged for a fifty- or even one-hundred-acre farm where the family could work out its destiny. But more efficient vehicles and better types of livestock housing were needed.

Up the new Post Road from New York and Philadelphia came huge red, white, and blue Conestoga wagons with canvas-covered hoods and bells jangling on six-horse teams. Evening gossip over a jugful of hot buttered rum revealed that the Pennsylvanians also had big barns that housed horses, cattle, pigs, and sheep with a winterlong supply of hay and grain in the mows above. The animals' manure, allowed to age outside the barn all winter, was spread across cropfields before springtime plowing. It gave the soil "a heap of growin' power."

The Quakers and Palatine refugees in Penn's Sylvania were evolving the most independent form of agriculture the world had ever seen: the family farm.

CHAPTER THREE

Genesis of the Family Farm

Glacier-fed by the Alps, the Rhine River tumbles out of Switzerland across West Germany and the flatlands of Holland into the shallow and violent North Sea. Despite feudalism, the residents of the upper Rhine valley developed a system of agriculture that enabled families to become self-sufficient in livestock, grains, vegetables, fruits, nuts, herbs, and wood. Europe's first printed books came from Mainz, capital of the Rhineland Palatinate. Martin Luther was a Rhine villager. The valley became the heartland of the Protestant Reformation. Consequently, its residents were relentlessly persecuted by the Holy Roman Emperors.

James I, the first Stuart ruler of Great Britain, betrothed a daughter to the King of Bohemia; a daughter of this marriage wed the Elector of Hanover. As Protectors of the Protestant Faith, Britain's rulers felt obliged to offer haven to the Protestant subjects of their German in-laws—and William Penn needed settlers for his colony in the American wilderness.

Penn, the wealthy son of a British admiral, had converted to the Religious Society of Friends. The Friends' opposition to all wars, to slavery, and to priests and ornate church ritual brought them the derisive nickname of Quakers. During 1681, in payment for a debt owed his father, Charles II granted Penn a royal charter to land "between the 40th and 43rd Parallels and extending five degrees west of the Delaware River." The king insisted that the territory be named Penn's Sylvania.

During the three generations since the founding of Jamestown, Plymouth, and Salem, the British immigrants had become as brutal as the Spanish, French, and Austrians in their persecution of "unbelievers." After packet ships delivered the news that Penn's Sylvania would be a Quaker colony and that its proprietor was pledging freedom of worship for all settlers, ministers thundered exhortations from pulpits in Boston, New York, Baltimore, Williamsburg, and Carolina's new capital city of Charleston. In New York and Massachusetts, ministers decided that Halley's Comet, which flashed by the earth that year, was a celestial warning about Quaker heresy; a day for "fasting and humiliation" was declared.

Tours of the Rhine valley, Switzerland, and Holland by Penn and his agents showed them the essentials for a self-sufficient agriculture. The first shiploads of English and German settlers to Penn's Sylvania carried sacks of clover seed, wheat, barley, and rye, as well as deckloads of horses, cattle, and sheep. While foundations were being laid for the first buildings of Philadelphia, the friendly Swedes, Dutch, and Finns who had homesteaded along the Delaware since the 1640s were invited to give demonstration talks on local biology, soil types, and weather patterns.

In contrast to the communal pastures and cropfields of New England, the tenant farms of the Hudson valley patroons, the feudalism of the South's plantations, and New Mexico's ranchos, Penn insisted on individual freedom for the farm. It was to be owned and operated by the occupying family. All cropfields and clover pasture had to be enclosed by fencing. All livestock must be earmarked or branded; if the owner's mark was not registered with a township clerk, a posse would be sent out to "take the animals up in estray" for re-sale. Harvests of hay and straw were to be mounded in midpasture, then covered with wood or thatch roofs so that the animals could self-feed during the winters.

By 1685, the colony was exporting horses and sawed timber to the Bahamas. Five years later, cheese, butter, lard, and pickled meats had been added to its West Indies provisioning.

The forests told Penn's Rhineland refugees where to locate their homesteads. Knowing, from back home, that hardwoods flourish on soils rich in limestone, men and boys searched until they found an oak or maple forest with an adjoining creek. As soon as a lean-to hut was built and enough forest chopped out for a crop of corn, wheat, cabbage, and turnips, oxen began hauling stones to the foot of a natural embankment selected as the site for the barn. By fall, logs from the oak, maple, cedar, or chestnut trees had been worked into beams and timbers. Meanwhile, the women began splitting chunks of hemlock and white pine into shakes (shingles).

James Westfall Thompson describes, in his *History of Livestock Raising in the United States, 1607–1860*, what kind of buildings these settlers put up.

> The German was sure to build a large, fine barn before he built any dwelling house for his family except a rude log cabin. This German, or Swiss, "bank" barn was, and still is, the best type of barn known. New England and Virginia created the plain "shed" barn, a simple structure sometimes connected with the house by a woodshed or other outhouse. The Dutch barn in New York and northern New Jersey was an immense improvement upon this. It was a spacious structure with ample mows and stalls.
>
> The German bank barn was like neither of these. Its basement was walled against a hill, and was used as the stable for horses, cattle, sheep and even hogs. The threshing floor was above the basement with [hay] mows on either hand. . . . A driveway led up to the threshing floor, and thence around the barn. Through trapdoors in the floor the corn or other feed

could be dropped from the wagons directly into the stalls below. [As a precaution against internal combustion] ventilators made of chimney pots were attached to the barn.

The Germans called this type of barn a *Holzsteiner* because it was built from wood (*Holz*) and stone (*Stein*). The overhang of the threshing floor and haymows provided shelter from winter snows and winds during the livestock's daily airing in the fenced yard. At one side of the yard, the straw bedding and dung from the stalls was piled for curing. In early spring, this pungent mixture was shoveled into carts, hauled out to fields that had been selected for the year's crop plantings, and hand spread. Blended with the soil by rains and plowing and harrowing, it re-energized the cropfields with nitrogen and essential minerals.

Constant supplies of natural fertilizers and a labor-saving livestock center were not the only advantages of the bank barn. "They keep their horses and cattle as warm as possible in the winter, by which means they save a great deal of their hay and grain," Dr. Benjamin Rush commented in 1787. "These animals when cold eat much more than when they are in a more comfortable situation."

With similar shrewdness, wives and daughters invented the glory of Pennsylvania Dutch cuisine. Cow and sheep milks were skimmed, churned, processed into sweet and salted butters, a dozen varieties of cheese, and bowls of "clabber" (cottage cheese) gloried with herbs. Cabbages opened the realm of slaw, sauerkraut, or cabbage boiled with meat. Poultry eggs could be kept fresh for weeks in a salt solution. Blackberries and other bramble fruits, ground cherries, choke cherries, young cucumbers, tiny onions, and chunks of cauliflower were blended with salt, honey, or vinegar in iron kettles suspended over a fireplace. The results were the "seven sweets and seven sours" essential to the day's big noonday meal.

Apples flourished on the gentle hillslopes between the Delaware and Susquehanna valleys, and both Quakers and Germans knew the multi-rewards from swarms of honeybees. Thus *Ap-*

felkuchen and *Streusel* were added to the American diet. Kitchen experiments showed that thin slices of apples strung on strings above the fireplace hearth could be dried to a leathery consistency. The Pennsylvanians called the result *Schnitz*. It was equally excellent for wintertime pies and *Kuchen* or for "gumming" by teething youngsters.

Most Quakers and Germans agreed with the taboo on tomatoes and potatoes, yet they developed delectable uses for a tomato cousin, the ground cherry. An annual that grows into a leafy bush, the ground cherry develops small spherical fruit, each enclosed in a thin calyx, that ripen to a golden yellow. Ground cherry pies and jams taste like peaches.

Sheep shearings and the fall slaughter of meat animals provided wool and leather to be home-processed into clothing, harness, shoes, saddles, gate hinges, snowshoe webbing, and scores of other uses. Since refrigeration was unknown, the week after butchering time provided feasts of sausages, shimmering blocks of headcheese, and that pork scrap and corn meal ambrosia called "scrapple." Aromatic links of braunschweiger, Lebanon bologna, and smoked sausages followed. Hams, loins, ribs, and shoulders began a fragrant year of "readying" after salt, honey, and pepper massages and a long hickory-smoke bath.

There was even multiple use for the blood of the slaughtered animals. It could be processed into spicy bloodwurst or it could be mixed with whey and hot lard to produce a durable red paint. Most barns were daubed with the blood-lard-whey mix. (Thus the red barn became the nostalgic symbol of rural America on greeting cards and movie sets.)

Slaughter-time also provided an essential ingredient for soap making. Animal fat mixed with the lye obtained by leaching wood ashes produces a firm yellow soap that can be perfumed with pine or dried flower petals. Some families grew the variety of pinkster called Bouncing Bet in herb gardens; the leaves of the plant produce a lather bubbly enough for a Saturday night bath.

Household furniture and most of the farm tools were hand-crafted from homegrown hardwoods and homecured leathers in the farmer's workshop. Women and girls transformed goose and duck feathers into billowy bed covers, and sweet grass and rushes into baskets of all shapes and sizes. Cured wood fueled the fireplaces.

The livestock provided work power and leathers and wool and meats, and their manure re-fertilized the croplands. These croplands then provided food for both animals and humans, completing a cycle of self-sufficiency that required no outlay of cash for mechanical power, fuel, or fertilizers.

The few commodities that were essential could be obtained through barter. The miller at the next waterfall up the creek ground corn, wheat, and rye into meal and flour. His fee was a small percentage of the grain wagoned in. The general provisioner at the crosstrails would swap eggs, cured hams, dried beef, apples, cabbages, and some of the kitchen specialties for the essential ingredients of gunpowder, some bullets and buckshot, a little bar iron, and the sea salt, saleratus, and spices necessary in the kitchen. Before holiday times, produce could be swapped for cotton yard goods, a yard or two of English ribbon, a jug of molasses, and a rockhard loaf of West Indies sugar. Self-sufficiency on the homeplace, plus barter, enabled the Pennsylvania farmer to be more independent than any agriculturist had been since the Caspian tribesmen imposed the horseman tyranny 4,500 years before.

After 1733, huge red, white, and blue wagons heralded Penn's Sylvania's techniques and self-sufficiencies from Georgia to Maine. In 1718, the Provincial Council in session at Philadelphia had received "a Peticion of several of the Inhabitantes of & near Conestoga setting forth the Great Necessity of a Road to be laid out from Conestoga to Thomas Moores & Brandywine." The sixty-mile lane through forests and across boulder-littered hills was completed in 1733, making possible the first appearance of the most remarkable wagon in American history.

The Conestoga wagon, as it was originally called, was similar to the freight and produce wagons that teams of "Great Horse" drafters hauled over the steep slopes of the Rhine valley and

Alpine passes during the Middle Ages. Presumably, a blacksmith in the village of Conestoga fashioned the first ones from homeland memories, with a Mennonite preacher as his relentless coach and groups of bearded farmers as final inspectors. The wagon body was sixteen feet long and boat-shaped. The body floor tilted down toward the center from each end, thus preventing freight from shifting on steep hills or in springtime's deep ruts. Because of the boulders and brush in the new road, and the necessity of fording streams, the wheels were huge, with rims two and a half to three inches wide and an inch thick. The rear wheels, higher than the front ones, were five and a half feet tall.

A white linen hood, pegged to hardwood hoops, arced over the entire body to provide shelter for the driver and freight. As a final flourish, the Conestogans painted the wagon body a bright Prussian blue and the giant wheels scarlet.

The wagon was drawn by a six-horse team, two abreast. An arch of four bells, identical in size and tone, was suspended above each horse's head. Small soprano bells jangled above the lead team. Medium-size tenor bells hung over the middle or swing team. Larger basso bells boomed from the arches above the largest and strongest horses, called wheel horses, who strode just in front of the driver and provided most of the power on the hills. Harness fittings were of shiny brass and decorated with red braid. And, during the post-harvest hauls of autumn, each horse sported a glossy bearskin robe across its back.

A single rein, called the jerkline, extended from the driver to the near lead horse. A short tug of the rein and the shout of "Gee" veered the team to the right. A long tug and the shout of "Haw" called for a left turn. The stop signal was "Whoaaa"; "Gee up" meant go.

"The economy of the Germans," wrote Lewis Evans in 1753, "has taught us the method of bringing produce to market from the remotest part at a small expense. Every German farmer in our Province has a waggon of his own. . . . In the Spring and Fall of the year, when it is here a vacation from farming, they load their waggon and furnish themselves with beasts and provender for the Journey. The Waggon is their Bed, their Inn, their everything. Many of them will come one hundred fifty miles without spending one shilling."

When, during the spring of 1755, testy Major General Edward Braddock sent agents across Virginia and Maryland to lease wagons for the baggage train of his expedition against the French entrenched at Duquesne and Niagara, he learned of only twenty-five vehicles that were fit for wilderness service. Braddock appealed to Benjamin Franklin, the new Postmaster General for the Northern Colonies.

A Quaker refugee from Puritan bigotry, Franklin was organizing a corps of post riders to make year-round deliveries of mail between Philadelphia and Boston. He ran off an armful of handbills announcing Braddock's need for wagons and guaranteeing that fair wages would be paid. Post riders jogged the notices to churches, blacksmith shops, and homes on the Pennsylvania Dutch frontier. Within two weeks, 155 fully equipped Conestoga wagons were at Braddock's camp. One of the wagonmen was twenty-one-year-old Daniel Boone, a Quaker born near Reading. Another driver was Daniel Morgan, the Jerseyman whose up-country riflemen would win the battle of Cowpens and lead the charges that won the battle of Saratoga for "those ragtag Continentals." The road that Lieutenant Colonel George Washington's militia chopped and graded across the Alleghenies that spring and summer was America's first wagon route to the West.

The drivers were forced to abandon the Conestogas after Braddock stupidly marched his men into a French and Indian ambush. A second train of Conestogas "gee-hawed" with the Forbes expedition of 1759 that cut a second road across the Alleghenies, captured Fort Duquesne, renamed it Fort Pitt, and gave Penn's Sylvania access to the Ohio River.

Weeks after the 1763 Treaty of Paris that surrendered Canada to the British, Benjamin Franklin—with a flourish typical of his suavity—launched a campaign for improvement of inter-colony highways. He took his daughter Sally to New York City, rented a one-horse chaise, and had a blacksmith fix an iron peg into the bottom of the vehicle opposite a wheel. Then a hardwood slat was pegged to one of the wheel spokes.

The slat clacked against the peg at each wheel turn. Franklin measured the circumference of the wheel, and short-divisioned the number of clacks per mile. Then the Franklins loaded armfuls of sharpened stakes beside their luggage and jogged off toward Boston. Franklin drove; Sally counted the clacks and shouted "Whoaaa" at the precise end of each mile. Franklin climbed down, scratched Roman numerals and capital letters on one of the stakes, hammered it into roadside dirt, and drove on.

Weeks later, a cart loaded with engraved slabs of stone creaked back along the trail from Boston. When the cart reached one of Franklin's stakes, the proper stone post was tamped in with its semi-spherical top eighteen inches above the ground. Engraved on the top of the post were the same mileage indicators that Franklin had scratched on the stake. Thus $\frac{NH}{XVI M}$ indicated that it was sixteen miles "to the clack" to New Haven. (That's how the Boston Post Road received its name.) Trains of red, white, and blue Conestoga wagons soon followed.

The excitement about the West that erupted after the 1763 peace treaty brought other triumphs for the Conestoga. The 1759 road built up by the Forbes expedition was widened and became the principal throughway between the Delaware and the head-waters of the Ohio. Wagon bodies were enlarged to carry three, even four, tons of freight. Processions of twenty to thirty vehicles averaged fifteen to twenty miles a day, and could make the round trip between Philadelphia and Pittsburgh in a month.

From the siege of Boston in 1775 to Cornwallis's surrender at Yorktown in 1781, Conestogas were the freighters of our regiments-of-the-line and state militia. Their red, white, and blue became a symbol of the long and desperate struggle for inde-pendence, and some historians believe this may have influenced the decision to make red, white, and blue the colors of our national flag.

Meanwhile, the British Admiralty tried to introduce the bank barn and the self-sufficiencies of the Germans' family farm in

New York's wilderness. In 1711, Queen Anne requested her ministers to find homes in the American colonies for three thousand Protestants from the Rhine Palatinate. The Admiralty, ignorant about botany in the American climate, decided to ship them to the Hudson Valley where they were to harvest sap from the pine forests and process it into turpentine, tar, and other ship stores.

The blunder was that there is not a turpentine-yielding pine within six hundred miles of the Hudson Valley. Nevertheless, the three thousand were set ashore midway up the valley and abandoned with some tools and provisions. The colony's government, they were assured, would find homes for them.

More than a thousand of the Palatines died from yellow fever, malaria, and starvation. In midwinter, one group struggled across the Catskill Mountains and settled in the Schoharie Valley. The rest lived in riverbank huts for almost ten years, until a treaty was made with the Five Nations Confederacy (now mistakenly called the Iroquois) for tracts of Mohawk Valley land west of Schenectady. There they became the Mohawk Dutch. Like their Pennsylvania kin, they built bank barns and big covered wagons and evolved self-sufficient farms. On the alluvial bottomlands of the Schoharie and upper Susquehanna valleys, they developed the most productive corn, wheat, and rye plantings of the Northeast. Mohawk Dutch Indian traders, called "bush runners," were prototypes for the heroes of James Fenimore Cooper's novels. The pungent cheddar cheese of the Mohawk Dutch, Liederkranz became famous from Boston to Long Island. (The cheese is named for a Mohawk Dutch singing society.) Communities took such nostalgic names as Palatine Bridge and Frankfort; the city names of Rhinebeck and Rhinecliff are memorials to the decade of suffering in the Hudson Valley.

The climate wasn't their only problem. When anti-tax protests of the 1770s fomented during our Revolutionary War, Scotch-Irish and English elitists in the Mohawk Valley convinced the Mohawks, Cayugas, Onondagas, and Senecas to remain loyal to Great Britain. Most of the Mohawk Dutch favored independence. They served with the New York militia and the regiments-of-the-line of the Continentals. In retaliation, Loyalist-Indian raids out of Fort Niagara massacred the women and children of valley villages and burned out the ripe grain fields of the Schoharie. General Nicholas Herkimer and hundreds of Mohawk Dutch died in the battles that in 1777 thwarted the British effort to conquer the valley.

Finally, in 1779, George Washington ordered a third of all his Continentals to join with New York militia in a burnout of the Indian homelands between what is now Rome and Niagara Falls. In the process of carrying out the order, the Americans would inadvertently discover a type of corn that became our favorite summertime vegetable.

The Clinton-Sullivan Expedition, as historians named it, razed the Indians' longhouses, chopped down fruit orchards, burned more than one hundred thousand tons of stored grain, and forced Indian survivors back to a "starving time" at Fort Niagara. Somewhere in the lovely Finger Lakes countryside, tradition says, soldiers discovered a variety of corn that was honey sweet and much juicier than field corn. Its ears were only six inches long; the cobs were so deep a scarlet that the water they were boiled in would permanently dye calico, wool, or linen.

No one knows where the white kernels of the new corn were first planted. The Massachusetts tale that "sweet corn" was first grown by a Clinton-Sullivan veteran at Plymouth has been disproven. Test plantings were probably first made in Mohawk valley, Pennsylvania, and New England gardens in 1780, since most of the expedition's veterans were farmers serving on three-month or one-year enlistments.

The first recorded reference to the corn appeared in Thomas Jefferson's Garden Book for 1810. No American President excelled Jefferson's breadth of curiosity or his devotion to gardening. Between 1805 and 1810, he built a terraced "kitchen garden" forty-five feet wide and a thousand feet long near his mountaintop mansion, Monticello. There he experimented with hundreds of edible plants, including several types of tomatoes and potatoes, and kept meticulous records of each planting, including an 1810 notation about "Sweet or shriveled corn in the NW corner, above Bailey's Walk." Seven years later, Timothy Dwight, the president of Yale University, wrote that "Maize of the kind called 'sweet' is the most delicious vegetable while in the milky stage of any known in this country."

"I regard all of these Indian sweet corns as tracing back to the Chullpi race of Peru," Paul C. Mangelsdorf, author of *Corn: Its Origin, Evolution and Improvement*, and paleobotanist at Harvard's Botanical Museum, wrote me in 1979.

> There is no evidence that any of the Indian tribes consciously crossed sweet corn with field corn to produce new varieties, but there is little doubt that hybridization occurred. Sweet corn was usually grown in small plots, but not well isolated from locally adapted field corn. There must have been sweet corn types segregating out of the crosses that resembled in some degree the field corn parents. . . .Whether or not the American Indian was a plant breeder in the sense that we know the term today, there is no doubt that the majority of Indian cultures did have sweet corn and that all modern varieties were derived from these.

Between 1780 and 1860, farmers succeeded in crossing the Iroquois sweet corn with field corn. This effort enlarged the ears and eliminated the scarlet dye of the cob. The kernels persisted in being creamy white, until a Greenfield, Massachusetts, gardener named William Chambers developed a variety with golden yellow kernels. During the 1880s, the Philadelphia seedsman, W. Atlee Burpee, bought the marketing rights for Chambers' seed and named the variety Golden Bantam.

By 1983 there were 650 open pollination varieties of sweet corn, plus thousands of hybrid varieties. The commercial land planted to sweet corn averages about 600,000 acres annually. From this, approximately 1½ billion pounds of the ears are marketed semi-fresh; another 5 billion pounds go into processing.

Many people are able to experience the greatest of all sweet corn delights every year when they twist an armful of ripe ears from stalks in the garden, hurriedly strip them, then plunge them into a kettle of boiling water. This July-to-September ecstasy is enjoyed in at least 90 percent of our 40 million home gardens.

The family farm was penetrating the South, too, between 1725 and 1800. There were three motivating forces: the independence of the Scotch-Irish; the invention of a Yankee schoolteacher; and George Washington's determination to introduce a more economical work animal.

The downfall of the Stuarts' regime in Great Britain brought shiploads of Scots to Georgia and the Carolinas. Most of them disdained the feudalism of the rice, tobacco, and indigo plantations and the turpentine and ship stores' camps on the coastal plain. Instead, they migrated beyond the rivers' fall-lines to the Appalachian foothills, where they discovered the feral herds of horses, cattle, and pigs.

Back in Charleston and Savannah the horse-wise immigrants had watched merchants and planters racing ponies on straight tracks a quarter mile long. Stocky but as nimble as jackrabbits, the ponies were called quarter horses and brought excellent prices at waterfront auctions. In the harbors, sloops and brigs loaded provisions for the West Indies plantations, where—it was common gossip—planters worked their horses mercilessly and took such poor care of them that replacements were necessary every year or so.

The Scotch and Irish soon developed a formula and tools to gather horses and livestock that would become legendary in Texas and the far West.

"Having selected a tract where cane and peavine grass grew more luxuriantly," John H. Logan relates in his *History of the Upper Country of South Carolina*, "the men erected in the midst of it temporary cabins and spacious pens. The pens were the enclosures in which to collect the wild stock for the purpose of

branding them. . . . The group was usually officered by a superintendent. . . . All of his sub-agents were active men, experienced woodsmen and unfailing shots at long or short sight
with a rifle. Finally a considerable area of land was cleared for
the cultivation of corn."

James Westfall Thompson compared the "cowpen" communities to "Miles City and Ogalalla in the palmy days of the western
cow country." Horse thieves and cattle thieves mingled with
honest men. Some of the pens contained two thousand cattle at
a time, as many hogs, and hundreds of horses. All of the stock
was branded with the cowpen's insignia. Colts were altered into
geldings and bull calves into oxen. A century and a half before
the "Rocky Mountain oyster" was jeeringly offered to green-
horns, bull calf testicles fried with wild onions were standard
fare in the cowpens. By 1750, the members of these crews were
routinely called "cowboys" from Savannah to the Potomac. (The
Spanish name *cimmarones* [wild ones] became the term for un-
branded animals.)

Quarter-path races, whip cracking demonstrations, bronc rides,
bundle-tie contests, and sharpshooting matches relieved the
boredom between roundups and trail drives in much the way
that rodeo games would develop in California and Texas.

Savannah and Charleston factors shipped horses, oxen, salt
pork, corned and smoked beef, leather, and other cowpen products to the West Indies. This surge of imports into the French-
owned islands lowered the prices the local *boucan* (wild bull)
hunters could ask, so some of them decided that a better, and
more exciting, livelihood could be swashbuckled from piracy.
But their victims continued to call them "boucaneers," a term
that Americans soon slurred into "buccaneers."

The feral stock of the Great Smokies bred so lavishly that trail
drives were pioneered to Salem and Wilmington, North Carolina. Soon they were extended into Virginia and, by the 1750s,
on to Baltimore, Philadelphia, New York, and Boston.

The most essential tool of a trail drive was the blacksnake whip.
It had a hardwood handle, preferably of cured hickory, a yard

long and two inches in circumference. A braid of leather ten to fifteen feet long was lashed to the tip of the handle by a linen cord. At the far end of the braid, a sliver of soft rawhide or boot leather was woven on. This tip piece was the "cracker."

A blacksnake whip, whirled rapidly above one's head, then flicked straight out with a simultaneous snap of the wrist, will cause the cracker to move so rapidly through an arc that it breaks the sound barrier and makes a noise as loud as a rifle shot. A good whipman can behead a rattlesnake from ten feet, trip a charging bull, or turn the leaders of a stampeding herd. Snapping a cheroot or pipe out of a friend's mouth, without touching the nose or lips, was a favorite cowpen showoff.

Hullooing and whipcracking through the seaport towns and across the tobacco and rice and indigo plantations, the drovers acquired a distinctive nickname derived from their whips. Townspeople began to call the drovers "Crackers." In time, the nickname would become a down-country sneer term for any farmer who wrested a living from mountain fields and forests, but it began as a term of jocular admiration, much as the term cowboy would emerge in the West a century later.

The eight years of the American Revolution cut off most of the export market for the South's tobacco, rice, indigo, and ship stores. In 1779, the British offered freedom to all American black slaves who would abandon their rebel masters and serve as sappers, wagonmen, and lackeys for the king. Thousands fled to the British encampments, served diligently, then migrated to Nova Scotia and Lower Canada with other Loyalists in 1783–85. In October, 1792, the first session of Upper Canada's new Parliament outlawed ownership of slaves in that vast territory. This action made it possible for runaway slaves to be smuggled up the Underground Railroad by the North's abolitionists to the "promised land" above Niagara Falls.

Many of the South's leaders, including Thomas Jefferson, favored emancipation and felt that the blacks deserved equal rights. Many of the South's most skilled craftsmen were black. Black cooks, black nursemaids, black carpenters and masons, black field workers, black grooms and wagonmen were the heart, blood, muscle, and soul of the plantation.

But in April, 1793, a young schoolteacher from Connecticut inadvertently perpetuated American slavery for seventy years. His name was Eli Whitney.

Whitneys had farmed beside the Boston–Springfield Bay Path for more than a century. Eli Whitney, Jr., was born December 8, 1765, two years after Ben and Sally Franklin had "posted" the road from New York to Boston. Family illness forced the boy to become the farm's handyman and tool tinker. He became so intrigued by the challenge of repairing old tools and building new ones that he won his father's permission to enter the new Yale University at New Haven and work for a degree as a Master Mechanick.

But job prospects were gloomy when he graduated in 1792. University officials persuaded him to hire out as a tutor on a rice plantation near Savannah, Georgia. The finest cabin on the packet ship he took south was occupied by Mrs. Nathanael Greene, ravishing widow of the general who had out-foxed Cornwallis and penned him in at Yorktown. Whitney became her shipboard favorite. When he learned in Savannah that the tutoring job had already been filled, she invited him to the plantation that Georgia had given her in tribute to the general.

Phineas Miller, manager of the Greene plantation, welcomed the opportunity of having a tool-wise guest around. The South needed a new crop, and there was a bang-up future in upland cotton—if somebody would just design a machine that could snag its seeds away from the fibers.

Planters on St. Simons and the other Sea Islands off Brunswick were becoming rich from crops of long staple cotton. The big bolls of these plants grew staples two inches long and as fine as China silk. Their black seeds grew loosely and dried so well that they could be rolled free from the fibers by using a *charkha*, an instrument from India that looked and worked like a wooden clothes wringer.

But sea island cotton wouldn't make a crop up-country. The

variety of cotton that would grow inland produced smaller bolls whose green seeds clung to the fiber like ticks to a hound. It took a slave a twelve-hour day to pull the seeds out of two pounds of the stuff. If Whitney could dream up a machine that would rake seeds away from the fiber of upland cotton, the South could raise more "tree wool" than the spinners of Europe ever dared dream about.

It took Whitney ten days to tinker up the first model of a cotton engine. He started with a sort of squirrel cage made from wooden slats set so close together that they almost touched. A handle extended out beyond a frame that had iron wires jutting up to the outer edge of the cage. Beneath the slats, a revolving brush was geared to turn when the cage did. The cage was filled with upland cotton bolls, then cranked. As the cage turned, the wires pulled cotton fibers out between the slats; the green seeds, still with wisps of fiber on them, continued to tumble inside the cage. The brush whisked the seedless fibers into a basket.

By April, 1793, Whitney had a horse-powered cotton engine that would clean fifty pounds of upland cotton a day. Mrs. Greene and Miller gave him funds so he could return North, obtain a patent, and find backers for a New Haven factory that would manufacture cotton engines.

The squirrel cage design was easy to copy. By 1795, more than a hundred bootleg cotton gins—the name cotton engine was shortened to cotton gin—operated in Georgia and the Carolinas; the South's export of cotton billowed from 1,601,000 pounds in 1794 to 6,276,000 pounds in 1795.

City speculators, younger sons of rice and indigo planters, and Charleston and Savannah factors began to study maps. By 1800, they were paying cash on the barrelhead for potential cotton land in Tennessee and Alabama. Cotton planters with processions of slaves and covered wagons filled with tools, bags of seed, and household goods began to invade the Mississippi's rich, black delta lands. Some of the wagons were drawn by long-eared, stubborn "mules." (This sterile cross of the donkey and the horse would become the most useful, and "plumb ornery," work animal of the South and West.)

George Washington, "Father of His Country," is also "father" of the American mule. When Washington retired to his Potomac Valley estate, Mount Vernon, in December, 1783, he resolved to devote the rest of his life to research for more effective livestock production. "The system of agriculture . . . if the epithet can be applied to it," he wrote from Mount Vernon to Arthur Young, editor of *Annals of Husbandry*, "which is in use in this part of the United States is as unproductive to the practicioners as it is ruinous to the landholders. Yet it is pertinaciously adhered to. To forsake it; to pursue a course of husbandry which is altogether different and new to the gazing multitude, ever averse to novelty in matters of this sort and much attached to their old customs, requires resolution, and without a good practical guide may be dangerous."

Washington's decision to "pursue a new and different course of husbandry" caused him to ask a shipowner friend whose vessels traded at Spanish ports to obtain "a good Spanish jack whose ability for getting colts can be assured." This shipowner told him that Spanish customs officials were under orders to "crush the testicles of all jacks exported out of Spanish territory."

Washington appealed to the Spanish consul in New York, who relayed the request to Madrid. During the summer of 1785, a jack and two jenny donkeys were landed at Portsmouth, New Hampshire, as gifts from King Charles III to "His Eminence, General Washington," then driven south over the post roads.

Washington's groom, Peter, named the jack Royal Gift. The animal stood fifteen hands high—taller than most stallions—and was proportionately sturdy in barrel and legs. But he adapted slowly to Virginia. That fall, Washington wrote his brother that Royal Gift "seems too full of Royalty to have anything to do with a plebeian race. Perhaps his stomach may come to him. If not, I shall wish he had never come from his Most Catholic Majesty's stables."

But by January, the jack was whinnying his acceptance of

Mount Vernon mares. On February 26, 1786, a Philadelphia paper carried Washington's advertisement that

> Royal Gift, a Jack Ass of the first race in the Kingdom of Spain, will cover mares and jennies the ensueing spring. The first for ten and the latter for fifteen pounds the season. . . . The advantages which are many, to be derived from the propogation of asses from this animal . . . and the usefulness of mules bred from a Jack of his size, either for the road or team, are well known to those who are acquainted with this mongrel race. For the information of those who are not, it may be enough to add that their great strength, longevity, hardiness and cheap support give them a preference to horses that is scarcely to be imagined.

Royal Gift had sired many foals by the time a jack named Knight of Malta and two Maltese jennies paced up the Mount Vernon driveway. With them a ship's captain brought a letter from the Marquis de Lafayette announcing that the animals were his gift and boasting that the jacks of Malta were "the best in Europe." Somebody leaked Lafayette's boast to the Spanish Ambassador. As a result, when Washington was presiding over the convention that drew up our Constitution, the Spanish Ambassador requested an audience and announced that "a surplus of jacks and jennies now exists in Spain and they can be delivered, in almost any quantity, to the United States at costs below the fifty dollars now being asked for a prime wagon horse."

During Washington's presidency, officials at the War Department decided it would be politic to buy some Mount Vernon mules for experimental use on commissary wagons and artillery caissons. But far greater demand came from the private sector— as a result of Whitney's invention of the cotton engine. The drudgery of clearing land for crops of upland cotton called for durable and disease-resistant animals. Hoof-and-mouth disease and other "critter plagues" had killed thousands of horses and oxen in the South's backcountry. But, gossip insisted, "a mule shakes off fevers as easy as a raccoon climbs a tree. And what's more, mules don't die until they're seventy-five—yes, even a hunnert years ol'." A $40 investment in a mule, then, would provide power for a lifetime of cotton crops; it could live on cottonseed meal and some hay.

Washington's promotion of the mule was one of the most timely hunches in American history. North and south, hundreds of thousands of Americans were gee-hawing west for freedom of virgin land. Cheap, durable work animals were essential.

Although "mulehead" and "mulish" came to mean the epitome of stubbornness, no work animal could match the mule's strength or durability. By 1850, more than half a million mules labored in the South, and Kentucky studs bred 65,000 animals a year. Mules from Mexico were standard equipment for wagon trains on the Santa Fe, Overland, and California trails. As agriculture pushed west, Missouri became the premier breeder of mules; "Missouri mule" became a national catch phrase. Between 1900 and 1915, the mule population of just three states—Missouri, Arkansas, and Oklahoma—rose to 1,315,000. Between 1,200,000 and 1,500,000 horses and mules died "in service" during the Civil War. More than 500,000 mules crossed the Atlantic to haul supplies and artillery during World War I.

Inability to pay long-overdue wages to army and navy veterans of the Revolution caused Congress to open sections of Ohio and Indiana for settlement as the Northwest Territory. The first wagon trains for the Ohio rolled out of Connecticut and Massachusetts during the summer of 1787. The wagon bodies were slimmer than those of the Conestogas. There weren't any arches of bells on the backs of the horses. But the white wagon hoods were in place. So were the huge wheels, the tool boxes, and the buckets of grease for lubricating axles. Fear of Indian attack in the New York and Ohio wilderness, plus Yankee reticence about "show off," caused the wagon bodies and wheels to be painted tan or dull green.

One of the expeditions assembled in Ipswich and Gloucester at the northern tip of Massachusetts Bay. Anticipating the plains of grass as "high as a horse's head for a thousand miles," the Gloucestermen called their Conestoga adaptation the "prairie schooner," after their own two-masted fishing boats. For almost a century, the prairie schooner would open new frontiers of land, flaunting banners of "Missouri or Bust!" "Colorado or Bust!" "California or Bust!"

Throughout the South, the rush for cotton lands forced Scotch-Irish stockmen and other determined homesteaders west into the mountains. Then plagues of tick fever, hoof-and-mouth disease, and other illnesses killed so many cattle and horses that hundreds of Crackers pioneered trails to Texas with their remaining quarter horses and Durham and Devon cattle; they soon adopted the name "ranch" for the family farm areas the Mexicans allotted them.

Others followed Daniel Boone's pack-pony trail through Cumberland Gap into the new state of Kentucky. Those who remained in the mountains bitterly resented the land exploiters and the feudal plantations. They defined freedom as "enough elbow room," used "we-uns" as equivalent to law, and heartily agreed with President Jefferson that "dependence begets subservience and venality, suffocates the germ of virtue and prepares fit tools for the designs of ambition." Eventually the nickname of "Cracker" became a plantation and city put-down for the proud mountain farmer, just as "forty acres and a mule" would symbolize the poverty and tribulations of the tenant farmer.

In the West, the family farm met challenges that even mule power could not overcome. Huge virgin forests shadowed valleys and mountainsides from the Susquehanna and Hudson rivers to central Ohio. Then, for a thousand miles, buffalo grass sent thick roots so deep into prairie loam that no wooden plow faced with scrap iron could penetrate them. Young, hungry cities like Pittsburgh, Cincinnati, and Louisville were developing at inland river junctions, while Boston, Philadelphia, Baltimore, Charleston, and the other older cities on the east coast demanded foods and fibers for their residents and for export. The forest, the prairie, and distant markets would inevitably turn the family farm toward dependence on iron, machines, and middlemen.

CHAPTER FOUR

Big Iron

From the St. Lawrence to Florida's Suwannee, a score of river systems drain the eastern slopes of our Atlantic seaboard barrier, the Appalachians. But down the western slopes of the Appalachians, only the Ohio sluices the runoff into the Mississippi. Water and trashwood snags swirl into the Ohio from the Allegheny, the Big Sandy, the Cumberland, and the Tennessee. Between 1780 and 1810, the 981 miles of the Ohio River valley became the boundary between the South's slave-powered plantation and the North's self-sufficient family farm.

New Englanders migrating to their land allotments in the new Northwest Territory traveled the Ohio River valley because, until the end of the War of 1812, British forces in Canada controlled the westward route up the Great Lakes. Their prairie schooners used trails across New York to the headwaters of the Allegheny River, where houseboats, appropriately named "arks," were built to carry wagons and livestock down rapids to the sandbars and snags of the Ohio.

Landseekers out of Pennsylvania, Maryland, Delaware, and

New Jersey used the Conestogas' road from Lancaster to Pittsburgh. The South's cattlemen and seekers of cotton land followed Daniel Boone's trail through Cumberland Gap or poled and roped arks and rafts down river rapids to Kentucky.

All the new West's pioneers were confronted by the dire problem of too much forest. For thousands of years, only storms, spring floods, and earthquakes had touched the forests that towered from the Great Lakes to the Gulf of Mexico in an arc often five hundred miles wide. Composting leaves and dead trees developed a rich brown topsoil. Trees and grass roots formed a subsoil sponge that absorbed rainfall and prevented excessive erosion. The spans of black walnut, hickory, chestnut, pine, and oak offered lavish summertime feeding and wintertime protection for bison, moose, varieties of deer, beaver, mink, and raccoon. Rattlesnakes, copperheads and other poisonous vipers favored the rocky gorges. Hundreds of varieties of berries, herbs, and wildflowers flourished in the forest's dim recesses.

Only rarely was there enough open space and sunlight to grow grains and vegetables or provide pasture for cows and horses. So fire, axes, and saws became the most essential tools of the pioneers. Fire was the quickest. Hundreds of thousands of acres of virgin timber were deliberately razed by fire. Scorched trunks became the lumber for cabins and barns. Tree limbs were trimmed and intermeshed into a type of zigzag fencing called "rattlesnake." Hickory made the best tool handles and chair rungs, black walnut and wild cherry produced the most attractive furniture, cedar built the most durable barns. The charcoal produced by the fires slowly fed minerals into the soil to enrich a few more years of bumper crops.

But without the roots of trees to bind together the particles of soil, erosion began. Rivulets, creeks, and rivers became murky with topsoil. Farmers and planters failed to follow the Pennsylvania Germans' method of replanting razed hillsides with fruit trees or shrubbery. Instead, they planted crops straight up and over hillsides. This left the soil without a sponge of roots during winter and spring. Melting snows dug gullies. Devastating

springtime floods and chocolate-brown rivers became, and remained, an American tradition. Topsoils that had taken millenniums to form rushed toward the Gulf of Mexico.

There were bumper crops, of course. Selling the surpluses was
the only hope for purchasing guns, ammunition, and "pleasur-
ables." The speediest trade route was down the Ohio and Mississippi to the French and Spanish bustle of New Orleans.

Rafts and keelboats carried the freight. The rafts were home-
built and could be manned by a crew of two. If they survived
the snags and whirlpools and sudden storms and river pirates,
they were sold for timber or firewood at the end of the journey.
In New Orleans, raft crews bought horses or donkeys to saddle-
bag their purchases, then walked home over a trail called the
Natchez Trace. Pirate gangs robbed and murdered many of them.

The keelboat was the only freight and passenger craft that could
be sailed, poled, and rope-hauled *upstream*. It averaged seventy
feet in length, had a ten-foot beam, and was pointed at each end.
The deckhouse held bunks, cargo space, and a tiny kitchen called
a "caboose." Two cleated boards, each a foot wide, hung out over
each side of the deck. These "running boards" enabled crewmen
using iron-tipped poles twelve feet long to literally push the boat
upstream. (The running boards on trolley cars and early automobiles took their name from this keelboat appendage.) Where
currents were swift and formed whirlpools, a gang was sent ashore
to tow the boat to calmer waters by use of a rope called a "cordell."

The "keeler" was "a lean and mean half hoss, half alligator,"
as adept at eye-gouging and groin kicks as he was with a cutlass
or a gun. His favorite costume was a low-crowned, broad-brimmed
hat of beaver felt; skin-tight breeches striped red, blue, purple,
and green; a homespun shirt; and a leather jacket.

The favorite drink of the keelers was an Ohio valley invention.
Pennsylvanians made a whiskey from rye, but rye was scarce in
Kentucky. So, during the 1780s, a Presbyterian minister decided
to use a corn mixture in his still. The result was a potent success,
which he named "bourbon" after the county where he circuit-
preached. Bourbon became the favorite "hard likker" of the South

and West. A jigger of it blended with sugar, mint, and ice made Kentucky famous as home of the mint julep long before anyone heard of Kentucky fried chicken.

Another itinerant preacher made a far greater, and multi-useful, contribution to the new West by introducing apple cultivation to Ohio, Kentucky, and Indiana. Born in Massachusetts in 1774, John Chapman studied for the ministry, then about 1800 resolved to spread the word about the values of interracial peace and the bounties of nature. A year's trek through frontier settlements convinced him that apple orchards were sorely needed.

Chapman learned that the Pittsburgh area had apple trees and cider mills. So, each fall, for the next forty years, the Reverend Chapman rode a skinny horse or mule into Pittsburgh to select seeds from the mash dumped out by cidermakers. He carefully sun-dried the plumpest and stored them in his saddlebags. Then, until the ground froze, he cleared plots at forest edges in Ohio, Kentucky, and Indiana and planted the seeds. From snowtime to blossomtime, he earned food and shelter by caring for the sick, leading prayer services, and presiding at the too-frequent funeral services for wives and children.

When his apple seedlings were knee high, he dug them up and saddlebagged them off to new farms. Sometimes he exchanged seedlings for packets of food or a piece of homespun clothing. Usually, though, he gave them away, asking only that the recipients listen to his talks about the graciousness of God's bounty and the urgencies for a brotherhood of all mankind. The Indians considered him a holy man and never disturbed his journeys. From Pittsburgh to the prairie edge in Indiana, the Reverend Chapman became beloved as "Johnny Appleseed." He died in Fort Wayne in 1845, leaving a heritage of orchards and apple recipes that have enriched the Midwest's cuisine for 150 years.

By 1810, more than 1,082,000 people lived west of the Appalachians; Kentucky, Ohio, and Tennessee became states. The greatest concern of these settlers was how to get their bumper-crop surpluses to market. The Conestoga road out of Pittsburgh was still the lifeline to the East; other routes were best suited for pack ponies. The British not only controlled the Great Lakes but were encouraging Indian tribes to ambush settlers and plunder their belongings. The bulk of trade, then, had to be downriver, but the round trip took six months—if you survived! Something had to be done, "real pert like!"

Kentucky's Henry Clay thought that another war with Great Britain might be the solution to clearing the way to the West. Urging his cause in Congress, he predicted that the Canadians would surely rebel against Great Britain and join the United States.

The Canadians, however, did not live up to Henry Clay's expectations. Hundreds of Loyalists who lost their American properties during the Revolution had fled north to the Upper Canada wilderness above Niagara Falls. So had the Iroquois, whose homelands in western New York had been razed by the Clinton-Sullivan Expedition in 1779. When the War of 1812 began, therefore, Loyalists and Indians had a score to settle. They quickly captured Detroit, then repeatedly defeated American forces in battles along the Niagara frontier and at the headwaters of the St. Lawrence.

In 1813, the battle tide began to turn. Troops led by Zebulon Pike, explorer of the Far West who gave his name to Pikes Peak, captured York (now Toronto), the capital of Upper Canada. A fleet built on the wilderness shore of Lake Erie enabled Captain Oliver Hazard Perry and crews of frontiersmen to defeat the British squadron that had ruled the four upper Great Lakes. The victories gave the United States a guarantee of "freedom of the Great Lakes" in the 1815 peace treaty.

Both the Perry victory and successive American victories near Niagara Falls were won with the help of a radically new type of gun invented by Eli Whitney. Whitney's new invention was as simple as his cotton gin had been, but the changes it motivated in American industry made it one of the most important discoveries of the nineteenth century.

The spur to the gun's invention was simple financial necessity.

After perfecting the cotton gin, Eli Whitney brooded in New Haven. Not only were bootleg gins destroying all hope of profit from his invention, but the factory he built for manufacturing cotton engines had burned down.

By 1798, however, the young Corsican general Napoleon Bonaparte had become dictator of France. Fearful for its overseas empire and faithful to the intermarriages of Europe's royalty, Great Britain became Napoleon's most relentless enemy. When French warships appeared off our coasts and shanghaied a few sailors from American merchant vessels, rumor spread that France was about to take Canada back from Britain—and then would invade the United States. Congress appropriated $800,000 for the purchase of cannon and "fifty thousand muskets."

Whitney read a newspaper article about the Congressional appropriation for the muskets and sighed. The army's arsenal at Springfield was able to manufacture only 150 muskets a year. Each part of a gun, from stock to trigger to barrel, had to be forged separately, then filed and polished until the pieces fit together. That was why a musket or rifle was as delicate as George Washington's wooden teeth. Whang it against a rock or let it become rusty and it was no good; it had to go back to a craftsman to be rebuilt. None of the parts were interchangeable. The right of the people to keep and bear arms, guaranteed in the new U.S. Constitution, didn't really say much when guns like that were the only ones available.

Weeks of trial and error convinced Whitney that guns could indeed be manufactured with interchangeable parts. He sent copies of his drawings to the Secretary of the Treasury with the request for a contract to manufacture ten thousand of the needed muskets.

Some members of President Adams's cabinet muttered in disapproval, but the contract was given, along with a five-thousand-dollar advance payment. The money enabled Whitney to rebuild his factory and to begin fashioning the necessary machine tools.

The first shipment of five hundred muskets was not delivered to Washington until September, 1801. Army inspectors and squads of militia gave the weapons a series of "bash-em-up" tests. Back to New Haven came the test results: "The finest muskets we have ever seen"; and "Any part of these guns can be replaced by a similar part from any other gun with a screwdriver and a few turns of the wrist."

The adaptability of the Whitney musket gave us an advantage over British infantry during the War of 1812. Whitney made the fortune denied him by the cotton-gin bootleggers. His startling concept of interchangeable parts also transformed American industry and launched the Machine Age. Before the Whitney musket, every part of every machine had to be hand-forged and hand-assembled. The engine and pulleys and sidewheels of Fulton's steamboat were made piece by piece, then ground and polished until they fitted together. Nails had square heads because each one had to be hammered out by hand. Horseshoes were hand-made by blacksmiths. But now, with this idea of Whitney's, machine parts could be cast by the hundreds or thousands from molds, trimmed and polished, then screwed together with a few turns of the wrist. The Colt revolver, the Winchester and Remington rifles, the new railroad engines—all used Whitney's notion. So did the manufacturers of hay rakes, shovels, pitchforks, sleds, and stagecoaches.

Down past new Cincinnati and Louisville during November, 1811, chuffed another recent invention, a steam-powered boat. The *New Orleans*, the new West's first steamboat, was financed and built by Nicholas Roosevelt (ancestor of both Theodore and Franklin D.). It was 116 feet long and powered by one of Robert Fulton's one-cylinder steam engines.

The night after the ship passed Louisville, massive earthquakes began to convulse the lower Ohio and central Mississippi valleys. Towns were washed away. The Mississippi changed its course. Islands sank and new ones oozed up. Reelfoot Lake was created in Tennessee. Preachers proclaimed that Roosevelt's "dragon-boat" had brought a curse by the Almighty. Mississippi navigation remained in chaos throughout the War of 1812. Safer and speedier transportation for the new West was not assured until Henry

Shreve invented the flat-bottomed sidewheeler steamboat in 1816.

The Great Lakes route to the West, now free from Canadian intervention, was open for steamship travel. Noah Brown, a Brooklyn shipbuilder, had blueprinted and supervised construction of Captain Perry's battle fleet from lakeshore forest during a bitterly cold winter. In the winter of 1817–18, Brown brought ship carpenters to Niagara to construct a two-masted schooner with paddlewheels amidship. Christened the S.S. *Walk-in-the-Water*, the vessel began the first steamship voyage of lakes Erie, Huron, and Michigan on August 23, 1818. Cleveland, Toledo, Detroit, Milwaukee, and Chicago became noisy ports.

To connect the new West with the cities of the East, New York began in 1817 its "big dig" of the Erie Canal from the Hudson River to Buffalo. Ohio mule teams also shoveled out a barge canal from Cleveland clear across the state to the Ohio River. Later, Michigan blasted the rocky passage for a ship canal to the solitudes of Lake Superior. Hard-eyed buyers for city wholesalers, land sharks, machinery salesmen, and marketing-for-cash soon followed.

The opportunities for more commerce, larger crops from larger farms, machines with easily interchangeable parts transported by the new steamboats and canals, the freedom of transit through the Great Lakes, the belch and growl of railroad trains, instituted a wave of patriotic fervor across the nation. Thomas Jefferson's devotion to classical architecture and the idealism of the ancient Greek Republic caused him to begin referring to the U.S.A. as "The New Greece." Public response was so enthusiastic that our 1816–40 period of social and economic development took the name of The Greek Revival Era.

While our ambassador to France, 1785–90, Jefferson "fell in love with"—as he confessed in letters home—the Graeco-Roman designs of ancient temples. He persuaded Virginia's legislature to use a Roman temple in Nîmes as model for the state capitol at Richmond, and was equally insistent on classical columns, domes, and gardens for the University of Virginia. During his presidency, Jefferson argued convincingly for Graeco-Roman designs of government buildings in the new national capitol, Washington. (A professor at Columbia University agreed with him. When given the task of choosing names for communities being established in upstate New York, he sprinkled the landscape with classical allusions—Troy, Ilion, Utica, Homer, Greece, and Ithaca—from the Hudson-Mohawk junction to Lake Erie.)

Deftly avoiding the fact that the ancient Greek republic depended on slave labor, politicians quoted Plato and Socrates as they proclaimed that the United States was the "New Greece—a revival of Democracy!" County courthouses and state capitols had to have a domed roof and a row of Doric or Corinthian pillars gracing their front porches. Village libraries were called athenaeums. Fervor for the New Greece stimulated community pride, enthusiasm for reading the classics, discussion groups, and even the concession that the theatre was not a device of the devil. The first magazines for farmers appeared. Rural horizons broadened; there were demands for better schools. Magazine and book learning hastened the adoption of the newly invented grain elevator and cast-iron plow.

The farmhouses that replaced the early settlers' log cabins had carved Greek pillars supporting the overhang of the piazza and were usually painted white with green or blue shutters. New barns were patterned on the Penn Dutch bank barns and daubed red. Big cornfields and pastures of timothy hay and clover allowed use of the Penn Dutch technique to fatten out cattle and pigs for the slaughterhouses in Cincinnati and Cleveland; soon Cincinnati shipped so much smoked and salted pork that it received the nickname of "Porkopolis."

The farms of the new West not only increased the yield they got from the cattle and pigs but also imported new varieties of farm animals. Henry Clay was the first to import England's finest beef animal, the Hereford, for his Kentucky plantation. Pennsylvanians developed the Chester County White breed of pig. New York's Robert E. Livingston wrote so glowingly about the merino sheep he had admired in Spain that Ohio and Michigan bankers agreed to lend up to a thousand dollars apiece for a ram and ewe shipped up the Lakes.

During this period, land in the new West began to acquire

value. There was often gunplay with squatters. Land sharks bought forested tracts of frontier for a few cents an acre, then parceled it off to newcomers at two and three dollars an acre. All in all, the Greek Revival era brought prosperity to the Ohio valley and the Northwest Territory. Despite factory-made wagons and rakes and cast-iron plows, farm men and women and children still depended on the skills of their hands; hired laborers were called "hands."

The agriculture that developed in the Ohio valley after the ravaging of its virgin forests established the Quaker-Palatine patterns of family farm as the best and most economical for our Midwest. Kentucky's hams, bourbon, horses, and tobacco, like Ohio's sage sausage, grape pie, apple butter, and the delectable Indiana gingerbread called "Hoosier bait," heralded the variety and prosperity of the region's farms and plantations. North of the Ohio River, farms averaged 150 acres per family. South of the river, the slave-powered plantation prevailed until the Civil War.

However, New Greece was for the young. The average lifespan was less than thirty-five years. Malaria, yellow fever, and typhoid lurked in the waterways. Infected raw milk killed thousands. Most of the heat from fireplaces went up the chimneys; pneumonia was commonplace. The few circuit-riding doctors knew no effective remedy against venereal disease. Almost-annual pregnancies weakened mothers' resistance against infections and tuberculosis. More than 30 percent of the babies died before they could learn to walk. Workdays stretched from sun-up to candlelight.

West of Fort Wayne and Indianapolis, nature posed a frightening challenge for families accustomed to forests, mountains, and bucolic valleys. Coarse, shoulder-high buffalo grass shimmered for more than a thousand miles, all the way to the blue-black thrust of the Rocky Mountains. This was the prairie, aftermath of a glacier that had straddled the northern half of the continent millenniums before. Its only contrasts were the zigzag stitching of cottonwoods, willows, and brush that hugged the banks of creeks and rivers. Each spring and summer, thunderheads scythed the black blades of tornadoes across its vastness; lightning fired its brown matting. In winter, snowstorms found room to become howling blizzards.

Unbelievably rich soil lay beneath the grass blanket, but the roots were so tough and so intertwined that no hoe or iron plow could penetrate them. The U.S. Patent Office issued 124 patents on designs, shapes, and castings for "prairie plows" before 1830—all of them were failures. One model required a team of ten oxen to haul its pointed wooden beam and two-wheel truck, but turned only a shallow furrow that grass sub-roots soon conquered. Plows made from cast iron proved to be back-breakers. Earth and roots clung to the rough surface of the metal. Every hundred feet, or less, it was necessary to stop the team, pull the plow out of the furrow, and dig away a sticky mass of roots and grass stems.

Steel finally conquered the prairie. John Deere, a Yankee blacksmith from Rutland, Vermont, migrated to Grand Detour, Illinois, in 1837, set up his anvil and bellows, and soon had waiting lines of wagons carrying plows with broken shafts, sheared points, or cracked moldboards. He decided to try covering a moldboard with a sheet of saw steel. It worked. By 1841, Deere had so many orders for steel plows that he gave up the smithy and built a plow factory in nearby Moline. Within a few years, Deere & Company produced ten thousand steel plows annually.

In opportune sequence, Cyrus McCormick arrived in Chicago during the summer of 1847. Sixteen years before, in a wheat field near his father's blacksmith shop at Walnut Grove, Virginia, McCormick had first demonstrated his invention of a wheat harvester. Powered by one horse, the machine's saw-toothed knife snipped ripe wheat off at the base of the stalks. The harvester was so successful that McCormick wished to build a manufacturing plant for it in the West. Within a month, bankers had pledged enough in loans for him to build the largest factory west of Pittsburgh. More than a thousand harvesters rolled off the assembly line in 1851.

Steel plows, patented grain drills, and McCormick harvesters were already changing the northern Illinois, Iowa, and western Missouri prairie from buffalo grass to corn and wheat in 1852. During the early summer of that same year a steamboat unloaded scores of crates that would also change the face of the frontier. The cargo, daubed with French legends, was greeted at the Missouri River docks of Fort Leavenworth by a train of fifty-two ox teams and covered wagons waiting to trek the shipment up the Overland Trail to Salt Lake City.

John Taylor, the person who shipped these crates, had been in France winning converts for the Mormons' Church of Jesus Christ of Latter-day Saints when he heard rumors about the prizes Napoleon Bonaparte had offered in 1809 for ways to offset the shortages imposed by the British blockade of French ports. Imitation coffee roasted from chicory, a method of preserving food by canning it, a candle that burned much longer because of its twisted wick, and saltpeter made from urine were among the French discoveries during 1810–14. But the technique that excited Bishop Taylor was a method for making sugar from the juice of the large white beets long used for livestock food.

Sugar cost a dollar a pound in Utah. Taylor wrote Brigham Young and the church councilmen to recommend that beet-sugar machinery and seeds be purchased. Back came an authorization, along with a letter of credit for $12,500.

Taylor's purchase was the shipment the ox train picked up at the Leavenworth dock. The gee-haw creak up the Platte and Sweetwater and through the agate gleam of South Pass took six months. The new sugar factory began its first boil-down in the late fall of 1853, but produced only a bitter inedible syrup. The frustrations continued for twenty-six years until, in 1879, H. H. Dyer perfected a technique for producing white or brown crystals and edible syrups in his laboratory at Alvarado, California. Thereafter, every mission colony established by the Latter-day Saints from Michigan to Oregon planted sugar beets and built a sugar house.

By the 1980s, our sugar beet crop has grown and now occupies an average of a billion and a quarter acres, with a fieldside value of $700 million—thanks to Napoleon, John Taylor, and the Latter-day Saints.

By 1859—when Republican strategists were brooding over Abe Lincoln as their next presidential candidate, and Dan Emmett composed a song he called "Dixie" for a New York City minstrel show, and John Brown was plotting a raid out of Kansas that he believed would finally free all of the South's slaves—the United States had divided into four agricultural "belts."

The Northeast, rooted in brown podzolic soil, had become a region of self-sufficient farms with grain fields, truck gardens, chicken yards, dairy cows, horses, hillside bands of sheep, families of foraging pigs, woodlots, and big-hipped barns.

From Pennsylvania to Missouri, farms of 100–250 acres specialized in corn and the new Lucerne grass (alfalfa), Poland China and Chester County White pigs, beef cattle, dairy cows, and thousands of horses and mules. During 1859, Mississippi steamboats paddled $6 million worth of flour, $14 million worth of pork, $1.5 million worth of bourbon, and hundreds of deckloads of machinery downriver to cotton, rice, and cane-sugar plantations.

As James Westfall Thompson reported,

> It was estimated in 1845 that southern planters had in the preceding twenty years expended $900 million in the north for horses, mules, cattle, sheep, hogs, hay and farm implements. Each year ten thousand horses were driven from the Middle Atlantic states into the south to stock plantations. . . . The south, because it raised only 10 percent as much hay as the north, had to buy feed outside its borders. . . . The old cowpens acquired a new lease on life. They became stands for the overnight care of thousands of cattle and pigs driven through each season from the north.

C. C. Clay of Alabama mourned,

> I can show you, in the older portions of Alabama and in my native county of Madison, the sad memorials and exhausting

culture of cotton. Our small planters, after taking the cream off their lands, unable to restore them by rest, manure or otherwise are going further west and south in search of other virgin lands which they may and will despoil and impoverish in like manner. Our wealthier planters, with great means and no more skill, are buying out their poorer neighbors, extending their plantations and adding to their slave force. The wealthy few, who are able to live on smaller profits and give their blasted fields some rest, are thus pushing off the many who are merely independent.

In the Midwest, a belt of corn, wheat, and livestock had begun to move up the river valleys of Kansas and Nebraska, although geographers warned that rainfall west of the Missouri was so undependable that the entire area should be labeled "The Great American Desert."

Wheat flourished in California, too, now that the madness of the Gold Rush was simmering down to mines and a hydraulic gouging of hillsides. John Bidwell sensed the region's richer future. A Missouri farm boy, Bidwell arrived by wagon at John Sutter's colony in the upper Sacramento valley in 1841. Awed by the botanic wonderland the Franciscans had created around their missions, he began to experiment with apple, peach, and plum orchards. When the cry of "Gold!" echoed in 1848, he packed off to the North Fork of the Feather River and, on July 4, made one of the big strikes of the year. He sold the claim and invested the profits in promising fruitland seventy-five miles north of Sacramento. His Rancho El Chico became a grandsire of California's fruit and nut industries, with 400 varieties of trees on the 1,800 acres of its experimental plot. The ranch also pioneered the state's raisin and olive production. Although he had developed several varieties of wine grapes, Bidwell ordered them plowed up when he converted to the Temperance Movement. (Years later he was the Prohibition Party candidate for President.)

But whether they grew grapes or corn or cotton or pork, the

producers of the nation's food and fiber were coming face to face with a form of techno-serfdom. Whitney's cotton engine and interchangeable parts concept, McCormick's harvester, Deere's steel plow, the Moore-Hascal threshing machine, Gibbons's grain drill—all constituted a calliope leading a parade of middlemen and "Big Iron" into agriculture.

Chicago's muddy sprawl at the foot of Lake Michigan was a noisome example of the new farm-plantation-ranch dependence on toolmakers, millers, meat packers, railroads, bankers, wholesalers, real estate speculators, and, inevitably, chain stores and exporters. Nevertheless, while vowing devotion to "our noble sons of the soil" and jerry-building a bureaucracy of "agricultural specialists," neither federal nor state governments would encourage a marketing system cooperatively controlled by producers or interfere with the machinations of what they preferred to call free trade.

Founded at the clay mouth of a river, Chicago by 1852 was a maelstrom of refugees from Central Europe's revolutions and adventurers heading for California gold when the first railroad trains from the East belched in. Livestock prices soared. Pens and slaughtering sheds were hammered up along the river. By 1854, hog and cattle prices from the Ohio to the Missouri valley were based on "Chicago offers."

A city ordinance sent the meat packers to a new location along the South Branch of the Chicago River, where the Union Stockyards grew into the nation's largest. The screams of dying animals still echoed back across midcity. The sky was usually black with fumes from lard-rendering vats, and the air pungent with the reek of decaying offal, rawhide, and clotting blood. The city council found it necessary to "flush the sluggish Chicago River by pumping water from the canal in order to cleanse it from the filth deposited by slaughterhouse men who so corrupt the water as to make it stink unbearably at every turn of the paddlewheels of the numerous steamers upon it."

Chicago's hunger called for more corn, more cattle, and more pigs after the refrigerator car was invented and meat trains began to supply eastern markets. St. Louis saw the opportunities, so the slaughterhouses and shantytown whorehouses of East St. Louis evolved. Des Moines, Omaha, Kansas City, Denver, and St. Paul followed the example. Dollar economy was in the saddle.

CHAPTER FIVE

Tenements and Middlemen

A gold "talent" in Homeric Greece was worth one ox. In both Latin and early Saxon, the same words were used for "money" and "cattle." Barter for agricultural products was the initial form of value exchange. But when cities began to huddle thousands of families behind grim walls, the urgency grew for middlemen professions to step in and negotiate between consumers and producers. Subsequently, money abandoned its agricultural roots and became pieces of metal or paper stamped with emblems and numerals. The United States reenacted this changeover from barter to cash-and-credit between 1815 and 1840.

Most agricultural trade during the colonial and post-Revolution periods was based on barter. The word "swap," meaning originally "to strike hands in a bargain," became so popular that it had a score of definitions, including "cheating" and "the semicircular buck of a wild horse." Farm products were swapped for essential metals, minerals, and imports. The South's planters exchanged tobacco, indigo, rice, and cotton exports for European furniture, clothing, and luxuries via the wholesale traders called "factors." (The word *factory* originated with them.) The Yankee swapped horses and cured meats in the West Indies for the sugar and molasses that enabled him to distill rum and enter the West African slave trade. Any coinage that came from these swaps was usually hidden away in the home or buried out back for emergencies or to amass as an inheritance.

The steamboats, canals, and railroads that penetrated the new West after 1815 not only transformed agriculture's economics from barter to cash and credit, but offered non-slave youngsters the choice of homesteading farther west or seeking hard-money employment in the burgeoning cities.

After 1790, inheritance of land became a major agricultural problem. Between 1609 and 1790, our national population reached a total of less than four million. Between 1790 and 1840, the United States population more than quadrupled to 17,069,453. But fewer than one million were recent immigrants. Most of the rest were farm and plantation bred. A "passel of kids" was the most economical way to obtain a labor force. Agriculture's children began helping with chores soon after they learned to walk and were considered capable of a good day's work by the time they were twelve. The British tradition of primogeniture persisted; property was inherited by the eldest son. Younger sons were on their own before they were sixteen. Daughters who survived disease, field work, kitchen work, snake bites, and the drunken brawls that erupted at county fairs and revival meetings were either married off before they were eighteen or fled to the nearest city to become seamstresses, waitresses, or whores.

The cities grew faster than Chester pigs on a corn-and-clover diet. The Conestoga freight road from Pittsburgh and the efficiencies of Pennsylvania farms enhanced the importance of Baltimore and Philadelphia as seaports. The Erie Canal's cornucopia of new West harvests helped turn New York City into a metropolis. Irish and German refugees from famine and civil wars landed at Boston and New York. (When the Civil War began in 1861, New York could rightfully boast that it was the largest Irish city on earth.) A half dozen cities mushroomed along the Erie Canal route. New England, with three cities in 1800, boasted of twenty-six in 1860. Philadelphia jammed 400,000 on its malarial thumb of land between the Delaware and Schuylkill rivers. Wilmington, Richmond, Charleston, Savannah, and New Orleans became trade and factory centers for the South. Cincinnati, fattened by butchers, tobacco, bourbon, and riverboats, so increased its real estate values that the twenty-three acres of land Nicholas Longworth took in swap for two copper stills in 1810 were valued at two million dollars in 1860. Toledo, Cleveland, Detroit, Milwaukee, Chicago, St. Paul, Minneapolis, St. Louis, Memphis, and Natchez—all added to the garish clamor along inland waterways.

A total of 140,000 manufacturing plants muddied the skies and waterways between Boston and Baltimore. Alongside them, tenement housing stretched to the horizons. Few of these gloomy buildings had yards or storage cellars or central heating or insulation or fire extinguishers. Many of the squalid rooms were without sunlight. Here, in walk-up apartments of one or two rooms, immigrant families and homesick surplus youngsters from the farms set up housekeeping while they worked out apprenticeships at factories, slung freight on the docks, stooped twelve to fourteen hours a day and six days a week over looms, sewing machines, drills, and ledgers.

The tenements functioned on a money economy. Few landlords would permit credit, and certainly none would barter for their dreary rooms. Shopkeepers would not permit credit until the applicant demonstrated that he or she was a solid citizen who could hold a job. There was neither room nor job-free time to garden, and no storage space or refrigeration for more than a one- or two-day supply of food. The new urbanites quickly learned that although our national currency bragged "In God We Trust," the economic edict was "In $$$ We Trust."

Some cities established cobblestoned areas where regional farmers could bring vegetables, fruits, cheese, butter, meats, homemade pies and jams and breads to sell from wagon tailgates.

These areas were also open to importers of citrus from Italy, bananas from the West Indies, and even occasional casaba melons packed in sawdust that had endured the voyage from Africa. Faneuil Hall Market in Boston was a redolent experience, as was Washington Market in lower Manhattan and the Reading Railroad's Terminal Market in Philadelphia. Pushcart vendors bought their supplies at these markets, then hawked them through tenement alleys at a 50-percent increase in price.

But most fruits and vegetables were available only in season. Between September and May, tenement diets were limited to cabbage, turnips, a few carrots, apples, nuts, fish, and a little meat. Most of the meat was salted or smoked. Although every riverbank and lakeshore north of Virginia had warehouses filled with hundred-pound cakes of ice buried in sawdust, this luxury was expensive; wagons rumbled it to the polished oak and walnut iceboxes in the kitchens of bankers, factory bosses, and merchants. Bacon, salt pork, smoked sausages, dried beef, liverwurst, bologna made from meat scraps and gristle, and scrawny chicken were the poor man's meats—with a rib roast of beef for Christmas and a salty ham for Easter.

Cow's milk, the urban housewife of 1800–60 believed, was normally a pale blue. Milk was too sensitive to summer heat, winter cold, and excessive jostling on dirt roads to be wagoned in from the farms. Consequently, it became a by-product of breweries. Beer, the oldest alcoholic brew, is processed from hops, malt, and reasonably clean water. The waste product of fermentation, called "slops," is excellent cow feed. In every American city, drovers brought cows in from farms and sold them to breweries. Sheds behind the brewery shielded rows of stanchions that faced wooden troughs connected to the brewery's stills. Once clamped in a stanchion, a cow stayed there until it died. And it subsisted on the lukewarm slops drooling out of the stills. Work gangs milked the animals twice a day, and occasionally shoveled and sloshed away their manure. The pails of milk were dumped into metal drums, sweetened with molasses, then thinned out with water until the mixture was a pale blue.

No one knows how many deaths city milk caused, but the way it was produced makes it probable that it caused as many deaths as yellow fever, malaria, typhoid, tuberculosis, and other killers of the nineteenth century.

Seasonal vegetables and fruits, salty meats, and blue milk were pretty much the range of choices in the diet of the urban worker. But dramatic innovations in food preservation techniques would soon improve both the variety and quality of the urban diet. A French baker, a British tinsmith, and the official surveyor of Texas pioneered the changes.

Nicholas Appert was the chef and owner of a bakery at Massy, near Paris, when Napoleon offered a series of prizes for ways to offset the shortages of imported supplies caused by the British blockade. Appert decided to try for the twelve thousand francs promised for a new method of preserving food. Experiments convinced him that sealing boiled vegetables in a jar prevented fermentation. He won the prize and used the money to build the world's first canning factory. The containers he used were wide-mouthed bottles that were sealed with chunks of Portuguese cork.

Appert's canned goods markedly reduced scurvy in the French army and navy. The British soon learned of the technique and copied it, but decided that iron cannisters coated with tin were more practical. William Underwood, an English migrant to Boston, was the first canner in the United States. He remained faithful to his homeland by labeling his containers of lobster, cranberry jelly, pickles, and preserves, "Made in England." During 1848, Nathan Winslow of Portland, Maine, successfully canned sweet corn for use on the two- and three-year voyages of whaling ships. Seven years later, processors in Baltimore canned Maryland sweet corn—which they labeled "Best Maine Corn"—then began experimenting with canned peas, carrots, plums, and peaches. In 1860, an Ohioan named Thomas Duckwell braved the prejudices against the poisonous love apple by marketing tin canisters of tomatoes. (Inevitably, Americans abbreviated "tin canister" to the familiar "tin can.")

The filthy blue milk peddled by breweries was abolished through the persistence of another pioneer in food preservation, Gail Borden. A native of upstate New York, a schoolteacher in Indiana, then a government surveyor in Mississippi, Borden wagoned his family to Texas to become the colony's official surveyor. He edited the Lone Star Republic's only newspaper during the war against Mexico, and by the time covered wagons bound for California began creaking over the Ox-bow Trail, he was agent of the Galveston City Company.

As he watched hollow-eyed men toss a filch of bacon, a ham or two, and sacks of wormy corn meal over a wagon's tailgate as vittles for the two-mile-an-hour journey across Texas and Arizona, Borden reached a decision: he would invent a non-perishable food that these travelers could take with them on their journey west.

Evenings at home Borden built a food drier to fit over the fireplace. Then he chopped strips of sun-dried beef, mixed it with corn meal and milk, and dried it stone-hard. Inedible! He started over again. Months of experimenting produced a dried beef biscuit that would store in a cotton sack without developing maggots. He invested all his savings in a company to manufacture the biscuit.

Borden Beef Biscuits brought so much praise from wagon trains that a group of provisions contractors for army posts in the Southwest began dickering for priority rights. Borden decided to take samples of the biscuit to the London Fair of 1851, where he might make contracts with suppliers for British colonies in Africa and Asia.

The biscuit was awarded a blue ribbon by the London Fair commissioners. Borden was discussing several contracts when a letter from Galveston informed him that the group of army contractors had stolen his formula, formed their own company, and, by means of political chicanery, had forced Borden's factory to stop production. He packed his trunks and booked passage to New York.

The sailing ship carried more than a hundred families of German, Swedish, and Irish immigrants eager for the riches of America. Borden found himself peering down from the hurricane deck at the shawled figures and feeling the same sadness he had experienced when he watched the forty-niners provisioning their wagons in Galveston. Some of these people would die from disease or polluted food and be buried at sea. Within a few weeks, the survivors would vanish into the grime of New York tenements or squeeze onto the plank seats of immigrant trains swaying toward Wisconsin and Minnesota. Most of them were pink-cheeked farm people, used to the rich milk of goats, milch cows, and sheep, to turnips and cabbages and greenstuff. What could be done to assure a healthier diet for these steerage immigrants and for a family huddled in a room on the fourth floor of a walk-up tenement?

In New York City, Gail Borden wandered from his hotel up Third Avenue to the pens and manure piles alongside the Bull's Head Tavern. This was the infamous auction yard owned by Daniel Drew. An upstate livestock buyer, Drew had made a fortune feeding salt to cattle, horses, and hogs during the plod into Manhattan and then, the night before they were to be auctioned, letting them guzzle all the water they could hold. The water sleeked the cattle out enough to sell them as prime stock. The manure odors of the auction yard blended with the sour stench that eddied from the Greenwood Dairies down the street, where two hundred cows were stanchioned beside a brewery slop-trough.

Again, Borden reached a decision. He hurried home to Galveston to salvage the remnants of his estate and explain his new goal to his family, then returned north to Lebanon, in the Berkshire foothills of New York. There, in gabled, barn-big communes, more than five hundred celibate Shakers were experimenting with methods and handicrafts to improve agricultural efficiency. They had already devised a way to test vegetable seeds so that a guarantee of the percentage of germination could be printed on each paper packet they marketed. Experiments with cheese making and canning methods were pursued in sunlit laboratories.

The Shaker leaders nodded after hearing Borden's idea and offered him bed, board, and use of their laboratories—without requiring him to join their church. Borden boiled and dried hundreds of pans of milk—then threw away the murky results. He curdled milk with vinegar, thickened it with flour, baked it with corn meal. At the end of three months he was no closer to a palatable preserved milk than he was when staring at the pitiful prisoners of Greenwood Dairies.

A Shaker chemist suggested that Borden try the vacuum pans that the community used to process sugar. That worked. Late in 1853, Borden was in Washington petitioning for a patent on condensed milk. A bureaucratic delay dragged on for three years, however, before the patent was granted in 1856. Jeremiah Millbank, a Wall Street broker, advanced funds to build a factory at Wassaic, New Jersey, and to install rows of vacuum boilers plus a tinsmith shop where cans could be hammered out and soldered.

By the time Brigadier General Thomas Jackson won the nickname of "Stonewall" during the Confederate victory at Bull Run, Virginia, and made it obvious—even to Congress—that the Civil War would rage for years, the Borden Condensed Milk Company was selling a thousand tins of condensed milk a week to New York and New Jersey grocers. A week after Bull Run, the War Department commandeered the firm's entire output "for the duration."

Meanwhile, housewives in cities had learned that cow's milk was not naturally blue. They demanded, and won, deliveries of fresh milk by railroad and steamboat. One by one, the brewery cowyards closed. Banks financed new creameries that established milk-collecting stations throughout New York, New Jersey, and Connecticut. Their one-horse carts, painted white, jogged shiny canisters of farm-fresh milk, crocks of cottage cheese, and tubs of salty butter to tenement and mansion and corner grocery throughout Manhattan, Brooklyn, and even Yonkers.

But the middlemen's usurpation of agricultural markets via the tin can, centralized processing, and shrill salesmanship about the great advantages of iron and steel farm machines eventually crippled the farmer's self-sufficiency and made him as dependent on money as the workers in city sweatshops and tenements. Town and village banks burrowed greedily into agricultural life. Interest rates of 20 percent were demanded for the loans farmers needed to modernize equipment, dig a well, buy a few of those new breeds of Red Guinea pigs or Shorthorn cattle. If crops failed during a dry spell, or news of an Eastern panic frightened the bankers, they snapped the loans back or foreclosed. Grocers, lumbermen, machinery salesmen—all charged 15 or 20 percent interest on overdue bills. The burgeoning Dollar Economy caused farm publications to warn: "A farmer should shun the doors of a bank as he would the plague or cholera. Banks are for traders and men of speculation and theirs is a business with which farmers should have little to do!"

Middlemen also caused conflict between the farm and the ranch types of agriculture after the Civil War. Impoverished by the Civil War, Texans had driven thousands of scrawny longhorn cattle through Indian territory to railroad sidings in Kansas and Nebraska. There the animals were fattened on high plains grasses. Soon cattle ranches were being established as far north as Montana.

Meanwhile, railroads were promoting the sale of huge blocks of trackside land the federal government had granted them. Their lavishly colored posters and the guest speakers they imposed on Sunday school picnics and town meetings promised prosperity and harmony for farmers who settled on the "virgin croplands of the Golden West." Thus the farmers' need for cropfields and the ranchers' need for open range met at the tracksides of the Union Pacific and the Atchison, Topeka & Santa Fe railroads.

Joe Glidden left a schoolteaching job in New Hampshire to earn a fortune in the golden West and was lucky enough to acquire a six-hundred-acre farm near De Kalb, Illinois. During a visit to the county fair in 1873, his friend Jabor Haish urged him to come on over for a look at the "crazy fencing" being exhibited by an Eastern blacksmith named Rose. Rose had snipped iron wire diagonally into three-inch pieces, then twisted each barbed piece around long strands of wire. The pieces could be pushed back and forth like the counters on an abacus. It wouldn't be worth a tunket in a prairie wind! But the idea of running barbs along a wire fence had potential as a protector of cropfields and a deterrent to open-range livestock.

That winter both Glidden and Haish tried methods for holding barbed pieces tight on a wire. Both men were granted patents, although their schemes for holding the barbs between two twisted strands of horizontal wire were similar. Two years later, George C. Baker of Des Moines patented a machine that automatically cut the barbs and wove them into the wire. Eastern steel mills bought manufacturing rights and began promoting "the barbed wire fence." Farmers responded with enthusiasm.

Farm by farm, the spiked stuff was hammered into the grasslands that ranchers were claiming as open range. Arguments led to gun fights and bullying tactics that writers for Eastern publishers would hyperbolize into "wars." Time and again, commanders of army posts had to send out cavalry or infantry units to enforce a truce. Barbed wire became a major influence on the cowboy and badman legends that novelists and movies built into an American saga.

But before long, cattlemen too accepted the efficiencies of the spiked iron wire. "Fence riding" became a monotonous cowboy chore. By 1890, barbed wire was so commonplace that it sold for $4.80 per 100 pounds in Utah. Windmills, steel plows, irrigation ditches, and barbed wire hastened the twentieth-century dust storms and topsoil erosion that would transform much of the trans-Missouri West into the Great American Desert the geographers had predicted in 1810.

Rusty scraps of barbed wire, rusty tin cans, broken bottles, broken machine parts, burlap bags, and earthenware jugs became routine litter on farms and along roads and creek banks. Lockjaw, blood poisoning, leg and arm infections, and disease germs multiplying in garbage heaps and barnyard litter took a greater toll of human life than all the cattlemen wars, cowboy shootups, badmen, Indian wars, and rattlesnakes combined.

Back in the cities, as middlemen intensified their control of agricultural production and distribution, advertising agencies extolled the glass bottle, the paraffined cardboard container, foil and plastic wrappings as essentials of sanitation and efficiency. But the "sanitary efficiency" became trash that littered streets, fouled waterways, and eventually became "fills" on swampland and sandbanks so that more walk-up tenements could be built.

Jim Carpenter summarized it one afternoon in 1970 as we stood atop the Continental Divide in Wyoming's South Pass. Beer bottles, plastic bags, rusty cans, wads of newspaper and foil fouled the massive base of Oregon Buttes. The Buttes won its name in the 1840s. About where we stood, the Overland Trail had split. Still visible wagon tracks arced northwest to etch the beginning of the Oregon Trail. Due west along Sandy Creek, other wagon tracks memorialized the Mormons' trail to their "promised land" and the route of the forty-niners to "golden California." When wagonmasters gee-hawed up the grassy valley to the Buttes, they pointed northwest and shouted, "Ho for Oregon!"

Jim had been a deputy sheriff in South Pass for three decades. He reminisced,

> When I first came up here as a kid, I could walk three or four miles to the base of the Buttes on big glowing chunks of Sweetwater agate, fossilized wood and jade. Didn't have to step on any grass. Walked on jewelry all the way.
>
> Science was still in kindergarten in those days. An automobile was something to gawk at. A lot of that litter over there hadn't been invented. But it was invented later. Then the tourists and the lapidary wholesalers drove in. They took all of the agate and fossil wood and jade and left that trash. One of our most awesome, and meaningful, historical shrines became a garbage dump. Science litters on!

I could only nod agreement. Between 1800 and 1860, our pioneering scientists and engineers struggled against religious prejudice and folklore to win public acceptance. They opened brave new vistas of physics, chemistry, mechanical power, sanitation, abundance for both agriculture and the cities. But the technology spawned by applied science brought erosion, poisonous fumes, litter, drought, as well as bombs powerful enough to turn the planet into a wasteland. Applied science also strengthened the middleman, crippled the individualism of the family farm, made self-sufficiency outmoded, and built up a plastic wall of segregation between the producer and the consumer.

CHAPTER SIX

The Birth of Natural Science

Ignorance was the initial, and greatest, despoiler of the American land's virgin richness. For two and a half centuries, the founding fathers and their land-hungry heirs ruthlessly burned forests, depleted the chemical wealth of topsoils, let hillsides and cropfields erode, saw livestock sicken and die and rivers turn muddy—all because scientific method was unknown. Throughout the development of the ranch, the plantation, and the family farm, no one knew about photosynthesis or microbes or vitamins or trace elements. The Alleghenies, the prairies, and the high plains were conquered and fenced before people understood the intricate interplay of sunlight, carbon dioxide, water, and minerals.

The decades between 1770 and 1860 saw the painstaking birth of natural science, but there was a bitter struggle with the preachers every millimeter of the way. The reasons for the religionists' opposition to an orderly science of nature are complex and reach back to pre-Christianity. It began with arguments about the physical age of the Earth.

In the royal gardens at Pella, Macedonia, in 341 B.C., Aristotle of Stagira lectured about history and earth lore. Using handfuls of sand and chunks of rock and fossil bones as exhibits, he stressed that our planet is ancient beyond comprehension and in continual change. The lectures inspired a lifelong friendship between Aristotle and King Philip's arrogant heir, Alexander. Discussions with priests and philosophers about state religions, regional biology, and geologic beliefs became routine for Alexander during his conquests from the Dardanelles to India. Summaries of these discussions, along with specimens of strange minerals, plants and animals, were sent by courier back to Aristotle in Athens. By the time Alexander died in Babylon from fever or poisons, he had become convinced that the Earth was at least two million years old.

Scholars of the Kingdom of Israel, using evidence they believed to be valid, later proclaimed that October 7, 3761 B.C. (adapted to our calendar) was "the final day of Creation." When Christianity, after three centuries as a heretic cult, was proclaimed the new state religion of Rome, priests decided that the Hebraic account of the Creation should be retained as the first book of the Bible.

The concept of recent creation of the Earth became entrenched in all branches of Christian worship. Deft explanations were therefore necessary when giant fossil bones, ancient stone axes, delicately carved gems, and massive pottery jars were turned up by plowmen or washed ashore by gales. The standard explanation was that all of these objects were made by the devil to deceive mankind.

The Florentine genius Leonardo da Vinci had to hide out for months after he wrote that "the waters of the Deluge could not have carried the live shell animals on its crest and thus to the tops of mountains. The oysters were fastened to the bottom of the sea, while cockles could not have traveled from the Adriatic to the mountains of Lombardy in forty days, since their rate of travel is only three to four *braccis* a day." His royal masters finally won a pardon for him from the Bishop of Florence, by explaining that da Vinci was a very imaginative fellow of artistic temperament.

A similar taint of atheism hung over Sir Walter Raleigh because his devotion to the examination of nature led him to the conviction that "reason must be elicited from fact." One school of historians believes that James I ordered Raleigh's beheading on October 29, 1618, not because he had disobeyed orders and razed a Spanish town on the Orinoco River the year before, but because his new *History of the World* was anti-Christian by alleging that "in Abraham's time, all the then known parts of the world were developed. . . . Egypt had many magnificent cities, and these were not built with sticks but with hewn stones."

Studies of Hebrew, Greek, and Latin manuscripts convinced James Ussher, Archbishop of Armagh in Ireland, that the task of creation ended on October 10, 4004 B.C. In 1650, he published the date as fact in his *Annales Veteris et Novi Testamenti*. Church of England prelates were so impressed that they ordered the Ussher creation date printed in the margin of all authorized editions of the King James Bible.

The Ussher date was officially accepted in the United States. Before and after the Revolution, no citizen who "challenged the authority of the King James Bible" could hold public office or serve as an officer in the army or navy.

In every community, from the Green Mountains to Georgia's Sea Islands, the preacher was socially powerful. In many places, since he was the only person who could read or write, the preacher was the scribe for letters and the interpreter of local and national laws. On weekdays, he taught the only school and arbitrated the quarrels and public behavior of the parishioners. On Sundays, he threatened hellfire and damnation from a lectern, with little regard for cogency or brevity. Naturally, he was suspicious of people who dabbled in alchemy, who questioned the age of bones and fossilized wood, or pried into the secrets of nature. Truth, he preached, was in the Bible. God created Earth between October 4th and 10th in 4004 B.C. and put everything in place exactly where and how He wanted it; any evidence of an older date had been put there by the devil to deceive mankind. Objective scientific research that suggested anything to the contrary was sacrilegious.

In 1706, the popular Boston divine, Cotton Mather, petitioned Great Britain's Royal Society for Improving Natural Knowledge. He was seeking funds to finance his research and writing of a book that would prove how the natural history of New England demonstrated God's will, as revealed in Genesis and other books of the Old Testament. He would title the work *Magnalia Christi Americana.* But Mather was suspect to the professors and noblemen who controlled the society. Mather was also an authority on Satanic possession; his oratory had fired the terror of witchcraft trials in Salem and other Puritan communities. The petition was brusquely denied.

Similar devotion by the clergy to the Bible as the supreme authority on Earth's botany, zoology, and environment, and to Ussher's guess of a recent Creation, frustrated research into the reasons for the annual recurrence of green leaves, the deterioration of repeatedly harvested soils, pollenization by bees, the ticks that killed livestock, and other intricacies of nature. Thus there was persistent migration from worn-out acres to other homesteads of virgin forest, meadow, or prairie. The forests were burned. Erosion caused deep gullies and muddy rivers.

One of the few preachers who dared condemn this rape of the continent was the Reverend Jared Eliot of Killingsworth, Connecticut. His valiant *Essay upon Field Husbandry in New England* was published in 1740. "When our fore-Fathers settled here," he grieved, "they entered a land which probably had never been ploughed since the Creation; the land being new, they depended upon the natural Fertility of the Ground, which served their purpose very well, and when they had worn out one piece they cleared another, without any concern to amend their Land, except a little helped by the Fold and Cart-dung, whereas in England they would think a Man a bad Husband if he should pretend to sow wheat on Land without Dressing."

As ardent an advocate of animal manures as the Quakers and

Pennsylvania Dutch, Eliot scornfully compared farmers who did not re-fertilize their croplands to "a man who drew money from the bank and put none back." Red clover and "goode grass cover" were his favored treatments to nourish poor soils and prevent erosion. He also advocated large plantings of turnips and carrots, both of which he found good provender "for man and beast."

The book had little effect on farm or plantation practices. But three years after it was published, Benjamin Franklin proposed the organization of an American Philosophical Society in Philadelphia that "could best serve mankind" by collecting and publishing data about "useful" American botany, zoology, and minerals, as well as "encourage needed inventions."

Penn's Sylvania's freedom of worship encouraged freedom of research as well. Botanists, chemists, astronomers, and physicians could probe the mysteries of nature more intently and serenely than they could have done under clergymen like Cotton Mather. Consequently, the society became our most significant pioneer and popularizer of natural science. The scholarly lectures delivered—and vehemently debated—at its meetings were published in its *Transactions* and distributed nationally. Funds advanced to the portraitist Charles Willson Peale enabled him to found the first American museum and even to challenge the Ussher date of creation by exhuming, assembling, and displaying the skeleton of a prehistoric mammoth.

Since members of the society often journeyed to Europe for professional conferences or to continue medical studies, close relationship was maintained with the universities and scientific societies of Great Britain, France, and Germany. When Sir Humphry Davy of London's Royal Institution described his isolation of potassium, sodium, and other minerals in an 1812 series of lectures on "Chemistry in Agriculture," the society was the first American organization to analyze and publicize Sir Humphry's conclusions.

Thomas Jefferson became a member of the society in 1780 and served as its president from 1797 to 1815. Historians have written so lavishly about Jefferson's other achievements that his dedication to botany and agricultural improvements has been neglected. Agrarian development was unquestionably the strongest lure of all for Jefferson's amazing inquisitiveness. "The greatest service which can be rendered any country," he wrote, "is to add an useful plant to its culture; especially a bread grain."

During his years as our ambassador to France, Jefferson explored agricultural techniques as ardently as he examined and copied Graeco-Roman architecture. Later, he had a "kitchen garden" 1,000 feet long and 45 feet wide dug and blasted into a terrace at the southeastern tip of Monticello's mountaintop. There more than 250 varieties of vegetables and 150 of fruit trees, vineyards, and "berry Squares" went into experimental growth. Many of them were European imports. Largely because of this agricultural experiment station and the 16,000 books about botany and agricultural subjects he acquired for his library, Jefferson's estate was $100,000 in debt when he died in 1826.

When Jefferson ordered Lewis and Clark to organize an expedition for exploring the Louisiana Territory immediately after its purchase from Napoleon Bonaparte, he sent Meriwether Lewis to Philadelphia for a "crash" course on botany, zoology, geology, and map-making by Peale, William Bartram, Dr. Benjamin Rush, Owen Wister, and other distinguished members of the American Philosophical Society. The plants and seeds Lewis and Clark brought back from their walk to the Pacific were grown and analyzed at Monticello and in the gardens of other society members.

Botany departments at Columbia, Yale, Harvard, and the University of Pennsylvania were all founded through the influence of the Philosophical Society's research and lectures. Societies for the Promotion of Agriculture were also founded in each state to probe mysteries of productivity and carefully navigate the Ussher whirlpools and Old Testament sand bars of the clergy. Thus individualists, as patiently dedicated in their fields as "Johnny Appleseed" Chapman was in his, slowly achieved public support for natural science, and began the transition from natural philosophy to the daring new professions of agronomy, botany, zoology, animal husbandry, engineering, and bacteriology. No career was more typical of the prejudices that had to be allayed and the changes that were achieved than that of New York's Amos Eaton.

Eaton was born on May 17, 1776, in a log and stone farmhouse at Chatham, New York, a day's cart-ride east of the Hudson Valley village of Kinderhook. The boy's eagerness for book learning so impressed the village's Presbyterian minister that he tutored Eaton in natural philosophy, geography, Latin, and Greek, then persuaded villagers to hire the nineteen-year-old as Chatham's first schoolteacher.

But the quest for learning soon lured Eaton to Williams College. At twenty-three, he had a B.S. degree, was enrolled for courses in botany at New York's Columbia University, and was earning his way as a student clerk at a law firm. Largely because of his friendship with Washington Irving, another student clerk at the firm, Eaton next became land agent for William Livingston, miserly cousin of statesmen Robert R. and Edward Livingston, who owned large tracts of tenant farms, chestnut forests, and leather tanneries in the Catskill Mountains.

Business trips through the mountains so intrigued Eaton about soil types, rocks, and plant life that, by 1810, he founded a Botanical Institution in the village of Catskill and offered courses for "all persons of both sexes, from twelve years old to sixty" in botany, mathematics, and astronomic calculations. But a year later, an argument over land ownership with William Pendleton, the attorney who had been Aaron Burr's second in the fatal duel with Alexander Hamilton, led to a charge of forgery. Eaton was innocent; Pendleton was slick. Eaton was sentenced to life imprisonment and shipped downriver in chains to Newgate Prison in New York City.

The warden of Newgate, William Torrey, had a son named John who was fascinated by botany and particularly eager to learn about the late Carolus Linnaeus's system of bionomial classification of plants, animals, and minerals. The warden grumpily presided over the first meeting between his son and the new prisoner, then decided it would be safe enough for them to hold discussions in his back office. John's progress and enthusiasm were so remarkable that the warden agreed to let Eaton also use the back office every day for scribbling out a book, *A Manual of Botany for the Northern States;* in return for this favor, Eaton could try his hand at straightening out the prison's account books.

By 1813, Torrey was bragging so much about Eaton at city council meetings that Mayor De Witt Clinton ordered Eaton brought to City Hall for a chat. Clinton was determined to become governor of New York and needed help. If the fleet that young Oliver Perry and that gang of Brooklyn Navy Yard roughnecks had put together could gun the British fleet out of Lake Erie, there was hope that this stupid war would end with assurance of unhindered American travel up and down the Great Lakes. After the war, then, it would be logical to build a barge canal up the Mohawk valley to connect the Hudson River to the Great Lakes. The result would be a tremendous trade with the West that could make New York the most prosperous state of the Union. But the dream could not be realized without demands by the voters for "Clinton and the Canal." Clinton needed a lecturer who knew geography and botany and was lucid enough to explain the canal's potential to farmers, millers, carpenters, shipwrights, butchers, and draymen in terms they could understand.

Perry and his roughnecks did win the Battle of Lake Erie. Freedom of the lakes was assured for Americans. A series of conferences at City Hall convinced Clinton that Amos Eaton would be ideal as his popularizer for the Erie Canal. An order from Albany, dated November 17, 1815, lost Warden Torrey his best bookkeeper and John Torrey his most revered teacher. (In 1838, Dr. John Torrey, Professor of Botany at Princeton University, published his *Flora of North America.* The first copy off the press went to Amos Eaton.)

Benjamin Silliman graduated from Yale a decade after Eli Whitney. At the request of the school's president, Timothy Dwight, he studied botany and chemistry with members of the American Philosophical Society. By 1815, Silliman's lectures on botany and chemistry at Yale were considered the nation's best. Amos Eaton was forty years old that year. He moved his family to New Haven, signed up for the Silliman courses, and worked evenings completing the manuscript of a botanical dictionary.

Clinton became governor of New York in 1817. He called Eaton to Albany to deliver a series of lectures to the 1818 sessions of the state legislature about the agricultural and industrial wealth of western New York and the Great Lakes basin that could be developed by means of the Erie Canal's mule-team and barge transportation.

"I become all things to all men," Eaton boasted in a letter to John Torrey. "I turn everything in science into common talk. I illustrate the most obtuse parts by a dishkettle, a warming pan, a bread tray, a teapot, a soup bowl or a cheese press."

The appropriation for the Mohawk valley canal squeaked through the legislature. Eaton's "common talk" so impressed politically powerful Stephen Van Rensselaer that he asked the scientist to deliver a summerlong series of lectures to generate support for a Lyceum of Natural History in Troy. These lectures were so successful that the lyceum was financed and Eaton became its permanent lecturer and chief collecting agent.

That fall, both Van Rensselaer and Governor Clinton pledged financial support for a second series of lectures dealing with "the specific applications of geology and chemistry to agriculture," to be delivered before the 1819 sessions of the legislature. More than half of the state's senators and representatives, plus scores of bureaucrats and lobbyists, became regulars and took notes about soil tests, cropfield enrichment, and chemical reactions. During the final lecture, a certificate declaring Eaton to be a master teacher was presented to him. The real reward came a week later when the legislature passed New York's first appropriation ($10,000) "for the promotion of agriculture and industry." (This appropriation and the subsequent funding of a State Agricultural Society preceded the federal government's founding of a Bureau of Agriculture by forty-three years.)

More "common talk" lectures delivered in New York, Vermont, and Massachusetts communities during the spring and summer of 1819 led to Eaton's appointment as professor of botany at Vermont's first school of medicine, Castleton Medical Academy. Then Van Rensselaer requested a geological survey of the hundreds of tenant farms his family owned in the upper Hudson valley. The survey became another trailblazer for scientific agriculture.

In his report to Van Rensselaer, Eaton said,

> I have attempted to meet your views by collecting materials for a kind of Agricultural Calendar, to direct the young and inexperienced farmer in regards to times of sowing, planting, harvesting &c. as well as the most approved methods for preparing his ground. Theoretical treatises on agriculture are found in abundance on every bookseller's shelves; many of which are rather calculated to perplex, than to instruct, the practical agriculturist. I have endeavored . . . to reject all theory and prepare a concise system founded wholly on the experiences of the labouring farmers. . . . I called on one, at least, in every neighborhood in all the towns; and I wrote down, in his presence, the methods of culture adopted by himself, and by his neighbors so far as had come to his knowledge. . . . I did not confine myself to crops of grass and grain, but I extended my inquiries to the subject of orchards, kitchen gardens, shrubbery, cattle, horses, sheep, swine, &c.

(Eaton's technique of kitchen interviews and the resulting farm-year calendar anticipated the founding of the county agent system by ninety years.)

Governor Clinton and Van Rensselaer next guaranteed underwritings for a similar survey of the Erie Canal's three-hundred-mile route, with Professor Silliman of Yale as Eaton's principal consultant. The survey began on the morning of November 11, 1822, when a wagon powered by one horse carried Eaton, an assistant, their camping gear and geologic tools up the towpaths around Cohoes Falls at the Mohawk-Hudson junction opposite Troy. Dedication to education must have obliterated Eaton's awareness of the winters in New York's upstate; the wagon had to be exchanged for a sled. Eaton developed acute laryngitis, pneumonia, and Western Lake Fever, but was back in Troy in mid-March, delivering lectures "for the accommodation of the young ladies in Troy Female Academy," later the Emma Willard School.

A flare-up of fever confined him to his Troy home when *The Van Rensselaer Canal Survey* was published in 1824. During his convalescence, Eaton brooded about the American future. Economic and social enrichment, he had long taught, could result from scientific knowledge about soils, rocks, and plants. But the few college courses available, the experiments and discussions conducted by the American Philosophical Society, and even his own common talk lectures were designed for adults. There should be a school where young people could receive training through performance for engineering, soil analysis, laboratory experimentation, land renewal methods, and other scientific principles.

Again, Van Rensselaer shared Eaton's enthusiasm for one of his ideas and offered endowments to establish The Rensselaer School at Troy. A letter to potential trustees announced that the school "would instruct persons, who may choose to apply themselves, in the application of science to the common purposes of life. . . . [The] principal object is to qualify teachers for instructing the sons and daughters of farmers and mechanics, by lectures or otherwise, in the application of experimental chemistry, philosophy and natural history to agriculture, domestic economy, the arts and manufactures."

Eventually renamed Rensselaer Polytechnic Institute, the school was the first American institution for technical and scientific training. Its initial classes were held during the first months of 1825. By the following October, observers from Union, Columbia, Middlebury, Amherst, Harvard, Princeton, and Yale were traveling to Troy to study this new technique in pedagogy.

Students during the school's first years included Theodore DeHone Judah, Joseph Henry, Asa Fitch, and Asa Gray. Judah built the first railroad in California, then surveyed the route for the Sacramento-to-Utah portion of the first transcontinental railroad and persuaded three Albany-Troy natives named Mark Hopkins, Collis Huntington, and Leland Stanford to finance its construction. Joseph Henry discovered laws of electromagnetism that made the telegraph possible, and later became secretary of the Smithsonian Institution. Asa Fitch, as New York's first State Entomologist, pioneered programs to control crop pests and diseases. Asa Gray was professor of botany at Harvard and compiled the *Manual of Botany* that became a standard reference work on flora east of the Rockies.

Eaton's use of canalboat seminars and cross-country explorations with his students constitutes the first use of the field trip as a legitimate element in an American school curriculum.

While Eaton pioneered scientific farming in the North, Edmund Ruffin struggled on his James River farm in Virginia to discover minerals and methods that would restore the South's cotton-eroded soils. Born a decade after Whitney's invention of the cotton gin, Ruffin became so fascinated by reading the new British books on agriculture that he was dismissed from the College of William and Mary for "inattention to studies." Unperturbed, he returned to the family farm and began experimenting with fertilizers that might re-energize the soils depleted by repeated plantings of cotton or tobacco. Neighbors permitted him to cart off samples of soil from cropfields, pastures, and woodlots, then guffawed about Ruffin's folly. The experiments convinced him that a combination of marl (a mixture of clay and fossil seashells) and animal manures, spread on cropfields at an average 157 bushels to the acre, would revive the land enough to produce good crops of grain.

"The area was an old eroded field full of gullies," he wrote about one of his experiments. "It had been abandoned 39 years earlier, and at the time covered by pines. After the pines were removed, the field was heavily marled and was coultered twice, in July and August. Following a crop of wheat, the soil was given a two year rest, then corn and wheat were raised consecutively, after which clover for hay was raised for a year. The crops were good, and at the end of the period, clover grew well in the bottoms of the old gullies."

Other tests with marl doubled the yield of cornfields, too. Marling, he proved, also controlled the erosion of topsoils.

Ruffin's *Essay on Calcareous Manures* became the most popular agricultural book in the South. This success brought him the editorship of *Farmer's Register,* a monthly publication that gave him a forum for his ideas on soil improvement techniques.

During the time Ruffin was making his investigations into how to improve the quality of soil, the most significant advances were coming from Europe. During the fall of 1840 a wispy apple-cheeked man in a frock coat delivered a series of lectures to the British Association for the Advancement of Science on "Organic Chemistry in its Application to Agriculture and Physiology." Justus von Liebig, a chemist from Bonn, Germany, summarized his discoveries in two sentences: "The primary support whence man and animals derive the means of their growth and support is the vegetable kingdom. Plants, on the other hand, find new nutritive material only in inorganic substances."

Liebig's experiments had demonstrated that plants obtain their carbon by breathing in the carbon dioxide expelled by animals and humans. His analyses of the contents of leaves, stems, and roots showed that every plant contains traces of nitrogen, carbon, hydrogen, and oxygen. The carbon came from the atmosphere, the hydrogen and oxygen mostly from water; but, he pointed out, the nitrogen must come from some other source. The presence of nitrogen, or the lack of it, made the difference between rich and weak soil, between big potatoes and runts, between wheat four feet tall and one foot tall.

John Bennet Lawes, a chemistry student, hurried back from the Liebig lectures to his father's estate at Rothamsted, twenty-five miles out of London, and began extensive field tests with nitrogen. By 1845 he was able to demonstrate that applications of a mixture of nitrate of soda with sulfate and chloride of ammonia on fields would produce magnificent wheat crops. He called the compound "super-phosphate."

The manufacture of artificial fertilizers containing nitrogen began before 1850 in Baltimore and Boston but the new products stood little chance on the open market against nitrogen-rich bird manure gathered from the cliffs of the Chincha Islands, off the coast of Peru. Rainless upthrusts of lava, the Chinchas were a favorite nesting and breeding haven for pelicans, cormorants, and gannets. Their excrement had baked into chalklike cliffs hundreds of feet high. Sailboats occasionally put in from the mainland so the sailors could chip off a few tons for farmers. Its fertility-boost for crops of local corn and potatoes was known to U.S. Embassy personnel in Lima, but no reports about it were sent to Washington until Ruffin's strident editorials, Liebig's discoveries, and the Rothamsted developments revealed the potential wealth of the bird-made cliffs. Soon requests for funds arrived to make a survey of the Chinchas' odorous cliffs. The survey, made in 1850, estimated total deposits of 12 to 20 million tons of bird manure, or guano.

The Peruvian government decided that the Chinchas' guano would be available for $50 a ton "at chuteside." Indian and coolie laborers were shipped out to the islands to gather guano, but they could not stand the ammonia stench for long. They had to work in thirty-minute shifts, blasting away pieces of cliff, then hammering them into chunks that could be wheeled to holding pens at the top of the cliffs. To load a ship, enough guano had to be rowed out to it to assure ballast. Then the vessel was warped in to the lava shore, anchored within reach of the canvas chutes dangling from the holding pens, and loaded.

American imports of guano soared to 200,000 tons a year; a third of it went through customs at Baltimore. Mixed in 5 and 10 percent proportions with lime and ordinary loam, it produced fabulous results. Cotton growers in the Carolinas claimed that guano increased their yield by 200 pounds per acre. Grain farmers saw it push taller, fatter cornstalks and sturdier oats and barley up from the earth. Vegetable growers of New Jersey, Connecticut, and the Hudson-Mohawk Valley reported larger crops and healthier plants.

However, guano was prohibitively expensive for gardeners and operators of small farms. Petitions against "the Peruvian monopoly" were drawn up and delivered to Congressmen. Daniel Webster had consented to return to public life and serve as Secretary of State. In 1852, a few days before his death, he strongly denounced Peru's claims to the island of Lobos, where more guano deposits had been discovered, and urged the President to order a cruiser of our Pacific squadron to Lobos to "protect American interests."

The cruiser was not ordered south, but Webster's ire and the outspokenness of President Pierce's report to Congress the following spring led to riots in Lima and other Peruvian cities. In 1856 Congress passed the Guano Islands Act, permitting American citizens to occupy islands containing guano deposits not claimed by other nations and to consider them possessions of the U.S.A. More than forty islands were occupied, triggering disputes with Great Britain and several Central and South American governments. The Civil War—and new, inexpensive formulas for chemical fertilizers—ended the guano fever and our usurpation of guano-rich islets.

Throughout guano fever and the introduction of chemical fertilizers, Edmund Ruffin continued to grieve at the depletion of the South's soils. No more than a fourth of the cotton and tobacco planters were heeding Liebig's discoveries and the new rehabilitation techniques. The other 75 percent continued to wear out soils, let wind and rain create gullies and muddy creeks, then move on to do it all over again on virgin land. "Choose and choose quickly!" he warned. "And remember, as my last warning, that your decision will be between your purchasing, at equal rates of price, either wealth and general prosperity, of value exceeding all present power of computation, or ruin, destitution and the lowest degradation to which the country of a free and noble minded people can possibly be subjected."

By 1860, Ruffin had become convinced that exploitation by

the cotton mills and machinery makers of the North was the basic cause of the South's soil erosion. His vehemence against Lincoln's election was so great that he asked for the privilege of firing the first gun of the Confederate bombardment of Fort Sumter. He worked zealously on army-supply problems throughout the Civil War, and when the news finally came of Lee's surrender at Appomattox, he put a pistol to his mouth and blew off the top of his skull.

The American Philosophical Society, teachers at universities, and the dedicated few like George Washington, Thomas Jefferson, Amos Eaton, and Edmund Ruffin began the transformation of American agriculture from land plundering to scientific rehabilitation. In the process, they pioneered our age of natural science.

Finally, in 1862, the federal government began to come awake to agriculture's problems.

CHAPTER SEVEN

"Guvmint"

The federal government's eighty-six years of apathy toward destructive agricultural practices and the emerging natural sciences was predicted in the second line of the Declaration of Independence. The line reads, "THE UNANIMOUS DECLARATION of the thirteen united STATES OF AMERICA." "States" was emphasized by capitalization, but "united" was not. From 1776 until 1861 the struggle over states' rights was vehement. During this time, a majority of states adamantly opposed interference in agricultural practices by a central government.

In his final presidential message to Congress, George Washington urged the creation of a Board of Agriculture to "collect and diffuse information." A bill was drawn up—and died in committee. Washington's promotion of mule power and the other livestock-improvement programs he pursued at Mount Vernon received no grants in aid from Congress. Thomas Jefferson's zeal for botany forced his estate into bankruptcy, but he received no aid or even any acknowledgment from Congress. The research of the American Philosophical Society was not encouraged by a congressional appropriation, and the group was not even given access to the Government Printing Office. The schools of botanical research founded at universities were supported by private fortunes and state funds, not by Congress.

Yet, insofar as the welfare of the land was concerned, state governments were as inactive as the federal government. No efforts were made to halt the massive burnout of virgin forests. Little encouragement was given to programs like Edmund Ruffin's to correct soil deficiencies. The mirage of limitless land continued to be as convincing to legislators as it was to most planters, ranchers, and farmers; there would always be prime land out yonder.

Committees on agriculture were appointed by the House and Senate of Congress in 1820, but they met rarely and did nothing. In 1836, when Henry L. Ellsworth became Commissioner of Patents, he made the drastic decision to request the Navy and State departments to cooperate by asking ship officers and overseas consulates to collect "new and valuable seeds and plants" for distribution to agriculturists. This boldness required congressional appropriations that rose to $300,000 a year by 1845. Thereupon, Senator John C. Calhoun of South Carolina, the fiery proponent of states' rights, pronounced the project to be "one of the most enormous abuses under this government."

Nevertheless, new varieties of muskmelon, grasses, and apples were obtained. But with them came the mildews and sperm of bugs, disease, and new varieties of weed. The Patent Office passed them all along to the land.

The only other involvement by the federal government in agricultural activity before the War Between the States was the Whiskey Rebellion. Significantly, it was caused by surplus production, excessive transportation costs, and a bureaucratic eagerness to collect taxes.

In 1791, the Conestoga wagon road east from Pittsburgh was the only commercial route between the new West and the thirteen seaboard states. The burned forest soils of the Ohio valley produced luxuriant crops of corn, but it was expensive to wagon the grain, or its meal, east or to raft and keelboat it down the Mississippi. The new bourbon whiskey offered a solution. A wagonload or boatload of kegs of whiskey yielded far more profit, and the "slops" from a whiskey still was noisily admired by pigs and cattle.

Alexander Hamilton, Secretary of the Treasury, was a strong advocate of a powerful central government that would be financed through taxation. He lobbied a bill through Congress for the collection of excise taxes—and one of the luxuries to be taxed was whiskey. Refusing to pay the tax, the farmers of western Pennsylvania and Kentucky drew up petitions of protest, threatening to "wing" any tax collector who showed up at a barnyard still.

President Washington realized that the new government must demonstrate the ability to enforce its laws, so, in 1794, he reluctantly ordered troops across the Alleghenies. There was gunfire; leaders of the rebellion were later pardoned. A decade later, Thomas Jefferson persuaded Congress to repeal all excise taxes, but they were reenacted during the War of 1812. Out of all this grew the folklore of "moonshining," the bootlegger, and 150 years of "feudin' " between "the Law" and unlicensed producers of "white lightnin'."

Between 1840 and 1855, the War with Mexico, California's Bear Flag Revolt, and revised treaties with Great Britain expanded the "united States of America" to include a two-thousand-mile strip of the Pacific coast and the wonderland of the Southwest. Railroads had been gandy-danced from the Atlantic to the Mississippi. Kansas and Nebraska prepared for statehood. Michigan financed the nation's first college of agriculture. Manufacturing and shipping were expanding so rapidly that, between 1790 and 1860, the farm population decreased from 89 percent of the national total to 75 percent.

In 1857, a waspish Vermont Congressman named Justin Smith Morrill introduced a bill that would allocate tracts of government-owned land to each state for financing a college of agriculture.

The bill finally got out of committee in 1859, was approved by the House and Senate despite strenuous objections by Southerners, then was vetoed because of President Buchanan's timidity about states' rights.

By the spring of 1862, the Union's back was to the wall. The armies of the Confederacy had outfought Union forces and threatened to gain control of most of the trans-Mississippi West. The only communication link with California—except the grim journey around Cape Horn or across the Isthmus of Panama—was the Overland Trail with its pony express and a single strand of telegraph wire. Even there, Mormons, pro-Confederate silver miners in Nevada, and Indians were all suspect.

Abraham Lincoln now decided to put into action his conviction that the best hope of the American future was freedom of land for the individual. Congress agreed. On May 15, 1862, Lincoln signed the bill to establish a United States Bureau of Agriculture. Five days later, he signed the Homestead Act, which granted 160 acres of the vastness west of the Mississippi to any person who would make an effort to homestead it over a five-year period.

A month later, after a Chicago convention wrangled a truce between eastern and western promoters, the Pacific Railway Act was approved. It granted the builders of the Central Pacific and the Union Pacific "vacant land within ten miles on either side of the lines for five alternate sections per mile . . . mineral lands excepted," plus federal loans of $48,000 per mile on 150 miles of mountain construction, $16,000 per mile on construction to the base of the mountains, and $32,000 per mile across the high plains of Nevada and Utah.

After such a giveaway, Morrill's act was a shoo-in and became law on July 2. Its gifts of government land to each state for founding a college of agriculture and mechanics was thirty thousand acres for each senator and representative, based on the census of 1860.

Iowa was the first state to take advantage of the Morrill Act. Iowa Agricultural College opened classrooms and an experimental farm at the village of Ames in March, 1869, with an enrollment of 253 students. The curriculum included: natural philosophy, chemistry, botany, fruit growing, horticulture, forestry, animal and vegetable anatomy, geology, mineralogy, meteorology, entomology, zoology, the veterinary art, plain mensuration, leveling, surveying, bookkeeping, "and such mechanic arts as are directly connected with agriculture."

"I began to tell the students what I knew about agriculture," recalled Isaac P. Roberts, the school's farm superintendent.

It did not take me long to run short of material, and then I began to consult the library. I might as well have looked for cranberries in the Rocky Mountains as for material for teaching agriculture in that library. Thus, fortunately, I was driven to take the class to the field and farm there to study plants, animals and tillage at first hand. . . . I fell into the habit of taking the students to view good and bad farms; to see fine herds and scrub herds in the country round about, even though we had to travel in freight cars. . . . One day, being short of lecture material, I went to the fields and gathered a great armful of common weed pests. Handing them around to the class, I asked for the common and botanical names and the methods of eradication. This experiment provided material for a week's classroom talks and led me to place still more emphasis on field laboratory work; walks-and-talks we called them.

When the reference shelves of the library failed him again, Roberts took the students to farms where horses had recently died, dug up the cadavers, and lectured on "the fundamental principles of horse dentition."

The same challenge of tiny budget and meagerness of reference materials confronted the United States Bureau of Agriculture during its early years. The Confederacy's determination to win the war by cutting off Washington from the rest of the Union almost succeeded at Gettysburg a year after the bureau was founded. Congress could not be bothered with such trivia as an adequate budget and manpower. The foundations laid between 1862 and 1870 for the bureau's expansion into the vast U.S.

Department of Agriculture are a tribute to the individual initiative of its remarkable director and chief gardener.

President Lincoln's advisors insisted on the appointment of Isaac Newton, a farmer-politician from Pennsylvania, as the first Commissioner of Agriculture. Although gossip said that Newton, in a moment of absentmindedness, suggested buying two hydraulic rams for the bureau because "I have been told they are among the best sheep in Europe," his gallantries toward the president's wife attest to his political sagacity. He not only escorted Mrs. Lincoln to spiritualist mediums and fortune tellers but proved his friendship in other ways; when New York store owners began to press her for payments on her extravagances, he helped placate them. Also, he is alleged to have acted as intermediary in buying back some of the "unfortunate" letters Mrs. Lincoln wrote to the White House's gardener.

Newton realized that the bureau was on a political choke-leash. The Committee on Agriculture of the House of Representatives controlled the bureau's budget. Although members of this committee were assumed to be experts on regional agricultural problems, they received the bulk of their campaign gifts from urban industries, wholesalers, railroads, and banks in their home districts and were under incisive lobbying pressures from these contributors. The farmers, on the other hand, did not have organizations or lobbyists. This condition, plus the knowledge that membership on the Committee on Agriculture could change every two years, kept Newton involved with negotiations on Capitol Hill and crippled bureau activity toward solving problems of agricultural production and distribution. (The 1863 budget of $87,792.96 enabled Newton to hire an entomologist, a chemist, one statistician, and a horticulturist to oversee all of the country's farms.) Thus, Newton's need for Mrs. Lincoln's friendship.

[The system of obeisance to the whims of congressional committees on agriculture would persist. It would encourage swarms of lobbyists in Washington, financed by both agricultural and middleman organizations. In 1984, it raises questions about the effectiveness of a choke-leashed U.S. Department of Agriculture in the oncoming era of genetic farming, technologic adjustment, acid rain, and domination of our food supply by middleman conglomerates.]

Newton also possessed a farm-grown shrewdness that enabled him to persuade the Committee on Agriculture to allocate swampy land east of the unfinished Washington Monument as the site for the bureau's offices and experimental gardens.

The North's victory in the Civil War and Lincoln's Emancipation Proclamation not only pledged social, and in some areas political, freedom to blacks, but signaled critical changes for the South's plantation system. The most obvious alternative for owners of large tracts of cotton, tobacco, and rice was adoption of the tenant-farmer system used by some of the corn and wheat growers on the prairies of Illinois, Missouri, and Kansas. Planters divided their one-crop lands into forty- or sixty-acre tracts. Each tract was assigned to a black or "poor white" family. The planter provided a mule, a plow, a few hand tools, and seed, and offered credit for the purchase of goods at the store he owned. After the harvest and sale of the crop, the planter deducted expenses and the family's store debt plus interest, and gave half the remaining pittance to the "cropper." The plantation's bookkeeping records were, of course, not open to the tenant's inspection. On most plantations, the one-room huts that had been slave quarters became sharecropper homes. This system was soon adopted from Virginia to California.

Neither Newton nor his successors suggested regulations to curb the greed of the carpetbaggers then ravaging the South or to guarantee greater freedom of initiative for sharecroppers. An effort by the Freedmen's Bureau, headed by General Oliver O. Howard, did propose a program for outright ownership of farms by blacks and poor whites; the program was killed by Congress.

But across the dirt path from Newton's office, in the bureau's Experimental Gardens, William Saunders performed green magic for agriculture's future. Born at Saint Andrews, Scotland, across the meadow from the world's most famous golf links, Saunders migrated to New England as a landscape architect. He won such distinction that he was chosen as the bureau's chief horticulturist, and he then took over the Patent Office's chore of evaluating the seeds and plants delivered by the Navy and State departments. As astute a gardener as Thomas Jefferson, Saunders developed fertile experimental plots in greenhouses, then began testing and hybridizing hundreds of plants, shrubs, and trees for regional adaptability. Apple trees were bred to withstand the droughts and blizzards of Kansas, Iowa, and Nebraska; black elms to flourish in the Nebraska sandhills; peach trees sturdy enough for Maine and Michigan winters.

During 1871 a messenger from the State Department brought in a damp package just received from our embassy in Brazil. It contained cuttings from an orange tree. The parent tree, the accompanying letter explained, bore oranges that were sugar-sweet and had no seeds. The variety had come from a sport plant discovered on Goa, a Portuguese possession off the west coast of India; now Brazil had groves of seedless orange trees.

Saunders nourished the shoots so successfully that he was able to send four young trees to California in the care of Luther Tibbets, a New York merchant who had decided that the golden state was the safest place to escape from his shrill wife. Saunders explained the importance of the trees to Tibbets and suggested that, if they adapted to the California climate, the fruit be called Washington Navel because the indented protuberance at the blossom end resembled a bellybutton.

Tibbets bought 160 acres of semi-desert near the village of Riverside, ran in an irrigation ditch, and planted Lucerne grass (recently renamed alfalfa) and grapevines along with the four trees. In 1879, a plateful of his Washington Navels won the blue ribbon at the county fair. The price of grafts from the trees rose from $10 to $20 to $100 each, and Washington Navel became the most popular orange produced in California and Florida.

Tibbets's orange trees were producing their first fruit when two hundred refugees from Russia's Crimea gathered around their leader at a New York pier-head and bowed their heads in a prayer of thanks for arrival in the land of freedom. When their luggage was winched down to them, the huskiest young men lifted out twelve square boxes that had been double-wrapped in sailcloth and sealed with red and black wax. The men formed a guardian circle around the boxes as they were carried to coaches that C. V. Schmidt, land agent for the Atchison, Topeka & Santa Fe Railroad, had assembled for them. During September, 1874, the group reached their new farmlands spanning Santa Fe trackage near Topeka.

The refugees were Mennonites whose ancestors had fled to Russia from religious persecution in Germany and who became prosperous farmers in the Crimea. In 1870, a rumor spread that Czar Nicholas II was readying a treaty with Bismarck's Germany that might invalidate the amnesty the Czar's father had pledged them. Schmidt was searching for settlers for the railroad's government grant land when he learned about the Mennonites' fears. He went to Russia, persuaded a delegation of the group's elders to come back to Kansas with him and see the swift brown rivers and rich prairie loam. The following year, the party of two hundred and their twelve precious boxes eluded Czarist agents and reached the United States.

The boxes contained thirty bushels of a pebble-hard, coral-colored wheat that the Mennonites had developed to withstand the gales and blizzards of the Crimean winter. Planted in the fall, the seed would send up emerald leaves as soon as the ground thawed and produced a harvest by July.

When news of this "winter wheat" reached Washington, Saunders begged enough seed to begin experimental tests at the USDA gardens and at several land-grant-college plots in the Midwest. By 1890, Saunders and the land-grant scientists had developed strains of winter wheat adapted to climate and soil patterns from Texas to North Dakota. The area took the name of the winter wheat belt. The only drawback to the grain was that its kernels were so hard that the burred stone grinders used in flour mills could not break them down to the snowy flour used by city housewives. Mills were forced to retool with steel grinders.

The Reverend Chauncey Goodrich of Utica, New York, had

taken the first steps to improve the hardiness and variety of American potatoes by requesting a shipment of wild South American potatoes from the U.S. Consulate at Panama. By the time the Civil War began, the reverend had crossbred eight thousand new varieties of potato, but made little effort to promote his discoveries. William Saunders set out test plots of the Reverend Goodrich's most promising varieties and persuaded the land-grant colleges of New York, New England, and Michigan to do the same. Decades of crossbreeding developed such mealy beauties as the Katahdin and established Maine's prairielike Aroostook County as our most famous potatoland. Further experimentation evolved a smooth-skinned creamy giant that was exquisite when baked; it flourished best in the loams of the Snake River valley and took the name of Idaho potato.

The Hatch Act of 1887 upgraded the Bureau of Agriculture to the Department of Agriculture, promoted the commissioner to secretary and made him a member of the President's cabinet. Saunders' greenhouses and gardens became the Bureau of Plant Industry. But throughout his four decades of public service, Saunders' payroll never exceeded 127 chemists, gardeners, field scouts, and secretaries. The importance of their work in increasing crop production and placating the middleman greed for more and more exports of farm products caused the Hatch Act to authorize federal funds for the development of an agricultural experiment station at each land-grant college.

"It shall be the object and duty of the State agricultural experiment stations," the Hatch Act ruled, ". . . to conduct original and other researches, investigations and experiments bearing directly on and contributing to the establishment and maintenance of a permanent and effective agriculture industry of the United States, including researches basic to the problems of agriculture in its broadest aspects, and such investigations as have for their purpose the development and improvement of rural life and the maximum contribution by agriculture to the welfare of the consumer." By 1891, every state had a land-grant college and was hiring personnel—too often through the demands of political bosses—for its experiment station.

America's meat export trade had grown from an $8-million total in 1860 to an $82-million total in the 1880s. But Texas Fever was spreading across the corn belt and killing thousands of cattle each year. Dr. Theobald Smith and L.F. Kilborne of the department's new Bureau of Animal Industry conducted studies that identified infected ticks as carriers of the fever. They prescribed dipping vats using chemical solutions that killed the ticks but did no harm to the animals except "stink'm up" for a few days. Some stockmen rebelled. There were burnouts and gun threats until pen users could prove that the dip was saving cattlemen $40 million a year.

In the summer of 1896, Iowa delegates to the Republican Convention protested William McKinley's nomination for President until he offered them the chance to name his Secretary of Agriculture. Their choice was a Scotsman named James C. Wilson who had served for years on the dictatorial House Committee on Agriculture.

Wilson and his constant companion, a five-cent cigar, moved into the USDA array of greenhouses, gardens, and rococo office buildings during March, 1897. He found a department employing 2,444 persons, with an annual appropriation of $3 million (equalling 7.8 cents per capita for our rural population). Meat exports, the lobbying of packers, the grievances of cattlemen and hog producers against rigged prices at the rail-junction stockyards had swollen the Bureau of Animal Industry to 777 investigators, clerks, and fieldmen—the department's largest unit. Only ninety-seven people worked for the Bureau of Biological Survey, responsible for all government planning and research for wild animals. (Bone and pelt hunters had practically eradicated the bison, elk, moose, and bear.) The Bureau of Chemistry had twenty employees. The Forest Service, charged with administration of all government forest lands and creation of a policy of timber conservation, had a staff of fourteen.

Wilson tilted his cigar and went to work. He was a good listener, a better flatterer, and a veteran of lobbyist wiles. "It is the aim of the department," he said in his annual report, "to bring the scientist to the help of the people, to ascertain what imported crop plants might be produced in our country, to search the world for fruits, grains, vegetables, grasses and legumes that might be found useful here, to secure new varieties of plants by breeding and selection, to control destructive diseases, to open new markets for plant products, and to improve methods of handling, shipping and marketing the things the farmer grows, especially in the more perishable crops."

Capitol Hill was argued into an appropriation for a corps of twenty-five "agricultural explorers," trained botanists who would search overseas for plants that might launch new types of agricultural production in the United States. Over the years, the cornucopia of goodness they sent home included soy beans, mung beans, seedless grapes, tung-oil trees, date palms, Smyrna figs, avocados (originally called alligator pears), pistachios, Japanese persimmons, kumquats, and new varieties of grain. Several of the new crops hastened California's transformation from cattle ranches and wheat farms to our largest producer of fruits, nuts, and vegetables.

Protective measures for wild game were sent up the Hill and to state legislatures for translation into laws. Railroad trains were rebuilt with exhibits of new machinery, better tillage practices, and new cover crops, then sent across the prairie and through the mountains; state-college professors and field agents gave lectures at each county-seat stop.

The Forest Service zoomed to a personnel staff of 4,127; a system of range patrols and conservation enforcement began to shape up. A thirty-five-year program of eradicating the deadly bovine tuberculosis in dairy cattle was launched. The Pure Food and Drug Act, effective after January 1, 1907, enforced use of the milk pasteurization process and inaugurated an inspection system for foods and drugs moving in interstate commerce. A corps of federal meat inspectors began to patrol the bloody labyrinths of the big packing plants in Chicago, Omaha, Cincinnati, St. Louis, St. Paul, and Des Moines.

After much editorial nagging by the Quaker-owned *Farm Journal*, a system of rural free delivery of the United States mail was pushed through Congress. A new Office of Public Roads experimented with gravel, macadam, and concrete topping for farm-to-market highways. New USDA experimental farms in Maryland and Virginia tested and crossbred for better breeds of beef, pig, chicken, duck, turkey. Blackleg, glanders, rabies, swamp fever, and other animal diseases all underwent the microscope-retort-drug-injection routine toward cure. The Spanish-American War brought new problems and new crop experiments for Puerto Rico, Cuba, and the Philippines.

The USDA's mail increased from 500 to 52,000 letters and postcards a week. The number of publications the department issued soared from 424 to 2,100 per year. When Wilson took office, only 41 bulletins for farmers had been issued in the department's 34 years. When he left, a total of 506 bulletins, discussing every phase of farm operation, had been printed and reprinted on the government presses, while 197 information specialists and secretaries hammered out more verbiage on "sidewinder" typewriters.

The seven years of Theodore Roosevelt's presidency were the liveliest that USDA would experience until Franklin D. Roosevelt's New Deal. President "Teddy" boomingly approved the circus quality of Wilson's promotion programs. As the gardens, orchards, and livestock of his Oyster Bay estate attested, he was a devoted agriculturist. After Upton Sinclair wrote *The Jungle* as an exposé of the filth, bad labor conditions, and miserly practices at Chicago packing plants, "Teddy" lobbied through the Meat Inspection Act, then "waved his Big Stick" to enforce it. (*The Jungle* has remained a "devil's book" to meat packers and their trade associations ever since!) Between 1902 and 1912, a series of wild life and rural life study commissions probed the mores of rural America, held long discussions on the whys and wherefores, and left impressive books and charts and brochures to collect dust on professors' shelves.

But Theodore Roosevelt committed political suicide in 1912 when he refused to endorse the nomination of William Howard Taft, formed the Bull Moose party, and enabled the Democrats to squeeze Woodrow Wilson into the White House. In his final report as secretary, written in December, 1912, James Wilson

boasted: "The department has both promoted and begun a revolution in the science of agriculture. The record of sixteen
years . . . begins with a yearly agricultural production worth four
billion dollars and ends with $9,532,000,000. . . . Beginnings have
been made in production per acre increasing faster than the
natural increase in population."

There were now 67 state agricultural colleges and 42 privately
endowed colleges graduating 30,000 "Ag majors" a year. Forty
of the colleges trained agricultural teachers for high schools. A
new system of appointing an agricultural agent, jointly paid by
federal and state budgets, in each rural county was being tested
in New York and Pennsylvania. A bill being readied for argument
before the House Committee on Agriculture would call for a
home-demonstration agent in each rural county, too, so that farm
wives and children could be prepared for the influx of electricity
and its array of household gadgetry.

Wilson's office windows gave him a view of the department's
massive South Building looming across the mall from the Washington Monument. When finished, it would sprawl across three
blocks, and would easily house twelve thousand employees. During his sixteen years, he had wheedled and harangued the annual
budget from $3,000,000 to $24,743,044, and, considering the
results, with a minimum of "pork barreling."

But had the colleges, the professors, the laboratories, the new
crops, the 506 bulletins, and the 197 information specialists been
too little and too late? Thomas Jefferson believed that democracy
could not exist under "city rule" because the larger cities grew,
the more individualism and self-sufficiency weakened. And
America's cities were growing faster and faster. Iron and steel
tools, the railroads' freight fees, and price fixing by middlemen
had catapulted agricultural producers from barter to cash and
credit. If the cities' new systems of electric lighting and automotive power were to penetrate the farm, ranch, and plantation
countrysides, agriculture's dependence on the middlemen would
increase, perhaps disastrously.

At the end of James C. Wilson's career as head of the USDA,

the sharecropper system of semi-slavery still persisted in the South; the region's dependence on cotton cropping was now being threatened by a voracious bug called the boll weevil. In the West, the farmer and the rancher had just about settled their feuding, but dust storms threatened each summer from the huge new fields of corn and wheat. Flour makers in the Mississippi Valley had discovered how to reclaim the bran and fiber coating that comprises two-thirds of a wheat kernel, mix it with some sugar, salt, and chemicals, and sell the mixture to livestock producers as prime feed. More middleman profits! Rivers continued to run murky brown. In the East and Midwest, overworked soil demanded more and more fertilizer. A bug that had been a fairly harmless native of Colorado developed such an appetite for the leaves of potato plants that it became a summerlong ravager and even managed to reach Europe and ruin potato crops there. Budget restrictions and congressional prejudices had banned any effort by USDA to encourage urban-rural communication, guarantee the producer a fair share of retail prices, or even correct those antiquated sneer terms of "hick," "rube," "redneck," "hillbilly," and "country bumpkin" used by urbanites.

Had USDA really solved agriculture's problems, or had too many mistakes been made before and since 1862?

One other question may have crossed James Wilson's mind as he stared for the last time across the mall where William Saunders' office and greenhouses used to stand. The most remarkable achievement of all USDA's years had germinated there, yet the department didn't dare claim it—out loud, anyway. The nation's first socio-political association of agriculturists was plotted in Saunders' office. During the 1870s and 1880s, the National Grange had raised considerable rumpus and, for a time, seemed to be humbling the arrogance of the middlemen. Now there were farmer organizations and farmer-owned cooperatives all across the continent. Could these win a fair share of retail prices and restore a degree of self-sufficiency for the agriculturist?

CHAPTER EIGHT

Team-Ups

If somebody with the legal skill and folkway wisdom of Abe Lincoln had transformed the "bee" into a sociopolitical movement during the 1860s or '70s, the fate of rural America might have been very different. But there weren't any more Abe Lincolns and the efforts of agricultural organizations to counteract the influence of industrialists, realtors, and bureaucrats have stumbled and fumbled since 1867.

The bee had been the most effective means of group action since the Pilgrim and Virginian landings. It grew from the belief that neighborliness involved the concept of "Do unto others as you would have others do unto you" and the ancient truism that two heads are better than one. In medieval England, "bee" was a synonym for "boon." The first colonial Thanksgiving dinner was a bee because it was an outpouring of neighborly cooperation by whites and Native Americans.

When colonial homes were built, neighbors brought in their tools and hand skills for a raising bee. From the meals prepared by the women came such delectable dishes as shrimp mull, cheese chowder, deviled crab, barbecued ox, and the New England boiled dinner. In late fall, after the corn had dried to bone hardness, husking bees were held in each family barn. (Whoever shucked an ear of predominantly red kernels won the privilege of kissing any member of the opposite sex.) Country preachers received meager salaries; twice a year there were preacher bees when every family of the congregation was expected to visit the parsonage with gifts of food and clothing.

Naturally, the cooperative zeal of the honeybee became identified with the neighborhood bee, just as it had been in Crete and mainland Greece three thousand years before, when replicas of the honeybee became popular on amulets, rings, and primitive paintings. The word *Deseret* in the Book of Mormon signifies "honeybee." The state seal of Utah features a conical beehive with a swarm of bees around it, emblematic of the industry of the people.

Sewing bee, quilting bee, threshing bee—all of them winnowed the miserly from the generous, ripened friendships, encouraged courtships, strengthened community pride, and served as cheery oases in the dawn-to-dusk demands of farm life. But they were homestuff. From 1610 until 1867 no effort was made to coordinate the bee's zest and neighborliness into an organization that would speak out for agriculture as a way of life in state and federal legislative halls or in the marketplace.

Oliver Kelley was a Bostonian who wandered the Midwest as a drugstore clerk, a newspaper reporter, and an Indian trader before he settled in as a field agent for the U.S. Bureau of Agriculture. Early in 1867 he was shipped off to the Southeast to investigate farm conditions in the ravaged heartland of the Confederacy. He returned north eager to relay his indignation to anyone who would listen. From Virginia to Texas he had seen carpetbaggers take up where planters left their silver mint-julep cups in 1861. Again, cotton spanned in vast green patterns across valleys and the black gumbo of the Mississippi's delta. The only difference was that the plantations operated on a sharecrop system that in some respects was worse than slavery. Up country, owners of small farms struggled wth eroding hillsides that would barely produce patches of turnip greens, runt corn, and enough peanuts, acorns, beechnuts, and pasture to feed two or three cows and a half dozen pigs.

Kelley soon learned that William Saunders, the bureau's horticulturist, shared some of the same feelings. Saunders, the gossip said, had "made some Congressional whiskers bristle" with his blunt comments on city control of the farmers' markets. He even dared to send a letter of congratulations to the New Hampshire Board of Agriculture when it resolved that "farmers are without power because they have never learned to act in concert," and urged its members to correspond with the Rochdale Cooperative in central England.

The Rochdalians were considered dangerous radicals by Congressmen and State Department officials who had taken the trouble to read about their achievements. A group of cottage weavers impoverished by low prices for their cloth and yarn and high prices for their food and supplies, they had formed a cooperative society with a strict code of profit sharing. Flour, rice, canned goods, cheeses, and equipment were purchased in large quantities so that the buyers could obtain wholesale prices. They pooled production of cloth and yarns the same way and sold them to tailoring establishments and London stores, thus eliminating the 10 to 30 percent fees of middlemen. (Both the Shakers and the Pennsylvania Dutch operated similar systems for their purchases and sales.)

Kelley crossed the mall one noon-hour and found Saunders eating lunch at his desk. The conversation became so vigorous that they decided to lunch together whenever work schedules permitted.

Saunders was adamant about the need for a national system of farmer cooperatives. From Maine to the new Scandinavian communities in Minnesota, he stressed, farmers had to sell crops at city markets at prices fixed by wholesalers. The farmers' prices for machines, wire, lumber, tools, flour, clothing, sheet iron, and nails were fixed by manufacturers and wholesalers. The agriculturist was selling at wholesale and buying at retail!

The situation could only get worse. Cities and their smoky clusters of manufacturing plants were growing. They would send more and more representatives to Congress and the state legislatures. Cities had to be collectivist; all of the residents were direly dependent on cash incomes. They couldn't be like farmers and fend for themselves for food and shelter and horse power and, if worse came to worse, for homemade tools. So there was kowtowing and bossism and be-nice-to-the-boss's-wife. The representatives elected by cities were usually lawyers trained to speak a jargon that few civilians could understand. Court decisions were based on legal decisions that had been made centuries ago by other jargon-droning attorneys.

Farmers knew how to be neighborly. They had bees for just about everything that required cooperative skills. How far from bees to cooperatives like the Rochdale? How far to a neighborly union that could match the powers of manufacturers and middlemen and railroad lobbyists and lawyers in the legislatures?

Kelley, four other USDA employees, and a New York State fruit farmer who happened to be in Washington on business met in Saunders' office on December 4, 1867. They agreed to form a farmers' organization that would be a secret order, something like the Masons. It would have a ritual, regalia, passwords, and titles, all with farm meaning. For the organization's name, they reached into French and plucked the word *grange* (from the Latin *granum*, or grain). The full title, as Saunders and Kelley suggested, would be The National Grange Order for the Patrons of Husbandry.

All the time, Saunders was in the midst of negotiations with the British Embassy to import eucalyptus trees from Australia. The leaves were said to be an excellent repellent against mosquitoes and other flying pests; there was every reason to believe eucalyptus would grow in California. But, for Saunders, the Grange took priority. He wrote a note of apology to the British agricultural aide, then began writing a constitution and by-laws for the Grange. Kelley wrote to newspaper editors, ministers, state boards of agriculture, and land-grant-college deans, urging the need for the Grange and explaining its basic principles.

Replies to the letters were so encouraging that Kelley resigned from the Bureau of Agriculture and began a coast-to-coast rail-and-wagon journey to organize Grange chapters and make the formal presentation of a beribboned charter to each one. The fees for the charters, he planned, would pay his traveling expenses. He buttonholed preachers, kissed babies, praised cooking, thumbed rides, sipped hard cider and bourbon with country editors, then spent evenings writing letters to legislators. When he won consent to form a Grange, he chaired the opening meetings, presented the charter, and used the charter fee to pay his fare to the next county seat. In Wisconsin, where taciturn Germans and Swedes would have little to do with him, he went broke and had to wire Saunders for fare to Minnesota.

For three years the Grange remained a shadow, with fewer than ten thousand members. Farmers thought it was a fine thing, belonging to a secret club with gleaming sashes for the officers and such titles as Master, Lecturer, Laborer, Cultivator, Harvester, and Husbandman. Lectures and discussion groups sounded needful, too. Maybe next year . . .

The French emperor, a Prussian politician, and a score of frightened middlemen inadvertently popularized the Grange. The traditional wastefulness of army commissaries, plus the West's new access to railroads, had caused the country's wheat production to rise from 173 million to 287 million bushels during the Civil War; oat and barley crops doubled. Grain traders guessed that European purchases would take all that could be produced. But, during 1868, political hackles began to rise from London to Moscow. In attempting to form a German empire from its ancient kingdoms and city-states, Prussia's Bismarck met the arrogance of France's Napoleon III. By the spring of 1869, war seemed certain.

In New York City during the same months, Jay Gould and Wall Street associates began to manipulate the gold market. Their plot failed. The stock market plummeted to the despair of "Black Friday" on September 24, with the usual trail of bankruptcies and suicides. Two months later, German armies rumbled across the Rhine into France. The price of No. 2 wheat dropped from $1.45 to 76 cents a bushel on the Chicago Exchange. The panic spread to corn and small grain-trading pits, to stockyards and packing plants, to feedyards, to the square gray towers of country elevators.

Bankers couldn't, or wouldn't, absorb the price collapse or lower the interest rates on short-term notes. Railroads wouldn't reduce the freight rate of fifty-two cents a bushel for wheat, St. Louis to Jersey City. Stockyards and grain-commission men found it cheaper to declare bankruptcy and go hunting for a while. Producers were burdened with losses; homes and machinery were foreclosed. Kelley, Saunders, and the other Grange founders began to hear a chant: "Let's try this Grange outfit." By the fall of 1872, more than a thousand Granges had been organized in the eleven Western states.

They argued on the porches and in the cloakrooms after Grange meetings, adjourned to the free crackers-and-cheese beside the grocery's checkerboard next afternoon. They didn't use the Grange name, but called themselves Independents, Reformists, Farmers, Antimonopolists. In Illinois, Iowa, Wisconsin, Minnesota, Nebraska, and Kansas they lobbied new laws empowering the state to control railroad rates within its boundaries and to appoint commissions that would establish uniform freight rates on all farm products.

Collis P. Huntington, the Troy, New York, saloonkeeper's son who once delivered Amos Eaton's weekly newspaper and was now the ruthless boss of Southern Pacific's empire, protested that "Grangers are a pack of communists." Jay Gould, already exceedingly skillful in borrowing railroads and banks, borrowed the accusation. Newspaper owners, having recently discovered that more profit could be made from advertising than from circulation fees, scribbled editorials about the threat to free enterprise.

Another financial panic in 1873 tumbled one-fourth of the nation's railroads into bankruptcy. The survivors' lobbyists sang such mournful choruses about "the poor railroads" and the "communist peril" that most of the state laws controlling rates were repealed by 1875.

The Grange kept growing, however, and by 1875 it had 20,000 lodges and more than 1.5 million members. Saunders, elected as the organization's Worthy Master, openly sponsored the Rochdale Plan of Cooperation in competition with industries and middlemen. Grain, cattle, and hog "pools" began to appear in prairie towns. Granges in Nebraska, Iowa, and Minnesota raised enough funds to lease grain elevators, stockyards, and shipping pens. Illinois Granges contracted to act as selling agents in Chicago, and announced a year later that they were providing savings of 20 percent for grain and livestock producers. The Iowa Grange boasted an annual saving of $365,000 for members through collective purchases of farm machinery.

At St. Louis, Chicago, Louisville, Omaha, ten-horse teams dragged lathes, forges, steel bars from rail sidings out to renovated barns and mills in weedy suburbs. The new signs over the doors said: Granger Harvester Company, Patrons of Husbandry Plow Company, Pomona Threshers, Inc. Grange Emporiums and Pomona Feedstores opened in villages to sell supplies "direct from the factory." Soon there were Grange Life Insurance, Grange Cheese, Grange Pork Products, Grange Weavers, Grange Ropeyards. In Chicago, the new firm of Montgomery Ward assessed the enthusiasm and launched America's first mail-order business "to meet the direct-to-consumer needs of the Patrons of Husbandry."

For a few years, while industry was recovering from the Panic of 1873, it seemed that Granger cooperatives had learned how to lead Wall Street's bulls on jute strings, to pet rattlesnakes, and to prove that Truth and Virtue prevailed in the United States. The delusion may have been the basic reason for the economic naiveté of a majority of the cooperatives.

Meager funds were appropriated for the cooperatives' advertising and other forms of sales promotion. Lobbying efforts in Washington and the state capitals were sporadic, with a tendency to be pompous. Preachers with a reputation for great sermons and veteran farmers with an itch to get into business were hired as managers and supervisors of cooperatives. Industrialists—hence bankers—continued to hold to the Huntington libel that Grangers were "a pack of communists."

The Montgomery Ward ploy of getting its mail-order catalogues into every rural home succeeded in underpricing most of the cooperatives. Moreover, the catalogue's paper was so soft that the publication hung on a hook in the outhouse as a most comforting alternative to the corncob. When drawings of shapely female forms in underwear were added to its pages, "The Montgomery" became a popular source of sex education for adolescents.

The Wall Street bulls and excellent growing weather returned during the 1880s. The winds were sweet with spring rains again. The dust storms didn't happen, nor did the midsummer plagues of grasshoppers. Livestock fattened in lush grasses. The corn and wheat belts produced big crops. Banks lowered interest rates. The Congress of the United States passed an act regulating interstate commerce. John Deere, McCormick, and other machinery makers began patent infringement suits against the small plants making Granger reapers, mowers, and plows, then flooded the market with "Spring Sale Specials." Meanwhile, Granger salesmen and managers who demonstrated business skills were lured off to jobs in private industry by offers of larger salaries and "a fine home only a few minutes' horsecar ride from your office."

The most meaningful victory of all for the middleman originated in the flour mills perched beside the Falls of St. Anthony at Minneapolis and St. Paul. When the Pillsburys and Washburns and Crosbys founded their mills there, they used wheels of burred stone to pulverize the complex wheat kernels into flour. (Consequently, wheat flour continued to be a tannish mixture of the kernel's oily germ, the white epidermis layer, and the bran "skin.")

But by the time the Civil War began, every city had a *nouveau riche* aristocracy of ship and railroad owners, wholesalers, bankers, and manufacturers intent on imitating the lifestyle and cuisine of Europe's aristocracy. One of their foibles was that the bread and pastries served on their Duncan Phyfe, Chippendale, and Empire tables must be made with snowy-white flour. White flour, however, could be obtained only by means of elaborate screening devices that winnow the wheat's epidermis from the brown wisps of germ and bran. Since the epidermis comprises only a third of the kernel, the two-thirds of vitamin-rich bran and germ became waste, so was sluiced into the Mississippi, polluting the river as it flowed south toward muddy junction with the Missouri. And the demand for white flour trebled after the Civil War.

At about the same time that white flour was growing in popularity, the first shipments of the new winter wheat were starting to come out of Kansas; it raised more hell than the competitive Granger mills. The red kernels of winter wheat were so hard that they chipped the burred stone grinding wheels before shattering into such tiny flecks that it was almost impossible to screen out the white epidermis.

Millers contracted with Edmund La Croix, a French-trained engineer, to solve the problem. La Croix perfected an air-jet system that suspended the powdered epidermis while the heavier bran and germ were escalated into the Mississippi. La Croix also insisted that the mills retool with steel grinding wheels.

White flour became so popular that the West's production of wheat rose to 2.5 billion bushels a year. Bakers learned how to introduce more air into bread; the average bakery loaf became as squishy as a moist sponge. After vitamins were discovered, white flours were "enriched" with dosings of malted barley, niacin, iron, thiamine, mononitrate, and riboflavin.

But the bran, germ, and husk of the wheat continued to pollute the Mississippi until C. A. Pillsbury of Pillsbury–Washburn Mills decided on an experiment. He ordered wagonloads of the wheat wastes out to his farm, then divided his beef steers, milk cows, and pigs into two lots. Lot One was to be fed the usual corn and silage diet. Lot Two would be fed entirely on wheat bran and germ wastage.

Lot Two animals gained weight as rapidly and were as healthy as the corn and silage feeders. At slaughter time, the wheat-wastage feeders of Lot Two revealed excellent marketing qualities. There was no longer any need to dump wheat bran and germ into the Mississippi. It could be sold back to farmers and ranchers as prime animal feed.

Selling wheat wastage back to agriculturists as prime feed that would compete with their home-grown grains called for imaginative promotion. The bran, germ, and husks were blended with cottonseed, bone meal, salt, and sugar. Orders were placed with cotton mills for bagging made from durable ginghams and muslins that farm wives could later sew into sheets, towels, or clothing. Advertising managers concocted such alluring brand names as Morepig, Cow Chow, and Beefmaker. Owners of grain elevators, lumberyards, and grocery stores were offered bonuses to retail the new prime feeds.

The feed-grains of the Granger cooperatives could not compete with the mills' feed without heavy investments, and were forced to close down. Lawsuits about patent infringement, the boisterous promotion of bargain sales by competitors, and the allegations of communism by industrialists and bankers caused hundreds of other cooperatives to give up. Between 1875 and 1890, active membership in the Grange skidded from 858,000 to 106,000. Meanwhile, dairymen and poultrymen and hog farmers paid profits to flour mills, bag makers, railroads, wholesalers, and retailers in their eagerness to buy the wheat bran formerly dumped into the Mississippi. (By the 1980s, livestock producers are paying out more than $17 billion a year for processed livestock feeds. The millers no longer find it necessary to use printed calico and muslin bags.)

In time, the millers also learned that housewives would buy bran flakes and toasted wheat germ, especially when they are displayed in lavish packaging on grocery shelves. Another market thus opened for the Mississippi "slops."

As the Grange membership dwindled, new farmers' alliances grew. Founded by the editor of a Midwestern farm publication, the initial Farmers' Alliance advocated political lobbying against railroad freight fees and the high interest rates levied on mortgages and credit buying. Thousands of homesteaders in the Mississippi and Missouri valleys joined. Southerners who dared oppose the sharecropper system in favor of cooperative enterprise formed a regional organization that also took the name of Farmers' Alliance but, because Civil War enmities persisted, failed to establish a united front with "those Northerners."

The bellwether of farmers' alliance popularity between 1885 and 1891 was a Kansas housewife named Mary Ellen Lease. Irish and irate, Mrs. Lease stumped farm meetings across the Midwest urging farmers to "raise less corn and more hell." She harangued for laws against farm foreclosures, claiming that banks and loan companies foreclosed on 10 percent of farms in Kansas each year. There must be federal legislation, she demanded, giving farmers the opportunity to make long-term loans at low interest rates. Railroad and telegraph systems should become government property. There should be networks of government warehouses where farmers could store grain, cotton, and tobacco, then receive government loan credits up to 80 percent of their crops' retail value.

Such strident calls for political reform caused farm alliance leaders to join with the equally strident Knights of Labor to form the Populist Party. The Populists held stormy conventions, polled a million votes in 1892, and in 1894 succeeded in electing thirteen of their nominees to Congress (seven Representatives and six Senators). Two years later, Populist endorsement of the stentorian religionist, William Jennings Bryan, assured him of the Democratic nomination for the presidency. The Republicans' McKinley beat Bryan in 1896 and again in 1900. The battle for a silver, rather than the gold, standard for the nation's currency was lost. The farmers' alliances collapsed.

Mrs. Lease left the Alliance and became a political analyst for the *New York World*, but her demands for agricultural reform continued to echo across the West; some of them became planks in the platforms advocated by the Democrats' candidates. She was in her late seventies when Franklin D. Roosevelt became governor of New York; she died the year he became President. Within two years, several of her old urgencies were being incorporated into the New Deal's farm program by Henry Agard Wallace, who grew up in Iowa where tall tales about "that Lease gal" were legion.

The Grangers' ideal of farmer cooperatives grew sturdier roots among California's navel orange groves. The new railroad refrigerator cars could carry crates of oranges from Los Angeles to Chicago in three weeks, with layovers for re-icing every other day. But orchardists were soon victimized by commission men and brokers—by the 1880s they were being paid a dime for a seventy-pound box of fruit that cost them five dimes to produce.

During November, 1885, growers formed the California Fruit Union, established a headquarters near the state capital at Sacramento, and set about the onerous task of achieving better prices and more uniform quality. Although out-of-state shipments totaled 160 million pounds in 1893, growers found that their income had not increased; their oranges had so little appeal for Easterners that markets were being glutted. A series of reorganizations produced the California Fruit Growers Exchange in 1903. Headquarters were transferred to Los Angeles, with branch offices in Eastern cities. After viaducts began to siphon snow water out of the Sierras, groves of oranges, lemons, figs, olives, and dates were pushed deep into the desert. There were years when less than a fourth of the crop could be sold.

At the 1907 meeting of the Exchange's directors, the decision was made to spend $10,000 "to advertise citrus fruit." The president of the Exchange, F. Q. Story, argued executives of the Southern Pacific Railroad into a dollar-for-dollar pledge to promote California oranges. Iowa was selected as the ideal test territory.

Across Iowa's rich countryside, New England and German migrants had developed a self-sufficient culture of corn, cattle, hogs, and poultry. Des Moines was a metropolis of eighty thousand population. Iowa's weather was a twin of Vermont's. The

Californians moved into the state with circus bombast. Advance agents of Southern Pacific put up posters announcing "Oranges for Health—California for Wealth" on billboards and barns from the Mississippi to the Missouri. The Exchange wangled free newspaper space by announcing a prize contest for essays and poems about California oranges and lemons. Lecturers offered women's clubs, church groups, lodges, and farm associations free speeches about California climate and the sun-kissed citrus groves, with a handout of tree-ripened fruit at the end of the lecture. Newspapers carried cartoons of a prim, flaxen-haired, lace-bloomered "Miss California" feeding an orange to a shivering urchin labeled "Iowa."

The trains carrying the fruit were painted orange and swathed in banners and bunting. They stopped at every grade crossing while an orange and a lemon were passed out to each person waiting. A deep, partitioned packing crate had been designed for exclusive use on the trains, each one labeled, "Ask for California Oranges in this style box." Full boxes, averaging a bushel of fruit, cost two dollars. Publicists and news reporters rode the Sun Kissed parlor cars attached to the trains and telegraphed daily human-interest stories, sprinkled with "kitchen tested" recipes for citrus desserts, drinks, soufflés, and sauces.

When the campaign ended, and Iowa hogs were grunting contentedly over the tasty peelings in their rations, the Exchange and the Southern Pacific sat down to analyze results. The Exchange had spent only $7,000 of its $10,000 advertising appropriation. Hundreds of repeat orders were coming in from Iowa grocers and produce dealers. The Southern Pacific's promotion department was receiving sacks of letters from Iowa farmers seeking more detail about potential homesites adjoining its Southern California trackage.

The Exchange appropriated a $25,000 budget for advertising in 1908. The name "Sunkist" was adopted for all Exchange citrus products, with each orange to be wrapped in tissue paper dyed sunset-orange. Then a silver "orange-spoon" was designed and offered to consumers at the super-bargain rate of "twelve wrappers and twelve cents for each spoon, postpaid." Ballyhooed on by orange wrappers, silver spoons, beribboned fruit trains, and offers of free electric orange-squeezers to drugstores and candy shops, the Exchange's gross rose from an annual $12 million to $58 million by 1920. The name of the cooperative was changed to Sunkist, Inc. During the same years, the population of Los Angeles rose to 576,000, with thousands of families bungalowed on Southern Pacific grant lands; the most popular event of the year was the Iowa Day picnic.

The Sunkist success became an example for farmer cooperatives and was significant in the transition of California to our most prolific producer of vegetables, fruit, nuts, wine, and specialty flowers. The botanical genius of a Massachusetts native named Luther Burbank, though, hastened the transition. A devotee of Darwin's theories about genetics and evolution, he developed a superior breed of potato before he was twenty-two, then, in 1875, decided to follow his brothers to California. The experiments he pursued at Santa Rosa during the next half century evolved an amazing span of green magic. His creations included: the Shasta daisy, the nectarine, a spineless cactus useful for cattle feed, and new varieties of tomatoes, asparagus, corn, squash, peas, and lilies. His eight-volume work, *How Plants Are Trained to Work for Man*, became a classic reference.

Almonds, grapes, figs, citrus, and olives had all been introduced to California in the gardens of the Franciscan missions. Hungarian, French, Italian, and English adventurers—at first lured in by the Gold Rush—realized the potential of California's commercial vineyards and orchards. Agoston Harazthy, a Hungarian, pioneered viniculture of European wine grapes in Sonoma county during the 1850s. Then, in 1871, Felix Gillet introduced soft-shelled walnuts from his native France to the hillsides of Nevada City. Another Frenchman, Louis Pellier, imported the first cuttings of prune plums.

A severe drought in the San Joaquin Valley during the fall of 1873 dried ripe grapes on the vines. Tradition has it that one Fresno grower picked his dried fruit and shipped it to a grocer friend in San Francisco. Stumped until he heard that a steamer had just docked from Peru, the grocer promoted the golden clusters as "a Peruvian delicacy" and sold all of them within a few days. Thus, folklore alleges, the state's raisin industry began.

William Thompson, an Englishman, obtained three cuttings of a seedless grape from his homeland, grafted them on a Muscat root, and initiated California's most popular green grape, the Thompson Seedless. Experiments during the 1890s proved that date palms, too, would flourish in the desert east of Riverside.

Like the American soils' adoption of British, Swedish, Dutch, French, and Spanish seeds in the seventeenth century, of German, African, Irish, and Welsh seeds in the eighteenth, the botanical introductions to California between the 1860s and 1880s were the result of international cooperation. But experiments and failures were necessary before cooperative marketing organizations could be developed for each product. The usual mistakes of inefficient management, faulty bookkeeping, and hapless sales campaigns were experienced. Sun-Maid Raisins, Sunsweet Prunes, Diamond Walnuts, Valley Fig Growers—all slowly developed as successful marketing cooperatives. In 1980, they combined as Sun-Diamond Growers of California. Net sales for the first fiscal year of the union totaled $502 million, with shipments of 290 million tons of dried fruit and nuts, of which 45,000 tons went to Europe.

Cautioned by memories of the Grange cooperatives and the political strength of middleman lobbyists, leaders of the marketing cooperatives for livestock, grain, cotton, vegetables, and seed producers undertook adventures in economic efficiency. Livestock-shipping associations, managed by veterans familiar with the price-fixing techniques of packer buyers at the stockyards, gradually replaced the 10-percent-commission men. Grain cooperatives built their own elevators, then negotiated with millers and feed manufacturers about price. Cotton cooperatives acquired their own gins and ventured into wholesaling the fiber, oil, and seed meal. Minnesota dairymen formed the cooperative that, through astute management and insistence on quality production, became Land O Lakes, the nation's most famous producer of butter and dairy by-products.

The Grange slowly recovered from its 1880 slump and again became a formidable promoter of cooperatives. In 1905, a Georgia farmer and part-time teacher named Charles S. Barrett began to organize a National Farmers Union. By the time he retired in 1928, it had a membership of half a million, principally in the cotton-impoverished South and the drought-plagued northern plains. A promotional plan devised to popularize the services of the government's county-agent system called for the organization of county associations of farm families. By 1910, these associations used the name of Farm Bureau and were forming statewide councils. In 1919, delegates from thirty-one state groups met in Chicago and founded the American Farm Bureau Federation.

Grange, Farmers Union, and Farm Bureau all became active in promoting cooperatives. One outstanding achievement was the founding of Nationwide Insurance by the Ohio Farm Bureau, under the guidance of Murray D. Lincoln, a shrewdly philosophical Yankee. Similarly, in New York, the Grange, the Dairymen's League, and the Farm Bureau co-sponsored GLF Exchange. Howard E. Babcock, as deft an idea man as Ohio Farm Bureau's Lincoln, guided GLF's growth, and it became the most influential farm cooperative in the Northeast. During the 1960s, GLF merged with other state cooperatives as Agway; annual sales exceeded $1 billion by 1980. Gold Kist, Inc., the most influential farm cooperative in the South, grew from the Cotton Producers Association that David W. Brooks, a teacher of agronomy in Georgia, shepherded through the Great Depression of the 1930s, then merged with poultry, peanut, and pecan producer associations. Farmland, Inc., with annual sales approaching $2 billion in 1980, grew from a $3,000 investment by local Kansas cooperatives to buying petroleum products wholesale.

By 1975, Wheeler McMillen estimated in his agricultural history, *Feeding Multitudes*, farmer cooperatives supplied 32 percent of farm fertilizers, 29 percent of farm-used petroleum, 20 percent of chemicals, 20 percent of seeds, and 18 percent of purchased feeds; but, he reminds the reader, "big though they seem, grain-selling cooperatives all together handle less than one-fifth of the production. Five giant private firms transact the rest of the grain business."

Today, although agricultural cooperatives have become economically important and scores of agricultural lobbying offices operate in Washington, with hundreds more in state capitals, the stumble and fumble persist. Only a few of the cooperatives have been able to assess enough funds to compete with the high-pressure advertising of middleman organizations in newspapers, magazines, and television commercials. Nor have cooperatives yet seen fit to compete against conglomerates by offering products with more natural vitamin content and flavor.

Unfortunately, farm organizations and their cooperatives succumbed to the crop subsidies and other federal "handouts" imposed on taxpayers by the New Deal of 1933–45 and continued by every Republican and Democratic administration since. Lobbying for federal aid became more important to organization and cooperative officials than developing effective programs to acquaint consumers and producers with their goals and advantages. Overall, naive public relations has often been a major defect of the agricultural cooperative.

The cooperative movement visualized by William Saunders and the Grange founders in 1867 offered farmer, rancher, and planter the opportunity, by group action, to retain a degree of self-sufficiency during the era when technology and its cash-and-credit economy was forcing producers toward a new form of serfdom. But most of the leadership between 1880 and the 1940s failed to comprehend the founders' goal. Promotional efforts focused on economics and dollar profits; speeches and publications failed to stimulate or educate a majority.

Political distrust was a second problem. The Civil War influenced most of the rural North to vote straight Republican and the South to become "rip-snortin' Democrat." Cooperatives held to these regional party lines until the Populists lured some Northerners to the Democrats' platform. After 1933, the lavishness of the New Deal programs caused more conversion to the Democratic fold in the rural North and West. As labor unions became politically adept, repeated efforts were made to unionize farmers and ranchers. The unions succeeded in organizing seasonal workers in the vegetable, fruit, sugar beet, and grain regions. The result was distrust within the cooperative movement; pro-Democrat and pro-labor cooperatives bickered with pro-Republican cooperatives, and Huntington's hoary libel of "a pack of communists" echoed again.

A third stumbling block has been the inability—or is it unwillingness?—of producer cooperatives and consumer cooperatives to work together. Consumer cooperatives, also patterned on the Rochdale technique of group buying, spread from Nova Scotia to our Midwest early in the twentieth century and soon gained ardent support from educators, social workers, and labor unions. Although a few leaders of producer cooperatives made valiant—and expensive—efforts to launch consumer cooperatives in rural areas, the two groups have always been wary of each other. Each group has continued to be suspicious of the other's "profit motives." The urgency for cash has destroyed the good neighbor aura of the seventeenth and eighteenth century "bee."

Despite these shortcomings, cooperatives helped agriculture to adapt during the great changeover from homegrown animal power to cash-and-credit machine power. The half century between the end of the Civil War and the outbreak of World War I was rural America's era of transition.

CHAPTER NINE

Transition

Railroads, tractors, and central markets were promoted as "civilizing" forces in American history—certainly, they were more appealing than Indian raiding parties, prairie fires, tornadoes, rattlesnakes, and balky mules. Yet, over the decades, they subtly crippled the American farmer's self-sufficient independence.

Between 1865 and 1915, farm and ranch and plantation were maneuvered toward total dependence on technology and its edict of cash and credit. The self-sufficiency of horse, mule, ox, and donkey power was abandoned for machine power and the expensive by-products of distant oil wells. Farm and ranch prices were fixed by professional gamblers in the cities' grain exchanges and stockyards. Tick fever, the boll weevil, potato bugs, grasshoppers, and other crop ravagers forced the first widespread use of such poisonous insecticides as Paris green. The need for more cash crops necessitated extensive use of chemical fertilizers on overworked soils. The rural preacher gradually lost his leadership to the educational upsurge caused by public schools, public libraries, Chautauquas, land-grant colleges, and easier access

to cities. Eagerness for advertising revenue persuaded farm publications and newspapers to promote more mechanization, hence
greater dependence on middleman manufacturers. Books, dime
novels, and then the movies sang a Lorelei song of rags-to-riches
in the cities.

There was little hope of escape either to "the good old days"
or to a golden future. Geographically, the agriculturist was cut
off at the pass by the wasteful practices of his predecessors and
the eagerness of poor Europeans to become rich Americans.
Between 1865 and 1880, Western railroads lured hundreds of
thousands of homesteaders to the land tracts the federal government gave them. By 1900 most of the Far West was being farmed
or ranched. Thereafter, the challenge was to "make a go of it"
where you are. The boundless land was gone.

The struggle to make a go of it was intense in the high-plains
region west of the Missouri valley and in the Southwest where
rainfalls averaged only ten inches or less per year (as against
the thirty-five to fifty inches average between the Atlantic seaboard and the Mississippi Valley). Wells had to be dug one hundred, two hundred, three hundred feet down to tap aquifers
whose renewal depends on snow-water seepage from the Rocky
Mountains. Windmills and irrigation became farm and ranch
essentials.

The ravage of Appalachian forests between 1780 and 1820 was
repeated in the Rockies. Railroad construction used millions of
hardwood ties plus scaffolding and bridge timbers. Promotion of
"golden West" homesteads along the "high iron" of Union Pacific,
Southern Pacific, Santa Fe, Great Northern, Rio Grande, and
Burlington created new towns—and a demand for lumber. Thousands of loggers wagoned off to mountainsides. They razed the
largest trees, burned the "trash wood," and left barren slopes.
Tree roots died, erosion began, and the Missouri River became
"Big Muddy." So did the Platte and Arkansas and Sweetwater
and Green and Yellowstone and Snake and Colorado. The Appalachian sequel of floods each spring and drought each summer
soon repeated itself in the Far West.

Excessive livestock grazing changed land patterns, especially in the Southwest. When Francisco Vásquez Coronado in 1542 led his search for the legendary golden cities of Cíbola, he followed the gorge of the San Pedro River, then passed the future site of Tombstone, Arizona. The San Pedro gushed crystal-clear water. Trout waited for bait in every pool, and some of them were "as big as blue channel catfish." Riverbanks and rocky fields adjoining were waist-high in gramma grass that was "almost as protein rich as wheat."

A gunfight that lasted thirty seconds on the afternoon of October 26, 1881, was exaggerated by dime novelists and movie makers into the Battle of the O.K. Corral, turning Tombstone into a world-famous tourist lure. My wife and I were Christmas guests in 1970 of Burton and Jeanne Devere at Tombstone's Rose Tree Inn, built by Mrs. Devere's grandparents in the 1880s. The Deveres are authorities on the region's geology, biology and history.

By the twentieth century, the San Pedro was a muddy trickle. The gramma grass has vanished. Mesquite, prickly pear, barrel cactus, agave rise in somber silhouette from horizon to horizon. Overgrazing by livestock killed the gramma grass during the 1870s and 1880s; longhorn cattle driven in from Mexico brought the seeds of the cacti and mesquite in their manure.

Similar transitions from bluewater-and-gramma to brownwater-and-erosion occurred all across the trans-Mississippi West as the need for cash crops and the urgings for more exports intensified ranching and farming.

Yet from all the perils and demands emerged a high living standard. The farmer's faith in democratic neighborliness, his willingness to work "eight hours in the morning and eight hours in the afternoon," achieved it.

"I still need to be convinced that one can be heinously deprived when the good earth and one's neighbors are all willing to answer prayers. The only secret—but necessary—ingredient is a little sweet-smelling sweat." This is the famous California author/historian Paul Bailey reminiscing about his childhood in Utah's Cache River valley.

Cash money being the scarcest of all commodities, barter and trade were essential for survival. Our staple groceries were purchased from the American Fork Co-op in exchange for fresh eggs, a side of home-cured bacon and fresh garden truck. A threshing machine rendered essential services to a hundred farms in return for a share of the threshings. Our home was a small hut. But the granary out back, housing Dad's yield from the threshing, was built of clean new pine, and spacious. Chipman's Star Roller Mill, a water-driven affair up American Fork Creek, rolled our oats and barley for cow, horse, swine and human food, and milled our wheat into a superlative whole-grain flour, taking a share as payment. As for Chipman's cotton flour sacks, when emptied and laundered they became, under the skill and ingenuity of a loving mother, the only kind of underwear and nightshirts I ever knew as a child. It took a lot of washings to fade out the big red star. I knew that American Fork girls wore panties made from Chipman's durable flour sacks, even to Sunday School. A wind gust would reveal the big red star.

Monetarily, we—like everyone else in the valley—would have been considered desperately poor. Practically everything we used, we raised. Seeds—God's own magic—were actually our wealth and ever renewing promise. If we were long on one thing, and short on another, it invariably balanced out by barter with our neighbors. Everything had a use. Nothing was wasted. A new suit could be acquired by trading for credit the sheared fleece from our sheep to the Provo Woollen Mills.

The most I ever knew in cash money was for Utah's two great holidays—July 4, Independence Day, and July 24, Pioneer Day—when we kids were issued fifteen cents for each occasion. But sneaky and resourceful, my brothers and I might cop a dozen eggs apiece from the hen coops. Uptown, eggs were always legal tender. My mother's butter or a roll of Dad's spiced bacon could underwrite one hell of a holiday.

The versatility of chores demanded rigorous work schedules on the 80-acre farms of New England, the 160-acre farms of Iowa,

the 2,000-acre "spreads" in California, and the 100,000-acre ranches
that hugged the Rockies from Montana to Texas. Horses, pigs,
and cattle required daily care, despite the preacher's admonish-
ment against "laboring on the Sabbath." Every field crop, sugar
beet to cotton, meant an eight-month drudgery of soil preparation, planting, weeding, and harvesting. And hailstorms, tornadoes, drought, and blizzards always threatened seasonal
catastrophe.

While the farmers of the mid-Atlantic seaboard required only
occasional repairs for their fieldstone homes and massive bank
barns, and New England's sturdy cedar and white-pine homes
and barns also needed only routine maintenance, farmers west
of the Mississippi were consistently faced with an urgency for
better homes and farm buildings. "On the western frontier, housing was so various as to defy description—dugouts, sodhouses
and cabins of all kinds," Edgar W. Martin relates in *The Standard
of Living in 1860.*

> In prairie states, where there was less wood for building,
> the first homes were dugouts or sodhouses. Typically, the
> dugout would be an excavation in the side of a hill, perhaps
> twelve by fourteen feet. In each corner was set a heavy forked
> timber; poles were laid upon these and (diagonally) across the
> four sides. Split logs or lumber was then laid upon the poles,
> upon which thick sods were placed to form a solid roof; some-
> times a piece of canvas would be stretched to form a ceiling.
> The floor might be puncheons or dirt pounded hard and cov-
> ered with cornhusk mats. Sometimes sidewalls would be built
> up of sods and there would be a log front. In later years, the
> dugout might have an interior of unplastered stone walls.

The sodhouse was more durable than the dugout. Frank W.
Cyr was born in a sodhouse in western Nebraska. Like many of
the youngsters who matured under the influence of farm neighborliness and long workdays, he progressed from farmhand to
ranch cowboy to schoolteacher. As director of rural education at

Columbia University's Teachers College, he developed the yellow school bus, pioneered using the long-distance telephone conference and television as educational tools and improving the small school's curriculum by means of technologic adaptations. His memories of a sodhouse childhood were cogent.

I'm still convinced that the sodhouse was the best architectural design for the prairie. The inside walls of our soddy were plastered against the sod, and the plaster held. I don't know why. The ceiling was sheets sewn together and nailed to the rafters. The rafters were saplings. The ridgepole was a heavy cottonwood log that extended the full length of the building and rested on the walls at each end. The walls were very thick. They were two runs of sod, with some loose earth in between. It was very solid, like stone. The rafters had rush on them, and straw on that, and then the sod on top of that. Grass grew on the roof.

Environmental changes for farm wives and daughters between 1865 and 1915 were as marked as the transition from hand skills to machine skills in farming. The movement for woman suffrage, born in a farming community in upstate New York in 1848, spread to Wyoming Territory in 1869; by 1913 women in twelve states had the right to vote. The founding of the National Parent and Teacher Association in 1897 broadened women's social life and cultural participation, as did the missionary societies and welfare campaigns organized by the churches. Road improvements, Studebaker wagons, the durable flivver enabled a Saturday shopping trip to town. Rural free delivery of mail began in 1896.

The New England pattern of locating a village's churches, civic offices, and shops around a Common moved west to become the courthouse square. The courthouse square usually had a park with gossip benches, flowering shrubs, and a few flower beds bordering its gravel or flagstone walks. At one end a rococo bandstand, painted white and with slender Corinthian pillars supporting its tin roof, served as podium for Fourth of July speeches, summer band concerts, Memorial Day ceremonies, the Easter rendition of the "Hallelujah" chorus from Handel's *Messiah* by the high school choir, and a shelter for the community Christmas tree. If a railroad ran through town, hoboes slept there and left empty flasks of "Mrs. Pinkham's Elixir," which everyone knew was one-third alcohol.

The brick or fieldstone courthouse with gilt dome dominated the square. It housed civic offices, a courtroom, police head-quarters, the volunteer fire department, a few basement cells and the public toilets. Across the square were two, three, four churches, each with a steeple reminiscent of an upside-down ice cream cone. Pharmacies, doctors' offices, pool halls, gents' furnishings, ladies apparel, shoe and hardware stores—all vied for space on or near the square. From Ohio to Wyoming, the courthouse square was flourishing by 1900. Give or take a few techno-gadgets, it continues in the 1980s.

The following reminiscence, by Delores Langren Neill, who grew up on a grain farm in western Iowa, echoes a familiar experience: the weekend trip to town.

> Everyone went to town on Saturday. The family was all squeezed into the car, along with a crate of eggs and any other produce we hoped to trade at the general store.
> There was an outdoor movie in the park, and round and square dancing in the Opera House, a large second-story room above the bank. The popcorn machine was in operation, too, on the park corner in front of the bank. It was bright red with a lacy border of gold and big windows. We stood on tiptoe, clutching our thin but all silver dimes, while Mr. Bryan scooped the white puffs into bags and sluiced on a quarter-cup of butter.
> A quart of buttered popcorn crunched on a park bench with the antics of "Our Gang" humming across the movie screen, a full moon that seemed to be stuck atop the Presbyterian church steeple, the whisper of a prairie breeze through the lilac bushes. No memory piece can match it!

Back East, the concentration of cities and industries between Portland, Maine, and Baltimore, Maryland, caused radical changes in the region's agriculture. The diversified farm became the specialty farm. Borden's pioneering of "white milk" distribution influenced thousands of farmers to concentrate on dairy production. Purebred Holstein and Belted Dutch cattle were imported from Holland, Guernseys from the Channel Islands, and sleek, fawn-colored Swiss from Switzerland. Dairy wholesalers built collecting stations beside the railroad tracks where farmers delivered the day's production each morning. Farm production of cheese was replaced by cheese factories in the villages; these, too, were eventually taken over by city-based wholesalers. Through the 1880s, the 770 million pounds of butter produced annually in the United States, though, was still made on farms, and most of it was churned in the Northeast.

Because of the railroads, diets improved in the cities' tenements and rowhouses. Onion, celery, lettuce, and beet fields evolved on farm mucklands. Cherries, peaches, plums—all the small fruits that canners could seal in tin and hucksters could sell up and down tenement streets—were grown along valley floors and ridges. Apple orchards heralded springtime across Massachusetts, New York, and Pennsylvania. Herman Chapin of East Bloomfield, New York, developed a fragrant apple with creamy-yellow flesh that didn't ripen fully until the fruit had been stored indoors for two or three months. He called the variety Northern Spy. City people could now have fresh apples during the sooty dreariness of February and March. A sport seedling discovered in an apple orchard in Dundas County, Ontario (Canada), produced a crisp, rose-colored fruit that also held its lushness in storage; the orchardist gave the variety his family name of McIntosh. Apples, dairy products, fresh vegetables, and poultry became the cornerstones of the Northeast's farming.

Trains and steamships also introduced the commuter and the "summer boarder" to rural areas. As railroad efficiency improved, workers in cities realized that they could regain fresh air and bucolic environments for their families by moving a few miles beyond the city limits. Railroads encouraged this decentralization by scheduling commuter trains to deliver workers to midcity terminals before nine o'clock in the morning and get them back to a suburban station before dinnertime. Farmlands were purchased by real estate developers. New villages sprang up beside the railroad stations. Suburbia's fifty-foot building lots, grass lawns, concrete walks, and shopping centers were not far down the line.

The "summer boarder" traveled farther to reach the quiet of the country. The Appalachians offered laborers, clerks, and shopowners the most reasonable escape to nature. Pennsylvania, New Jersey, and Delaware workers chose the Poconos. New Englanders headed for the Green and White Mountains, the Berkshires, and Maine. The Catskills and the Adirondacks became New York's playground, Memorial Day through Labor Day. The Catskills were the favorite retreat for the millions huddled in New York City's tenements. (Until 1900, the Catskills were called "The Irish Alps" by vaudeville comedians. After 1900, they became "The Jewish Alps.") Most of the hillside boardinghouses treated guests to evening entertainment of singers, comedians, and tap dancers booked out of New York City. Performers in these boardinghouse shows nicknamed them "The Borscht Circuit." The boardinghouses offered local farmers new markets for fruit, vegetables, dairy products, and meat; farm women and children helped family budgets by taking summer jobs as maids, cooks, waitresses, bellboys, caddies, and porters.

Immigration also influenced farm life between 1865 and 1915, not only in the Northeast but all across our chunk of the continent. Construction jobs on railroads, canals, and pipelines brought Irish, Germans, and Italians to the Northeast; many of their offspring became farmers or produce dealers or food wholesalers. Similarities to the climate and topography of their homelands brought Scandinavians into Wisconsin and Minnesota. New copper, iron, and coal mines required the skills of Welsh, Cornishmen, and Greeks. The sugar-beet fields, fruit orchards, and canneries of the Pacific slope used Oriental and Mexican labor.

Each national group made contributions to farm life, particularly to its cuisine. Italian immigrants popularized their devotion to pasta, tomato sauces, spicy salami, brisk wines, cheeses for grating, and the prolific green squash we renamed zucchini.

Corned beef and cabbage, soda bread, meat stews with potatoes in them are a heritage of the sons and daughters of Eire. Bologna, liverwurst, frankfurters, sauerkraut-with-hocks, rye breads, and fragrant cheeses extol the Germans' skills and frugality. Limpa bread, boysenberry jelly, smorgasbord, and the adaptable rutabaga are gifts of the Scandinavians. Cornish pasties and Welsh saffron breads are still specialties around the mine pits of Michigan, Wisconsin, Colorado, and Utah. Chile con carne, tortillas, and a host of other corn-based foods were imports from Mexico, but chop suey and chow mein are a Chinese-American invention unknown in China. Figs, grape leaves, feta cheese, halvah, squid, artichokes, and the garden's spectacular anemone were introduced by Greeks.

All of these foods reached agricultural America between 1865 and 1915. They implanted an awareness of international folkways and problems that, in turn, made a Saturday afternoon stop at the new public library a routine and quickened the eagerness of many youngsters to go off and see the world.

The railroads, public libraries, and better educational opportunities began the South's slow transition from "forty acres and a mule" to machine power and a degree of racial equality. Blind obeisance to King Cotton and distrust of the "Damyankee" made that transition more difficult.

During the Civil War, cotton production had crashed from 4.5 million bales a year to 300,000 bales. In the 1870s, the demands of the mills in the North and in Europe pushed harvests back up to 1, 2, then 3 million bales. But, with slavery outlawed, there were four or five tenant farms for every one owned by its operator.

An obvious result was the massive migration of ex-soldiers and ex-slaves to the North and West. Two-thirds of the bridge crews and track gangs building the transcontinental railroad west of the Missouri were Southerners; co-workers called them "galvanized Yanks." Later they became homesteaders, miners, or merchants in the tin-roofed trackside towns.

Some of the most famous cowboys of this period were blacks.

(Bill Pickett, the greatest rodeo star of all, and one of Will Rogers's coaches,was a black.) But few of the black settlers had any respect for farm life—they preferred the freedom of ranch or town. As steamboat roustabouts, cowboys, train porters, barbers, day laborers, soldiers, and bandsmen they introduced the world to the folk music that their slave forebears had composed as solace against "the troubles."

"From their dancing, singing and jigging came the 'blackface' minstrelsy," reminisced Laurence C. Jones, founder of the famous Piney Woods School near Jackson, Mississippi.

> Many of them progressed to the vaudeville and musical comedy that dominated the stage of the United States for three quarters of a century. This flowered to jazz and ragtime, to popular dance idiom, to the matchless balladry of "the blues," secular work chants, folktale ballads and "sinful" songs that constitute by far the greatest body of folk music enriching American heritage.
>
> And there was an even more important and significant contribution that went unnoticed until after the Civil War. This was the superb "spiritual" first recognized by an army officer, Colonel Thomas Wentworth Higginson, of one of the Negro regiments during the [Civil] War, who encouraged William Allen to collect such songs. Not until the Fisk Jubilee Singers began singing them in 1879, however, was the spiritual's uniqueness realized, and its extraordinary folk genius revealed. . . . Time has proven what the spirituals really were— a religious vitalization of Christianity and the Bible that, along with their use of humor, reflected the most serious and intimate aspects of the Negro in his life-sustaining hope of heavenly salvation and earthly freedom. It saved his spirit from breaking, and was also a triumph of folk art.

Demands for a "New South" echoed across the region after 1865, but most of them were calls for more industry, especially cotton mills. The superior technology of the North, as the South's leaders knew, was basically responsible for the Confederacy's defeat; regional rejuvenation, therefore, must come through machines and factories. The shame of tenant farming and racial segregation, the perils of worn out soils and erosion, became challenges for the educators.

Thomas Green Clemson, a Philadelphian, prospered as a mining engineer, married the daughter of South Carolina's fiery John C. Calhoun, then inherited Calhoun's mountain estate, Fort Hill. At the outbreak of the Civil War, he was corresponding with federal officials, urging government involvement in training schools and experiment stations for agriculture. The development of the U.S. Bureau of Agriculture and the land-grant college system closely followed his 1861 recommendations. He bequeathed the Fort Hill property to the state and most of his fortune to a fund for establishing an agricultural college. The result was Clemson College, one of the most fruitful developers of a "New South" for agriculture.

Booker T. Washington, a Virginia black, labored against racial biases as well as illiteracy in generating self-respect and economic independence for his people through industrial training courses at the Tuskegee Institute he founded in Alabama. In an ill-equipped laboratory at Tuskegee, slave-born George Washington Carver discovered 325 dietary and industrial uses for peanuts, 118 for sweet potatoes, 75 for pecans, a score for soy beans, as well as a process for making pigments from clay and iron, and numerous industrial uses for cotton waste. He anticipated the mobile laboratory by outfitting wagons with equipment that could be home-made, then mule-teaming these wagons from farm to farm to demonstrate more efficient methods of soil conservation and diversified crops that would provide healthier diets.

The University of North Carolina had offered new horizons to students from its beautiful Chapel Hill since 1795 but, like other educational institutions throughout the South, found that the wealthy preferred to attend European or Yankee universities. The land-grant allotments financed North Carolina State at Raleigh in 1889, followed nine years later by creation of the Biltmore Forest School, the nation's first training center for forest studies.

Wintertime short courses and correspondence courses passed along the new soil improvement, crop, sanitation, and dietary advice gleaned by the professors and their associates from field tests, trips to conferences, and acute devotion to the libraries. The Farmers' Institute, an annual offering of speakers sweetened by music competitions and the sputtering projection of free movies, became a North Carolina State tradition.

Occasionally, in imitation of the Sunkist–Southern Pacific promotions, colleges and railroads cooperated in outfitting the Education Train. It chuffed from village to village with exhibits of "the latest and best," plus a lounge car filled with professors and publicity staffers. The green-magic replacements for cotton that resulted included apples, peaches, citrus, and chickens as well as a long overdue appreciation of the sweet potato and peanut.

Slaves had always grown sweet potatoes, okra, watermelons, and peanuts in the garden plots allotted to them on plantations. They provided the initial seed for the popularization programs launched by colleges after 1880. The few references to "sweet potato pudding" and "candied sweet potatoes" in colonial cookbooks were a result of black salesmanship, since they did the planters' cooking. The Cherokee and their black slaves introduced the "goober" as far west as future Oklahoma during the 1840s. Union soldiers learned to like goober peas during 1863–64 when provision wagons failed to keep pace with their marches. Although a Missouri physician is alleged to have been the inventor of peanut butter, the long familiarity of both blacks and California Chinese with varieties of peanut soup and peanut dip makes this unlikely. In any case, roast goobers' popularity soared with the popularity of baseball after 1865.

The redolent Smithfield ham was a postwar happenstance— Virginia farmers discovered that meat from pigs that had foraged in harvested peanut fields had extraordinary flavor. The peanut, watermelon, okra, and sweet potato offered new markets for farms and plantations eroded and worn out by successive cotton crops. By the 1980s, the South's peanut production exceeded 2 million tons a year and its sweet-potato production averaged 600,000 tons.

Apples first became a profitable crop for the South at the foot of Virginia's Blue Ridge. Their culture moved slowly south as new varieties were developed for the warmer climate. Peaches soon followed, with South Carolina and Georgia as prime producers. Florida had learned citrus culture from the Spanish and by 1873 was shipping oranges in quantity as far north as New York. The sugar-cane industry revived in Florida, Louisiana, and south Texas. Tomatoes were being shipped from Tennessee to New York by 1887.

The popularity of the peanut encouraged the marketing of the creamier nutmeat from the pecan tree. A native of the South, the pecan flourished as far north as Arkansas and Indiana. Its lumber had long been a favorite for hardwood floors. Creole cooks in Louisiana invented the praline and pecan pie. The nut shells were easier to crack than the competitive black walnut, butternut, and hickory of Northern forests. Pecan orchards began to replace cotton fields from Georgia to Texas. University specialists offered advice on necessary insect sprays and fertilizers and on the development of marketing cooperatives.

As medical research provided more data about vitamins and the dietary causes of pellagra, hookworm, and other prevalent diseases, demonstration lectures on the wider use of collards, kale, turnip greens, swiss chard, and herbs were added to the program of the Education Train.

The hardwood forests of the Appalachian ridges provided oak, walnut, beech, ash, and other fine-grain timber for mountain craftsmen specializing in classical reproductions of furniture. But pine dominated on the coastal plains of the South and yielded so much turpentine, tar, and other naval stores that North Carolina took the nickname of the "Tarheel State."

Charles H. Herty, a Georgian, perfected a simpler method for tapping turpentine pines, then moved on to become president of the American Chemical Society. But the pines still fascinated him. He returned to Georgia, financed a laboratory and, after years of experimentation, developed a method for making newsprint, bags, and cartons from pine pulp. His method initiated a tree-farming industry that absorbed thousands of small subsistence farms, but provided employment for foresters, loggers, chemists, pulpmakers, and salesmen. By the 1980s, timberlands in the South built root shields against erosion into 207 million acres, as against 59 million acres for all other farm crops.

In 1873, when seventy-nine breeds of chicken were available, the American Poultry Association was formed. As cities and villages grew and highways improved, some of the South's farmers experimented with flocks of White Leghorns, Plymouth Rocks, Rhode Island Reds, and a weekly chicken-and-egg route in town. There were multiple perils of disease ahead, but from 1880 to 1910 producers of the Carolinas and Georgia pioneered an industry that by 1960 would provide two-thirds of all the broilers consumed in the nation.

USDA experts in animal husbandry solved the tick-fever decimation of beef herds; nevertheless, Texans and Floridians had begun to import the hump-backed zebu cattle from Asia. Unlike European breeds, the zebu has sweat glands, so it can better withstand the tropical summers of the Gulf Coast. Also, through the centuries, it has developed greater resistance to disease. Experiments in crossbreeding developed the Brahman and other breeds that transformed the Gulf Coast and Florida grasslands into prime cattle country. During the same decades, experiments by universities and the USDA led to citrus and vegetable plantings; citrus soon became the state's leading crop. By the 1980s, Florida grew five times as many oranges, ten times as many grapefruit, and two and a half times as many tangerines as California, plus approximately 300,000 acres of vegetables.

The pioneering efforts in fruits, vegetables, timber, peanuts, sweet potatoes, and pecans from 1865 to 1915 would assure a new South for Southern agriculture after World War I. The farmers and planters who first tried out the new methods and new crops were given a fitting epitaph in 1960 by Hodding Carter, the Mississippi editor and author, in his essay "Statues in the Square!"

I would erect somewhere in the South, preferably deep in the Lower Mississippi Valley, another statue, as anonymous and as representative as the graven Confederates of the court-house squares, but unlike these, neither armed nor uniformed. This figure would be clad in the work clothes of a farmer. . . . His face would reflect the toil, the frustrations and the sufferings of a people who have passed through a succession of ordeals . . . of flood and decimation by malaria and yellow fever; the ordeals of military defeat and of political grinding down and agricultural ruin and long poverty. The eyes of this unknown and soldierly warrior would be fixed upon the far horizon of the frontiersman; and in the set of the shoulders a sensitive observer would perceive the glory of an indestructible people.

Carter's essay was about the South, but his memorial is equally appropriate for the Baileys, the Cyrs, the Olsens, and the other 5 million farm and ranch families who braved the social and economic transition of 1865–1915.

The first American-made automobile was built in Springfield, Massachusetts, during the spring of 1892. Caterpillar-tread-type tractors first plowed and harrowed farmland in 1904. The 1.5 million horses and mules shipped overseas during World War I would signal the grand finale of three centuries of self-sufficient power on our farms, ranches, and plantations. After 1918, horse stalls and mule sheds would be rebuilt as garages and toolsheds; the animals would go off to slaughterhouses. In 1902, McCormick Harvester and its principal competitors merged into a single conglomerate named the International Harvester Company. The conglomerate then bought up factories to enable it to mechanize not only grain fields but also other areas of the farm, giving the firm a line of machines "to sell the year round." Radium, x-rays, vitamins, and pasteurization were discovered by scientists. For the first time, urban population exceeded rural population. Yet, throughout it all, the agriculturist of 1865–1915 retained his faith, labored "eight hours in the morning and eight hours in the afternoon," and earned "the glory of an indestructible people."

CHAPTER TEN

City Rule

"**I** think our governments will remain virtuous for many centuries as long as they remain chiefly agricultural," Thomas Jefferson wrote in 1813. "When we get piled upon one another in large cities, as in Europe, they will become corrupt as in Europe and go to eating one another as they do there."

By 1913, when Woodrow Wilson moved into the White House, a majority of our population was "piled up on one another" in large cities, and these urbanites were "eating one another" via technology, economic controls, and political bosses. New York City had stuffed in 4 million residents, more than the entire population of the United States in 1790. Chicago, with just 35,000 people in its 1860 mud, now had 2 million. Irish, French-Canadians, and Poles swelled Boston to 600,000, an increase of more than 400 percent since Lincoln for President banners flapped on the Common. San Francisco, with only 35,000 at the height of the Gold Rush, clustered 400,000 around her Nob Hill mansions and Grant Avenue's Chinatown. Atlanta, with 5,000 when Sherman's troops marched through, was a railroad boomtown of

100,000. Railroads, steamships, and factories caused Omaha, Los Angeles, New Orleans, Minneapolis, the two Portlands, and Baltimore to grow faster than dandelions after an April shower. As Jefferson knew, the pattern was as old as the pyramids and the Parthenon. Greece, Rome, Carthage, Spain, France, England—all experienced feverish rushes to the cities. Consequently, the value of land within their walls soared; tenements, narrow streets, meagerness of botanical life, dire dependence on foods grown outside city walls made selling food within the city a "shrewd business." It was a fairly simple matter for merchants and noblemen to organize control over the distribution of harvests. Bossism and bureaucracy became a way of life.

The United States bumbled down the same road because of the way in which technology developed. Throughout the nineteenth century, all forms of machine power favored centralization. Steamboats and steamships operated over fixed routes, with cities developing at deepwater ports and at heads of navigation on major rivers. Railroads operated on T-rails; terminals and division junctions became sites of growing cities. Factories had to be built within horse-haul of railroads or steamship piers, while factory and office workers were forced to live near their places of employment. Inevitably, museums, theatres, department stores, newspapers, banks, and universities "followed the crowds." Aggressive publicity campaigns—including the steady grinding-out of the Horatio Alger type of rags-to-riches fiction—lured American youth from farm and ranch and plantation into cities.

The keynote of the urban program of reorganization for agriculture was announced on February 11, 1860, at a meeting of the Philadelphia Society for the Promotion of Agriculture by Craig Biddle, son of the promoter of the Bank of the United States and, like Alexander Hamilton, a partisan of centralization. "The fact has at last gone home to the cultivator of the land," Biddle alleged,

> that to live he must increase not his farm but the yield of his farm. Land is at last dearer than labor or manure, and these

it is that he must buy if he hopes for profit. . . . At the present, the man who has spent most on experiments on all points of agriculture is Mr. Mechi, a London tradesman and alderman. He starts with the assertion that "whatever does not pay in agriculture is not an improvement," and tests all his operations by that stern standard, the balance sheet. This he publishes and thus gives warning or affords an example to his neighbors. This is what we want here.

Adherence to Biddle's conviction of improving only for profit, plus the advantage of expensive machines that traveled on water or T-rails, enabled bankers, manufacturers, wholesalers, and other "middlemen" to centralize economic control over professional agriculture. By 1913, Boston investors controlled most of the nation's wool and lamb markets. Los Angeles and Miami dominated citrus production. Chicago became the "brawling bully" of grains and meat. New York City influenced national milk and poultry production. New Orleans and Savannah manipulated cotton plantings. San Francisco reigned over the vegetable, grape, wine, and olive production of California. Kentucky and North Carolina cities prospered because of tobacco. St. Louis became monarch of the mule market and livestock-feed processing. Minneapolis reigned on as Flourtown.

The growth of mechanized power for agriculture followed the same pattern. International Harvester headquartered in Chicago. Automakers centralized their operations around Detroit, and tiremakers in Ohio cities. Gasoline-makers built skyscraper headquarters in New York City, Philadelphia, and Houston. Bankers and stockholders provided enough funds for lavish, but not necessarily truthful, promotion campaigns. Their lobbyists glibly persuaded USDA to mutter about "the rights of free trade" and sit on its hands.

The technique of political control that developed in each of the cities was necessary, according to the Biddle "law" of improving for cash profits. In obeisance to technology, these political organizations became known as "machines." New York's

Tammany Hall was the most notorious. Chicago, Boston, New Orleans, San Francisco—every city developed Republican and Democrat machines astutely influenced (and sometimes financed) by banks and factories and trade associations. Ward leaders doubled as benefactors of the poor, spies, vote buyers, bullies, and publicists. The terms *ward heeler* and *political hack* entered the language during this period.

Most candidates for public office were machine-approved. So were the workers on city, state, and federal payrolls. Corporation lawyers, Ivy League professors, petroleum heirs, department-store owners, Wall Street brokers, and real-estate millionaires became Congressmen and Senators. Their interests focused on scientific progress, industrial growth, and more powerful cities. Few of them had more than a casual interest in, or understanding of, the problems of agriculture.

Coincidentally, after 1870, a belittling prejudice against the agricultural professions was initiated by city vaudeville houses and theatres, then perpetuated by the movies. Comedians portrayed the farmer as an ignorant miser. The traveling salesman always outwitted the farm parents, then frolicked with a daughter who just as inevitably displayed acute nymphomania. Singers of country music dressed in baggy overalls, calico dresses and sunbonnets, held hands on their stomachs when guffawing, chewed tobacco, and knew no words of more than one syllable; their singing implied that everyone outside the city limits suffered from adenoids and had black teeth. Musical comedies and Broadway hits depicted farmhands as sex-starved illiterates. Pulp magazines and movies created the folk image of cattlemen as gun-happy barflies, and ignored the ravages of malaria, yellow fever, raw milk, tuberculosis, and venereal disease, conjuring up instead deadly gun duels with nonexistent outlaws or Indians. Newspaper columnists and sob-sisters scooped "sleepy," "quaint," "drowsy" from their adjective bins when writing about farms or the countryside. The shout of "Hey, rube!" became the rallying call for circus employees when trouble threatened.

The most prevalent derogatory terms for agriculturists were

invented in the cities. The term "hick," derived from "hickory," originated in Cincinnati in 1821. "Hayseed" originated in 1889 in Boston. "Rube" was fashioned by Chicagoans in 1896 from the given name of "Reuben." The sneer term of "hayburner" for a horse first appeared in 1921. The use of "boondocks" as a derogatory term for the countryside is a by-product of the Spanish-American War. Soldiers who fought against Filipino nationalists in 1898 borrowed the Tagalog word *bundok*, meaning "hill country," mispronounced it "boondock," and applied it to anything beyond a city's limits.

Perhaps these slurs were invented because most city residents of 1860 to 1900 had farm or ranch backgrounds; the "funning" was intended as a mental aspirin for the headaches of urbanism. In any case, they helped shape a class barrier between city and country, thus abetting the aggressiveness of the middleman and the creation of that "plastic curtain" between rural producer and urban consumer.

Neither public school nor university curriculums were designed to improve urban-rural communication. Vocational courses in agriculture were restricted to high schools in farming areas. Although the liberal arts originated in pre-Renaissance Europe as a series of courses "suited to the studies of freemen," its meaning became so warped by pedantry that even the land-grant colleges barricaded the liberal arts from the "practical arts" of agriculture, nursing and "Mechanicks." As a result, science, economics, and sociology courses focused on technology, factories, and cities; history courses were choke-reined to military campaigns and political strategies. Librarians banned the rural realism of Mark Twain's *Huckleberry Finn*. Kindergarten teachers continued to inflict "Old MacDonald Had a Farm" on trusting toddlers. Publishers frowned on manuscripts about rural life that didn't have at least four shootouts, a whorehouse, or a family of interbred "Jukes" in it.

Urban attitudes, sneer terms, and the deftness of urbanized lobbyists put agriculturists on the defensive—and kept them there. Still, in the 1950s and '60s, reporters who were sent out to learn "farm opinion" had to overcome the reticence of the agriculturists and to dissipate protests of "What do you want my notions for? I'm just a dumb farmer."

Persistence of the insinuation that the agriculturist was, by and large, a member of an inferior social class played a role in rural acceptance of the technologic gadgetry that began to transform the countryside after the Civil War. Railroads, ponderous threshing machines, barbed wire, windmills, silos, milking machines, stationary engines—as well as the household wonders of pianos, telephones, kerosene stoves, and sewing machines—were all welcomed as advantages that could ease the sixteen-hour workdays and bring the countryman's status closer to the privileged city dweller's. Only a few people pondered the thought that all of this cash-and-credit purchasing was threatening agriculture's self-sufficiency and might lead to a strange new peasantry of dependence on machine-makers and fuel-suppliers.

Passage of the Smith-Lever Act in 1914 offered a new source of help toward "the better life with machines."

German submarines prowling Atlantic shipping lanes, and poignant Allied publicity about "the barbaric Huns," were inching us toward declarations of war against the Hohenzollerns and the remnants of the Holy Roman Empire soon after the Smith-Lever Act became law. The bill funded a network of county agents who would consult with farmers and ranchers about more efficient production methods. Urbanites in Congress had voted for it because of the certainty of war and the probability of an all-out campaign stressing that "Food will win the war!"

A secondary chore for county agents would be to encourage the formation of more 4-H clubs. Sporadic efforts to organize study and recreation clubs for farm and ranch youth had been made since 1850 when Horace Greeley, a New York editor and presidential aspirant, financed a corn-growing contest for boys in upstate New York. The name "4-H," coined in 1913 when a national club was formed with pledges of support by farm organizations, stood for "Head, Heart, Hands and Health," and was based on the membership pledge that promised, "I pledge my head to clearer thinking, my heart to greater loyalty, my hands to larger service, and my health to better living, for my club, my community, my country and my world."

War demands and public approval of the pledge to "Make the World Safe for Democracy" caused farmers to rip open an additional 40 million acres of land for cropping before 1919. Neither county agents nor USDA objected to the fact that 25 million of the acres were on prairie where rainfall averaged less than ten inches a year and windstorms were frequent. Chicago packers paid $6.32 per hundredweight for hogs when the war began; by 1919, they were paying $41.90 per hundredweight. Cotton rose from 7 to 34 cents a pound. Butter, cheese, and milk prices doubled. Wheat rose to $2.20 a bushel. Artillery and commissary needs sent more than 1.5 million horses and mules overseas, at farm prices of $200 per head and up. The "silk-shirt years" saw land prices in the Midwest soar to $400, then $500, and finally $600 an acre. Banks and wildcat loan firms worked overtime on applications for "enough money to buy one of those tractors." (Owning a tractor, however, also meant buying a tank to hold a truckload of gasoline, building a new tool shed, and shipping mules and workhorses off to the "bone market" at the county seat.)

The war brought some weird semantic changes for what the farmers produced. Sauerkraut became Liberty Cabbage. Salisbury Steak replaced hamburger on menus. A few years before, the New York cartoonist Ted Borgan nicknamed the frankfurter on a roll sold at baseball games a "hot dog." Patriotism banished frankfurter and popularized the name hot dog. German rye bread became American Rye. Braunschweiger suddenly was liver sausage.

If farmers received more money for their crops, much of it went to pay an inflated overhead. Freight costs rose 211 percent. Feed and fertilizer costs doubled. Wages paid to hired help in 1914 totalled $700 million; in 1920, they were $1,600 million. Farm and ranch investments in machinery rocketed from $328 million to $1,150 million a year. In six years, the national tax bill went from $624 million to $1,497 million.

President Wilson was still haranguing Congress to approve his League of Nations plan when the bust came. Thanks in large part to American machines, seed, and livestock animals, Europe quickly put her croplands back into production. Argentina dumped surpluses of meat and grain on North Sea and Mediterranean docks. Chicago corn prices plummeted back to 68 cents a bushel and wheat to $1.44 a bushel. At New Orleans and Savannah auctions, cotton went begging at 14 cents a pound. Mule and horse dealers petitioned for bankruptcy. Agriculture's gross income for 1920 dropped by $4 billion.

That same year, the Mexican boll weevil completed its deadly journey across the South to the Georgia and Carolina coasts. By depositing its eggs in the pre-blossom "squares" of a cotton plant, the worm aborted the plant's production of cotton bolls. No pesticides would slow the weevil's voraciousness. It ended the reign of King Cotton from the Sea Islands to Arizona and as far north as Virginia and Arkansas. As the Atlanta editorialist George H. Aull summarized, "The boll weevil has achieved what man has failed to achieve through one hundred and ten years of 'common sense,' great oratory, high tariffs, the continent's grimmest war and the impoverishing hatreds of Reconstruction." More and more tenant farmers took to the roads and searched for employment in cities. The new land industries of fruit orchards, tree farming, peanuts, dairying, and beef production, however, flourished.

Two acts passed by Congress during 1921 and 1922 sought to slow down agriculture's march to the bankruptcy courts. The Packers and Stockyards Act was intended to correct the meat packers' domination of stockyard prices by establishing a corps of federal inspectors at the central yards and enforcing a system of sales-price reporting. The Act also ordered packers to sell their investments in the yards' operating companies. But within months, Swift, Armour, Hormel, Rath, and the other meat giants opened auction barns at county-seat towns, then bought most of their animals there. This ruse lowered the demand, hence the "official" price, at the central yards in Chicago, St. Louis, Omaha, and Kansas City. It also crippled the federal inspection system, because the county-seat auctions were not interstate operations. The Capper-Volstead Act exempted farm cooperatives from the antitrust laws of 1890 and 1914. Thus Land O Lakes, Sunkist, Diamond, and other cooperatives had opportunity to expand interstate. By 1930, there were more than 12,000 marketing and supply cooperatives.

Throughout the Harding, Coolidge, and Hoover administrations, farm prices dropped, operating costs increased, and sheriffs patrolled the auction sales of evicted families. "During the decade 1920–29," the economic geographer O. E. Baker deduced, "about forty percent of the youth who started to work in factories, offices and stores of the cities came from farms. The net migration from farms during the decade was 6.3 million. If it cost $2,500 to feed, clothe, educate the average farm child to the age of fifteen, then this migration represents a contribution of roughly fourteen billion dollars."

The same decade saw the annual budget of USDA soar to $150 million a year, with a work force of 22,189 clerks, typists, bureau chiefs, scientists, plant hunters, home economists, food inspectors, statisticians, pamphleteers, and speech writers. Although there were outcries of "boondoggle" and "pork barreling" from both farm organizations and urban politicians, the department's researchers, working methodically with university scientists, were pioneering drastic changes in both agricultural production and national diet. Their 1900–30 research developed awareness of vitamins, calories, trace elements, pasteurization, frozen foods, and soil chemicals. They also pioneered disease-control methods and new crops, as well as new uses for crops. They built upon the rural transformations made possible by automobiles, farm to market roads, electricity, and airplanes. None of the achievers of socio-economic revolution became household names but they, too, deserve acclaim as folk heroes of the twentieth century.

Biochemists had long suspected that vegetables, grains, fruits, and meats contain minute quantities of chemicals essential to human health. In 1906, the English researcher F. G. Hopkins first isolated evidence of one of these chemicals. Six years later, in collaboration with Casimir Funk, a Polish biochemist, the chemical was isolated. Funk coined the word *vitamin*, meaning "essential to life," for the substance. The outbreak of World War I brought Funk to the United States, where he became an American citizen. Throughout a half century of research here, he identified Vitamins B_1, B_2, C, and D and wrote about their importance for the prevention of deficiency diseases.

In 1912, Joseph Goldberger, a researcher for the U.S. Public Health Service, demonstrated that a deficiency of nicotinic acid in the diet of Southerners caused the dread disease pellagra. He prescribed peanuts, wheat germ, yeast, and organ meats in the diet as preventatives.

Drug and chemical manufacturers added research laboratories to their factories. Universities, USDA, and public health agencies all focused research and publicity on the "vitamin mysteries." Vitamin pills, vitamin sprinkles in white flour, and urgings to eat "more fruits and salads" rapidly followed.

As food processing became centralized, stockholder demands for more profit, disgruntled workers, and balky machinery made consuming processed foods as risky as a Saturday night stroll through San Francisco's Barbary Coast, New York's Bowery, or Chicago's Skid Row. Flinty pebbles were concealed in cans of pork and beans. Ground charcoal was mixed into tins of pepper. Dead flies and roaches floated amidst segments of stem in tins of vegetables and fruit. The tangy, dark blobs in sausages were mule meat. Hair and chips of bone appeared in hot dogs. Bags of sugar contained liberal sprinklings of sand.

Harvey W. Wiley, an Indiana farm son, was chief chemist at USDA. Excessive use of adulterants in the processed foods that he and his co-workers analyzed impelled him to argue for introduction of a Pure Food and Drug Act in Congress. He finally won in 1906 and was appointed the new bureau's administrator. Despite bitter opposition by processors' lobbyists, he succeeded in winning appropriations for federal inspectors at food-processing plants. The struggle for better sanitation, fewer adulterants, and more complete labeling of contents on processed-food containers has continued ever since.

Flies and mosquitoes were discovered by army doctors to be

the creatures responsible for the thousands of deaths from malaria and yellow fever among workers on the Panama Canal. Leland O. Howard, an Illinois farm son, was chief of the Bureau of Entomology at USDA. Knowing that flies could spread these and other diseases, he received permission to begin a "Swat the Fly" campaign, popularized the fly swatter, and contributed to the development of eucalyptus sprays and flypaper tapes. In 1916, Clarence Birdseye returned from a fur-buying expedition to Labrador determined to adapt food freezing to year-round use. (He knew that electrical firms already manufactured refrigerators that could make ice cubes and sherbets.) Birdseye settled in Gloucester, hometown of the schooner, and began experimenting with freezing fish filets. He was so successful that, in 1924, he became one of the founders of General Foods. In 1949, he perfected the anhydrous method that greatly reduced freezing time for foods. The home freezer and the frozen-food industry burgeoned as a result of Birdseye's pioneering efforts.

Experiments that would influence consumer purchases and eventually frustrate the federal government's efforts to curb farm overproduction began when Edward M. East, George H. Shull and Donald F. Jones independently decided to explore the mysteries of the corn seed. All three were plant geneticists. East was at Harvard and Shull at Princeton, while Jones did his analyses at the hilltop agricultural experiment station outside New Haven. When their investigations began in 1912–15, the average yield on the 110 million acres of the Midwest's corn belt was 25 bushels per acre. Their laboratory discoveries provided details that encouraged decades of field experiments with inbreeding and controlled pollenizing. The result was hybrid corn, first commercially marketed about 1925. The hybrids raised per-acre production fantastically; the current record is 352.6 bushels per acre. Although corn-belt acreage has been halved since 1912, the crop total currently averages about 6 billion bushels, a 400 percent increase over the 1912 harvest.

A tour through the South caused Hugh Hammond Bennett, a chemist with USDA's Bureau of Soils, to plead for government support of a program to slow down soil erosion. Indifference by farm organizations as well as Congressmen frustrated his recommendations for 25 years. But during the summer of 1935, dust storms out of Kansas, Nebraska, Oklahoma, and Texas darkened Washington and filtered yellow and red grit on the Capitol, White House, and city streets. Congress frantically approved a bill establishing a Soil Conservation Service, with Bennett as director. The ensuing programs against "flooding, erosion, inadequate drainage, poor water supply, sediment damage, woodland improvement, more fish and game production" led to conservation laws in every state and to the creation of the National Association of Conservation Districts. By 1980 the NACD, with headquarters in League City, Texas, had more than 3,000 district groups composed of men and women who volunteer their services "to help save the land." It was estimated that more than 2 million landowners used soil conservation practices. But despite federal expenditures of more than $200 million a year, the erosion of American topsoil remains as devastating as it was in 1935. Government insistence on more foods for export, and farmer frenzy to wrest a profit from excessive production costs and low market prices, have been, and still are, the cause.

Despite agriculture's acceptance of technology, scientific discoveries, and an educational system that enabled farm youth to contribute to the nation's well-being, the agricultural depression intensified through the 1920s. A succession of droughts in the Midwest contributed to the slump, but the basic cause revolved around the costs of machinery, fuel, insecticides, fertilizers, and processed feeds, which were using up most of the money the agriculturist received from harvests.

An essay, anonymously submitted to the American Farm Bureau Federation in 1921, was enthusiastically endorsed and distributed nationally as a pamphlet. The essay, "Equality for Agriculture?," challenged: "Why do we have to pay four hundred bushels of corn for a wagon that we used to buy for one hundred and fifty bushels, or one hundred and fifty bushels of corn for a suit of clothes that formerly cost fifty bushels? And why is ham sold at retail throughout the country at six times the price per pound of live hogs, when the normal ratio is three and a half to one?" The essay called for a system of "parity prices" for agriculture, to be policed as rigorously as the federal inspectors policed food and drug sanitation.

"Equality for Agriculture?" influenced introduction of a bill in Congress that would finance a USDA bureau of super-salesmen for farm surpluses overseas; a sales tax levied on processors and shippers would be paid to farm and ranch producers. The bill passed Congress. Calvin Coolidge, however, vetoed it in 1926 and again in 1928.

Authorship of the pamphlet was traced to George N. Peek and General Hugh S. Johnson, both officials at John Deere's Plow Company. Twelve years later, General Johnson would become the director of Franklin D. Roosevelt's National Recovery Administration (NRA).

Arthur Hyde, former governor of Missouri, was President Hoover's appointee as Secretary of Agriculture in the spring of 1929. Both Hoover and Hyde were committed to a policy of greater federal aid to agriculture. "Agricultural-producer bargaining power," Hyde declared, "must be strengthened through cooperatives, the supply of agricultural products stabilized, and a scientific land-use policy developed. In addition, the marketing for agricultural products must be broadened by finding new uses for them. . . . Transportation maladjustments must be corrected."

Hoover appointed a Federal Farm Board that included executives of outstanding farm cooperatives as well as processors and railroaders. Congress granted the board a $500 million revolving fund so that low-interest loans could be made to cooperatives. Crop surpluses of wheat, corn, cotton, cheese, and butter would be bought by the government and placed in storage. It was the most realistic relief program conceived in the 67 years since the founding of USDA.

But it was too late. Steel and auto sales dropped sharply during August, 1929. The British boosted their loan rates to 6½ percent.

This, for reasons comprehensible only to bankers, caused Europeans to reduce American purchases. Between October 23 and November 13, a price collapse in the stock market wiped out $30 billion in capital values. Banks failed. Unemployment rose from 4 to 15 million. Summer-long droughts withered the Midwest and South. Grasshoppers ravaged crops in the Missouri Valley. Mortgages on thousands of farms were foreclosed. The auctions that followed set off riots and gunfire. Through the dust storms and parched fields, the new landless headed toward hope of jobs and "anyway, some green growth to smell again" in California and the Pacific Northwest. It was a repeat of the forty-niners, but this time they rode in flivvers and trucks and had to beg, buy, or steal gasoline and oil every hundred miles. Editors would give these banished farm families a name, "Okies."

On November 8, 1932, Franklin D. Roosevelt beat Hoover in the Presidential election by an 8-to-1 margin. One of the most vociferous critics of Hoover's agricultural policy had been *Wallace's Farmer*, an Iowa magazine. Its third generation editor/owner was Henry Agard Wallace. Although political strategy had brought his father the Harding appointment as Secretary of Agriculture, Henry A. changed parties, supported Roosevelt, and won the 1933 appointment as head of USDA. Within a week after reaching Washington, he assembled a conference of agricultural experts to submit proposals for drastic policy changes.

That June, cotton growers were pledged government payments for plowing up every fourth row of the 1933 plantings. In August, hog growers were offered "double the market price" for each pregnant sow or small pig sent to slaughterhouses; more than 6 million pigs became "tankage," a high protein livestock food; 100 million pounds of edible pork were made available to welfare agencies.

By midwinter, state and county committees had been organized to implement the objectives of an Agricultural Adjustment Administration. Popularly known as the "Triple A," this new USDA adjunct was authorized to "secure voluntary reduction of the acreage in various crops through agreements with producers and by using direct payments for participation in acreage control programs." Wheat, cotton, field corn, hogs, rice, tobacco, milk, and their by-products were specified as "basic commodities." Funds for the payments—they totaled $100 million in 1934— were to be obtained through processing taxes on foods and fibers that would, of course, be passed on to consumers as higher retail prices.

The New Deal, program by program throughout 1933–35, promised central government responsibility for adequate living standards to every citizen, without the racial, religious, or ethnic prejudices that had long sullied our social behavior. The distinguished columnist Carl Rowan recently reminisced on "the sense of hope and pride it gave me when a federal grant to our school meant that I was going to get a huge three dollars a month for raising and lowering the school flag every morning and afternoon."

That payment to a sensitive and highly intelligent black boy also demonstrated a basic premise of the New Deal pledge. Adequate living standards were promised in return for physical or mental effort. The hundreds of thousands of unemployed youths put on the payroll of the Civilian Conservation Corps "earned their keep" on conservation projects by planting trees, building trails, cleaning garbage and sediment out of creek beds, building roads, and correcting erosion. Art projects not only gave opportunities to painters, engravers, and photographers, but their creativity broadened cultural appreciation in villages as well as cities. Writer projects exhumed local history and brought new pride to hometown heritage.

In all of these work projects, the paramount rule was reward for personal effort. The Triple A initially held to the same concept. It borrowed the parity-price idea from Peek and Johnson's 1921 pamphlet and established 1914 as the "parity base" for the ratio between farm and ranch income and outlay. Federal payments, abetted by taxes on processing and marketing, would restore the same ratio between fieldside prices and operating costs that had existed in the year World War I began. Once

again, 50 bushels of corn would buy a suit of clothes and 150
bushels would buy a trailer wagon for the tractor. In return,
producers would reduce crop acreage and livestock herds, and
instead grow more alfalfa, clover, soybeans, and other "green
manure" crops to revitalize undernourished fields.

But processors and other middlemen challenged the legality
of the processing taxes that would help finance Triple A. They
took their arguments to court and in 1936 won a Supreme Court
decision that Triple A was unconstitutional. Wallace reacted with
another conference of farm experts and appeals to Congress.
Finally, Congress passed the Soil Conservation and Domestic
Allotment Act that shifted a second Triple A's emphasis to "soil
conserving crops and the methods designed to conserve soil resources." This time the processing taxes were squelched; all farm
and ranch payments were to come from the federal budget.

A large loophole in the Wallace program was that payments
to producers were based on acreage rather than on yield. Owners
of tenant farms and of the 1,000- to 10,000-acre grain "spreads"
in the West succumbed to the temptation to "milk Uncle Sam."
Hybrid corn was tripling and quadrupling the corn harvests. New
varieties and techniques gave spectacular increases per acre in
wheat and cotton. It was a simple matter to increase production
on the best acreage, plant legumes and grasses on the worst, and
collect Triple A payments! Crossbreeding with European types
of pigs and cattle by the experiment stations, a clearer understanding of vitamins and balanced feeds, and more sanitary housing made similar increases in milk and pork production possible.

Local politicians welcomed Triple A, like other New Deal
projects, as a matchless power tool. They were the ones who
"nominated" the township committeemen that would negotiate
contract agreements with producers, approve the multiple-copy
forms, and presumably check on plantings and harvests. The
Triple A offices at county seats were staffed with file clerks,
secretaries, stenographers, librarians, chairmen, and "consultants"—each worth two to six votes at election time. County
offices reported to state offices who reported to Washington.

Centralization was so acute that a project such as a township reservoir for storing irrigation water would not be approved until it had been examined by one or more teams of "experts" sent out from Washington.

The second AAA was recognized as a failure by 1938. Wallace, with approval by Congress, substituted as his program "the ever-normal granary," an adaptation of the government storage plan devised nine years earlier by Hoover's Farm Board. Triple A was given the power to fix the acreage allotments on basic crops. In times of surplus production, Triple A could restrict sales by marketing quotas. In times of crop failure, it could make parity payments to growers. During the crop-surplus years, loans would be advanced to producers, whose crops would then be stored in government warehouses "until needed." By 1940, there was enough wheat and cotton in storage to supply processors and exporters for two years.

Millionaire processors bought farm magazines and re-rigged their editorial policies to advocate "preservation of individual enterprise" and decry "the outrageous boondoggling in Washington." Radio programs sponsored by middlemen, like their newspaper advertisements, sang the same refrain.

The operating costs of USDA rose from $279 million in 1932 to $1,293 million in 1939; its payroll fattened to 79,430 full-time employees. Surveys showed that 42 percent of all farms and ranches were being operated by tenants, with their parity payments going to urban owners. Efforts to raise the living standards of tenants and sharecroppers only quickened the importation of Mexicans, Filipinos, Japanese, and East Indians as cheaper manual labor for canneries, orchards, and field harvests of the West and South. Processor lobbyists squashed Wallace's plan to grade-label all canned goods under a standard system of qualities that would be established by government inspectors.

Thomas Edison's pioneering had, by the 1930s, produced hundreds of types of electrical machines for homes, stores, and industry. But power companies contended that extension of their power lines to farms and ranches would not be profitable; by

1935, only one-tenth of our farms and ranches had electric power. Wallace won White House support for creation of the Rural Electrification Administration. REA approved federal loans, at only 2 percent interest, to farmer cooperatives for the construction of dams, generating plants, and power lines. The results included the huge Tennessee Valley Authority (TVA), the Grand Coulee project, and hundreds of other government-financed cooperatives designed to store water, check soil erosion, and provide power to rural areas. Later, REA's funding facilities were transferred to non-government lenders that had federal guarantees. By 1980, more than 99 percent of farms and ranches had electric power. The home freezer usurped the root cellar. The electric stove ousted the bulky kitchen range. Agriculturists added "electrician" to the technologic skills that machines had forced on them since 1865.

Henry Wallace's popularity won him the Vice-Presidency in Roosevelt's third term. By that time, Hitler had conquered most of Europe and had sent his Luftwaffe off to bomb Britain. During March, 1941, Winston Churchill appealed for $500 million worth of American farm products to be shipped to Britain through the Nazi blockade of U-boats and dive bombers. In April, Congress passed a Lend-Lease Act. Camouflaged convoys, shepherded by our destroyers and cruisers, zigzagged toward the Hebrides and Irish Sea ports. After Hitler turned on his Soviet ally and attacked Leningrad and Moscow, the convoys extended their journeys to Murmansk. Our participation in another world war was inevitable. On December 7—a Sunday—the Japanese pushed us over the brink by a sneak attack on our Pacific fleet anchored in Pearl Harbor, Hawaii.

USDA resurrected the World War I slogan of "Food will win the war." The AAA committees became Agricultural War Boards. Farmers and ranchers were exempted from the military draft and urged to all-out production (but with their gasoline and steel rationed). As in the last war, millions of marginal acres were ripped open and planted to grains or cotton. New irrigation ditches gurgled the reserve water out of reservoirs and aquifers. Purchase of chemical fertilizers and insecticides doubled and tripled. The droughts of the "dust bowl" years were over, but billions of tons of topsoil had swirled away in the dust storms of the 1930s. Rising prices for harvests persuaded most farmers and ranchers to complete the mechanization of their holdings. Cowboys began patrolling fence-lines in trucks and jeeps. The trail drives to rail sidings became truck hauls. Crop-dusting of insecticides by airplane became so common that Flying Farmer clubs formed; pastures were bulldozed and graded into landing fields for their biplanes. Both the automobile and the airplane had borrowed the term "horsepower" as a term for measuring the strength of their engines, but the horse itself was transformed, in public imagery, into a racetrack "gee gee" or a family pet.

Wallace's plan of subsidy payments as a reward for reducing production of major crops continued after the war—but never quite made the grade. In the wheat, corn, cotton, and tobacco fields, as in the dairy barns, science outpaced the acreage cutbacks by persistently increasing the yields per acre. Nevertheless, farm organizations became convinced that "guvmint" could solve their problems, with the result that they became vociferous lobbyists for more and more and more federal funding.

The New Deal, and all succeeding administrations, failed to see that agriculture's problems could be solved by a return to self-sufficiency, *with* the machine. The government never offered subsidies to finance auto, truck, tractor, and tire factories owned and operated by farm cooperatives. Congress never got beyond the speech-making stage in encouraging the development of a moderately priced engine fuel from farm crops—although all alcoholic drinks and industrial alcohols are processed from grains, berries, and roots. One major reason for this governmental evasiveness was the processors' anguished outcry—embellished by the prose of advertising agencies—about the "freedom of the marketplace." Another reason was the social and political power gained by labor organizations during and after the New Deal years. Aligned with both groups were industry's stockholders calling for higher profits. As a result, the agriculturist continued to buy machinery, fuel, fertilizers, insecticides, and livestock feeds at retail prices, then sell harvests at wholesale prices held down by perpetual crop surpluses.

High costs, low prices, and machinery that could plow, weed, and harvest huge tracts of land caused a post-war frenzy of farm expansions. Aggressive producers borrowed funds to buy the "For Sale" property of neighbors who were "over fifty" or preferred an "eight-hour job in town." The agricultural population dropped to just 15 percent of the nation's total. Farm sizes grew to 400, 800, 1,000 acres, and were dependent on specialty crops and the quantity of machines. The goal was "grow more and pay off your bills." In most cases, this approach was no more successful than the subsidy payments.

The harbingers of hope that did appear during and after the New Deal were homemakers in both the cities and the countryside. The molecular probing into vitamins, proteins, and hydrocarbons by Hopkins, Funk, and other medical researchers convinced wives and mothers that drastic changes were needed in their menus. There wasn't much "sweet-smelling sweat" in the modern worker's day. Even farmers performed much of their work sitting down. Yet, meat-and-potatoes, fatty bacon, breakfast pancakes, fried foods, and sugary desserts were still the mainstays of most Americans' diet. Americans became obese. The obvious solution: fill them up with high-vitamin, low-calorie foods.

They began with lettuce. The fast diets that followed brought new major crops and regional specializations into agriculture.

CHAPTER ELEVEN

The Fast Diets

In 1926, the Womans' Association of the Union Church in Hinsdale, Illinois, assembled their favorite recipes in *The Union Church Cook Book*. Gracing the first hilltops west of Chicago's mud flat, Hinsdale was home to steel executives, owners of window-shade mills and auto-parts factories, and officials of meat-packing companies; it was considered a suburb of conservative sophisticates. Of the cookbook's 190 pages, 110 were devoted to bread, pastry, and meat recipes. The Salad section of ten pages detailed twelve varieties of dressing and twenty-five salads. More than half of the salads were based on mayonnaise or gelatine; only three of them included onion. Lettuce was used merely as a decorative base for the "jellied ring" or banana-pineapple-maraschino-whipped cream glories. "An Italian Salad" recipe called for sliced tomatoes, olives, onions, oranges, and warned, "Arrange on individual plates, as it is messy when tossed together in a bowl with dressing, as the Italians do."

A decade later, in 1936, Fannie Merritt Farmer published a new edition of *The Boston Cooking-School Cook Book*. Its 838 pages, too, were dominated by meat, pastry, bread, and sugary dessert recipes. But Miss Farmer was sufficiently alert to vitamins and proteins to include 45 pages devoted to Salads and Salad Dressings. Of the forty-three dressings she recommended, twenty-seven were "the French type," made with oil, vinegar, herbs, and "a sliced clove of garlic to be discarded before serving." Her preface to the Salads section urged that a "green salad" be served with both luncheon and dinner. She recommended four varieties of lettuce plus chicory, watercress, spinach, dandelion, and parsley as "base for the green salad." In all, she detailed eighty salads.

This growth in salad awareness between 1926 and 1936 was a significant leaf of American history—a green leaf that initiated sixty years of fast diets and also established lettuces, peppers, mushrooms, garlic, celery, tomatoes, parsley, and herbs as major agricultural crops.

Borrowed from Europe and the Near East, the salad had been a springtime tonic, summer side-dish, and winter "dainty" since the Salem and Jamestown settlements. After 1912, technology and biochemists transformed it into the best—and, initially, the cheapest—method for slimming sedentary America back to the "lean and lanky" models of the frontiersman/cowboy/Uncle Sam tradition.

Lettuce is believed to have originated as a weed on the green prairie that the Nile nourished in its swirl through the Egyptian desert; priests used wild lettuce in religious rituals. The Greeks associated lettuce with their Olympian gods. Romans ate raw lettuce, doused in oil and vinegar and salt, to lighten the stomach as a prelude for meat and starch gorgings. The word *salad* has its root in the Latin word meaning "to be salted."

William Shakespeare established a metaphor for both lettuce and the salad when he had Cleopatra brood about "my salad days, when I was green in judgement." Columbus brought lettuce seeds to Haiti. In pioneer New England and Virginia, lettuce was mixed with the leaves of horehound, burdock, and sage as a "springtime physick." But the plant required cool nights and

April showers. In the June heat, it began to produce seed; the frilled emerald leaves filled with a bitter white fluid.

In the antebellum South, the redbud tree, the region's most spectacular harbinger of springtime, was called the "salad tree" because its burst of rosy blossom announced the imminence of dandelions, wild onions, mint, young milkweed, and lettuce for the annual salads. *The Williamsburg Art of Cookery*, a compilation of eighteenth- and nineteenth-century recipes from Virginia, contains only one recipe for a green salad and two recipes for "Boiled Dreffing."

"We had a row of green and reddish lettuce in the garden and ate it," Dr. Frank Cyr recalled of his sodhouse childhood in Nebraska. "There were collards and lambs' quarter, too. But there weren't any salads."

"There were mustard greens and pigweed greens and native herbs for Brigham tea," Paul Bailey mused of his Utah youth. "Freely provided by the Utah terrain was the sego lily, now the state flower. Actually, it was a sort of wild onion. Gathered green and stripped, it became a sweetish salad. Left alone, it flowered into beauty." But in Utah, also, the salad bowl reigned only from March through June.

When I was a preacher's kid in the Catskills and Hudson Valley, salad was a Sunday dinner item: a fairyland barge of half a canned peach with a blob of whipped cream, peaked by a maraschino cherry on a pool of parsley. Garden greens and side-yard dandelions were "greens," but not "salads."

"Sometime in 1926, Mother got involved in an Extension Club and really went gung-ho on balanced diets, vitamins, and so forth," Paul Zillman recalled about his farm boyhood in central Missouri.

> From there on out, we had it—but good! The only lettuce available then was Black Seeded Simpson. As head lettuce, it doesn't work too well, and it gets too warm too quickly in the spring. But we consumed it, along with the green beans, carrots, beets, onions, and cabbage Mother raised. After the gar-

den froze out in the late fall, she'd serve up celery, Chinese cabbage, turnips, sauerkraut, and canned goods from the root cellar. There was always some of it on our dinner plates. Dad could get away with eating what he liked, but my brother and I had to clean our plates. My brother still doesn't like green vegetables too much. As for salad on a separate plate, I can't recall having that until I went to college.

Florida and California have semi-tropical climates that sustain citrus, fig, and mango groves. Both states had large populations of Spanish and Italian heritage. Their salad awareness was two thousand years old. They knew that the climate would also permit year-round production of the lettuces, celery, tomatoes, peppers, onions, and garlic essential to a salad. The largest potential market for salad crops was the megalopolis between Boston and Baltimore. A railroad freight car needed nine days for the Los Angeles to New York trip, and four days from Miami to New York. But a refrigerator car would retain a semblance of freshness for two, even three, weeks. (You could always play it safe by picking the produce before it was ripe!) Bank loans for the rip-up of Florida's Everglades and for sluicing more Colorado River runoff into California's Imperial Valley were justified by the biochemists' announcements that a cupful of shredded lettuce contains only fifteen calories and two units of carbohydrates, with minute traces of protein and fat.

By the 1930s, city markets sparkled with mounds of Simpson, Boston, and Romaine lettuce, fennel, endive, watercress, tomatoes, scallions, red and yellow onions, and celery. Oriental and Italian vendors sprayed their displays with water and arranged them in geometric designs. Out through the tenements, vendors announced bargain prices for battered or wilted surpluses, along with pots of geraniums, chives, oregano, and rosemary for windowbox or rooftop gardens. Chain stores promoted "salad kits" that contained a bottle of wine vinegar, a tin of olive oil, shakers of pepper, paprika, and garlic salt, plus a glass miniature of a cocktail shaker. From November through April, clerks at "deluxe" groceries performed a daily chore of opening crates and stripping slimy outer leaves from California lettuce, rinsing the pale-yellow centers, then arranging them on beds of green confetti. The centers sold out front—and at an excellent profit— as "hearts of lettuce."

When mildew and rot infections crippled the California lettuce crop, botanists were called in to produce blight-resistant hybrids. Their creation was a pale-green sphere that looked like cabbage and tasted like damp papier-mâché. A publicist devised the name of "Iceberg" for it. Massive plantings and the use of Mexican, Japanese, and poor-white labor on field crews enabled Iceberg to underprice other lettuces.

The influx of Europeans and Orientals as well as the mechanization of the fruit and vegetable and seafood industries helped turn San Francisco into a city of gourmet delights. Cupola'd restaurants along Grant Avenue featured Peking duck, spicy pork, mung-bean sprouts, water chestnuts, ginger root, and bamboo shoots. DeMaggio's restaurant, down near Fisherman's Wharf, made the creation of a Caesar Salad a picturesque ritual of pounding garlic, cheese, anchovies, raw eggs, and oil into a paste, then tossing it with snipped endive and lettuce. Mexican restaurants served up corn, garbanzo beans, taco, and frijole as salad creations. Oakland became internationally famous among gourmets as the home place of Trader Vic's. The Palace, the Fairmont, the Saint Francis, and the Mark Hopkins were all known to travelers for their fine food and splendid salads. A trip to the farmers' market was as essential for a visitor as the cable car ride up Nob Hill.

Fredric A. Johnson was one of the city's devotees of salad consciousness. He owned a seat on the San Francisco Stock Exchange but spent much of his leisure time experimenting with herb gardens in his backyard. One afternoon he returned home early, followed by a truck carrying his desk and office equipment. "When I told my wife that I had sold my seat on the exchange and intended to pioneer herb growing in California," he told friends, "she looked at me for a moment, shook her head and said, 'You're crazy! When do we get started?' "

Encouraged by conferences with Extension Service botanists and agronomists, the Johnsons explored farming areas from Vancouver to Tia Juana, then contracted for experimental plantings of paprika peppers, basil, dill, rosemary, sage, marjoram, and other zesty components of a salad dressing. Trial and error, with steadfast cooperation by agricultural scientists, eventually produced quality crops. Meanwhile, techniques for drying and milling the herbs were being tested in San Francisco. The final premarketing step was design of an attractive container for retailing the product. The one adopted—and still used—was a round glass jar four and a quarter inches high, with a snap-on plastic shaker top and a metal screw-on lid. The adhesive used on the brown-and-red label dissolved when soaked in hot water, thus making the container reusable by spice-shelf devotees. Under the trade name of Spice Islands, the Johnson condiments became internationally famous and initiated California crops that have a current annual revenue of $100 million.

Reductions in most family incomes during the 1930–39 Depression were so severe that vegetables, fruit, and nuts became dominant in the national diet. In addition, our entry into World War II prompted an increase in vegetarianism after the government instituted meat and fat rationing with food stamps and appeals for "meatless days." Exorbitant advertising campaigns by food processors and the new supermarkets brought so much revenue to magazines and newspapers that publishers added "food editors" and "home economists" to their staffs and installed "model kitchens" beside the cubicles of the editorial department. These new staff members and their equipment churned out thousands of pages of rehashed recipes and saccharine verbiage stressing the ease and "health building goodness" of meatless meals. Consequently, lettuce, onion, garlic, tomato, celery, and herb farming flourished—and retail prices increased.

There were religious and animal-welfare adherents, too, who were promoting a change in the American diet. Buddhist and

Hindu immigrants followed all-vegetable diets. Humane societies protested the cruelties of meat-packing plants, as well as the rough-and-tumble of the cowboys' rodeo events; many members expressed their resentment by promoting the all-vegetable diet.

During the 1840s, a Methodist minister named William Miller in upstate New York had denounced Wesleyan doctrine and founded the Adventists as a sect that would subsist on a vegetable diet. Reorganizations of the Adventists evolved the Seventh Day Adventist Church. The Seventh Day Adventists financed community hospitals, welfare missions, and dietetic laboratories. Their technicians devised caffeine-free beverages, tasty cutlets made from vegetable glucose, and other meatless entrees. Will K. Kellogg, a devout Adventist in Battle Creek, Michigan, experimented with the ancient Indian method for popping corn and invented cornflakes. His products soon generated competition by processors of puffed wheat, puffed rice, toasted wheat germ, and similar products. Advertising programs stressing the cereals' contributions to health and fitness caused the American breakfast to veer away from the traditional bacon and eggs, grits, pancakes, homefried potatoes, and the finish-off of apple pie.

Vegetarians were instrumental in founding health-food stores that specialized in dried fruits, nuts, herbs, herbal teas, vitamin pills, whole-wheat flours and crackers, fruit-flavored candies, and chocolate substitutes made from the "locust beans" of the carob tree, a leguminous evergreen adapted to Florida and California. Health-food stores popularized the phrase "natural foods," but failed to identify what "unnatural" foods were. This semantic dodge was soon mimicked by the chain stores' use of "farm fresh"— which didn't tell the consumer when or where the product had been harvested.

By the end of World War II, the salad was a staple of the American diet. Restaurants installed salad bars where customers could choose from an array of lettuces, pickled beets, garbanzo beans, tomatoes, onions, cottage cheese, chopped celery, grated cheese, and croutons—and then drown their plateful in dressings that were 50 percent fat and sugar.

The new streamliner trains specialized in fancy salads, too. The premier Washington to Chicago express of the Baltimore & Ohio railroad was the Capitol Limited, a government and lobbyist favorite because its schedule permitted a full working day before the "Aaall Aboard!" from Chicago's Loop or Washington's rococo Union Station. The Capitol's dining cars featured a salad bowl a yard wide. It was mounded with a mixed green salad gemmed by half-inch cubes of blue cheese. The stewards vowed that the bowls had to be refilled three and sometimes four times each dinnertime.

Southern Pacific's sleek Sunset Limited featured crabmeat and Oregon's Tillamook cheese in its salads. Waiters on the Burlington's California Zephyr served a salad featuring Colorado's mammoth peaches before presenting the diner with broiled Rocky Mountain trout shimmering on a bed of Utah parsley. The Great Northern's dining cars did much to popularize the Idaho potato and the Pacific Northwest's fruits, just as the Sante Fe's Chief promoted the dates and citrus of Arizona and California by its salads.

By 1980, American farms produced more than 6 billion pounds of lettuce on 232,000 acres; our 40 million home gardens grew at least one row of lettuce. The commercial lettuce crop, centralized in California and Arizona, had a fieldside value of $576 million. This, plus home production, put Peter Rabbit's favorite nibble far past the billion-dollar total. The Black Seeded Simpson grown in home gardens in 1926 is still marketed, and another score of lettuce varieties have since been developed by geneticists and are available in seed catalogues. But chain stores continue to favor the tasteless Iceberg and feature it at half the price of succulent Boston, Redleaf, Buttercrunch, or Oakleaf.

Two-thirds of the 2 billion pounds of tomatoes grown for the "fresh market" in 1980 came from California and Florida. Our commercial garlic crop—despite prejudice against its redolence—bulged from 50 million pounds in 1965 to more than 200 million pounds in 1983.

But the ideal of slimming Americans through salads was doomed by the post-war promotion of superfatty snacks. Mechanization enhanced the national habit of "snacking" after 1900. Every drugstore installed a soda fountain where mammoth "banana-split" sundaes would be skidded down the marble counter in exchange for an all-silver quarter. The Sunday afternoon drive out into the country often ended at an ice cream "parlor." The Earl of Sandwich multiplied the business of the medical profession with the simplicity of his slabs of protein wedged between two spongy slabs of carbohydrates. High wages, the gourmand tastes acquired by millions who served overseas during the war, and a growing indifference toward home cooking pointed the way to a new fast diet that began in 1945–46 with the popularization of pizza.

During the summer of 1923, Leopold and Blanchette Arnaud were houseguests in Rome. Leo was Dean of Architecture at Columbia University; Blanchette was a distinguished authority on primitive art. Both were gourmets whose culinary enthusiasm probed the complexities of food history. "One evening our host suggested that we dine at a new and exciting restaurant," Leo related. "The restaurant, it seemed, served varieties of cheese, meat and vegetable pies that were made from old Neapolitan and Sicilian recipes. We had a delicious meal. It was the first time that Blanchette and I had ever heard of pizza!"

The migration of pizza from Naples to Rome in 1923 is a landmark in the 1945–60 development of a new American cuisine: the fast-food emporium. Southern Italy had begun experimenting with tomato recipes soon after the Spanish introduced the strange plant from South America. "Pizza is a very simple way to use up leftovers," Neapolitans explain. "The basic condiments are cheese and tomato. The crust can be flaky or bready, thick or thin. A scrap of ham, a little sausage, a mushroom or two, a wave of garlic and oregano, and you have a topping."

Although pizza initially influenced only small segments of our agriculture, its sudden popularity west and south of New England and New York literally set off a "chain" reaction—hamburger chains, fish-and-chips chains, pancake chains, fried-chicken chains, as well as a greasy flood of french fries, potato chips, corn chips, and frozen dinners. Heart disease and diabetes increased. The incidence of obesity increased. The plastic curtain between producer and consumer became more opaque.

The role of the delightful pizza in all of this melee was little more than that of an innocent Italian Riding Hood, with a basket of goodies, entering America's industrial jungle at a time when the wolves were restless and hungry. As Americans have ruefully learned, the primary motive of industry is to earn a profit. The beneficent foundation that lavishes grants on universities, researchers, artists, and television networks is usually the escape hatch for a corporation seeking a "shelter" from excessive government taxation. The huge manufacturing facilities that developed during World War II had to adjust to peacetime production, or we would be faced with the usual post-war depression. War veterans had experienced French, Near East, South Seas, and Chinese cuisines and had grown to detest the commissary monotony of canned pork, "vitamin bars," and dried-egg concoctions. Thus, with $$$ as their insignia, promoters launched an era of excessive sugar, excessive salt, and excessive fat, served fast in tile-and-plastic chateaus.

Before World War II, the boardwalks of Coney Island, Atlantic City, Revere Beach, and other surf-and-sunburn refuges for urbanites were walled with hot dog stands. By 1950, the "Coney Hots" and "Texas Dog" purveyors were being replaced by pizza parlors. Soon competitors were promoting hamburgers, seafood boiled in fat, crisp-fried chicken, submarine and "poorboy" sandwiches, umpteen varieties of ice cream, salty sausages on salty biscuits, and salty salami on hard rolls.

The hoary specialties of regional cooking were also integrated into a new nationwide cuisine. New England's favorite, fried soft-shell clams, became a commonplace "Wednesday special" at restaurants in Oshkosh, St. Joe, Great Falls, Wolf Hollow, Spokane. The South's overfried chicken became "Kentucky Fried." Louisiana's sugary pecan pie invaded the "French cuisine" restaurants of Wisconsin, Idaho, North Dakota—often with ghastly results.

The hamburger—dripping cottonseed oil, then drowned in catsup that was twenty-nine percent sugar, and swathed in a rubbery "vitamin-enriched" bun—became America's favorite lunch, along with a papercupful of french fries dredged in salt.

The Gulf Coast's delectable shrimp cascaded into kettles of cottonseed or corn oil to become gummy-brown masses of "butterfly shrimp," from Portland to Portland. Mexico's fiery chile con carne migrated out of Texas into "chili parlors" of the East and South, intimidated by home economists' squeals for "less pepper." Sacks of fried corn chips followed. So did tortillas, fried beans, tacos, and stucco haciendas winking neon invitations to such places as Gringo's Downfall, The Gay Aztec, and Rodriguez Hideaway.

Food processors and chain stores quickly imitated the trend, thanks to the Birdseye discovery of quick-freeze. The chrome and white-enamel splendor of frozen-food bins came to store aisles and were filled with plastic sacks of french-fried potatoes, Chinese fried rice, Japanese stir-fry vegetables, Mexican-fry tortillas, fried Hungarian peppers, New York fried steaks, Texas fried beans, plus regiments of ready-to-eat entrees, pies, cakes, and pastries, all liberally laced with salt and sugar.

Per capita consumption of sugar soared from 40 to 129 pounds per year. Salt consumption rose as alarmingly. Three out of every five calories Americans ate were from fats and sugar—and still were in 1983. Forty percent of our population were overweight; 75 percent snacked on salty and/or sugary fast-foods while watching prime-time television.

Through all of this, pizza bubbled on. Nutritionists recommended its use as an "economical and nourishing entree" for the School Lunch Act adopted by Congress in 1946. Its chameleon-like adaptability allowed a broader range of flavors than the hamburger–fish stick–herbed chicken competition.

One of pizza's most spectacular achievements was its influence on mushroom farming. Before the pizza conquest, mushrooms were a rare treat to most Americans. City restaurants with continental aspirations served a sparse sprinkle of mushrooms on porterhouse steaks and filet mignons. Italian groceries sold dried black mushrooms from the Alpine foothills—at Alpine prices. The Boston–Philadelphia–New York carriage trade luxuriated in mushroom stuffing for Thanksgiving turkeys. The farm-wise gathered wild morels and puffballs, then butter-sauteed them. But newspapers gave page-one play to amateurs who had guessed wrong about wild mushrooms and died writhing at the dinner table. The mushroom was as rare to most people as the French truffle and the Russians' salty black sturgeon eggs.

A modest mushroom industry did exist in the suburbs of Philadelphia. It was a by-product of the horsecars that clanked along Broad and Chestnut before Mr. Edison's curiosity produced the trolley car. The generous droppings of horsecar teams, plus those of the Percherons and Belgians hauling beer and freight wagons, became a civic embarrassment. There weren't many gardeners; nearby farmers had their own manure providers. Then a Scotsman, whose name has been carelessly lost by historians, recalled that horse manure is the best medium for growing mushrooms. Mushroom cellars, aromatic with composted horse manure and straw, burgeoned in Kennett Square and other Philadelphia suburbs.

The popularity of the mushroom grew with the popularity of the pizza. Its enhancement of salads, soufflés, and cocktail dips forced chain stores to stock it. By 1966, our mushroom production had reached 165 million pounds annually, with a cellar-door value of $58 million. By 1978, mushroom farmers in 26 states produced a 452-million-pound harvest, with a value of $360 million, an increase of almost 300 percent in 12 years. (Horse manure remains the best growing medium; the reason is still a scientific mystery.)

However, middleman greed has encouraged increasing imports of lower-priced mushrooms from Asia and Europe. Between 1970 and 1980 these soared from 11,253 to 41,899 metric tons per year, with Taiwan, Korea, and Hong Kong as the largest shippers. These canned stems and caps continued to underprice American production costs and, by the spring of 1983, raised the spectre of bankruptcy for many American producers.

Pizza-munching also increased the popularity of the plum-shaped Italian tomato, tomato paste, and Parmesan and Romano cheeses. The national appetite for cheeses had increased steadily since 1900, mostly because of the low prices for pasteurized cheddar. The pizza's medley of flavors encouraged greater cheese sophistication and persuaded grocers to stock their shelves with Italian, French, British, Dutch, Danish, Swiss, Greek, and Canadian cheese varieties, as well as their American imitations. Between 1965 and 1980, per capita consumption of cheeses made in the United States rose from $9\frac{1}{2}$ to $17\frac{1}{2}$ pounds, and our annual imports of foreign cheeses rose to 12 million pounds.

By the time "Kentucky chicken" sizzled onto the great pizza trail, the changes underway in chicken production were as drastic as the technologic move from the village blacksmith's shop to a Detroit assembly line. Automatic incubators replaced the broody hen with crates of fertilized eggs delivered by the mailman. Block-long buildings, automatically heated and lighted, replaced the chicken coop and its chickenwire yard. Factory-blended feeds and the invention of vaccines and antibiotics to control diseases reduced the growing time of a broiler from ten to seven weeks. Coincidentally, egg production of hens rose from an average of 83 a year in 1909 to 225 in 1981.

These efficiencies were soon adapted to the assembly-line concept. Cockerels destined for the race to broilerdom are sorted out from young hens as they move by workers on a conveyor belt. When the hen is five months old, it is placed in one of thousands of wire cages of the "egg house." A belt moves slowly in front of the cages to the plant's cleaning and packing rooms. The hen stays in the cage for one year, with daily feeding and watering. Her sole duty is to lay eggs. The eggs roll down an incline to the moving belt. At the end of the year, the hen is loaded into a truck and hauled—often hundreds of miles—to a packing plant, where she is processed into soup, pot pie, canned meat, bonemeal livestock feed, and pillow stuffing.

The assembly-line technique permitted chickens and eggs to underprice red meats and be exploited as "loss leaders" by the supermarts. Per capita consumption of chicken rose from 33 pounds per year in 1965 to more than 41 pounds in 1980. However, in the same period, egg consumption per capita dropped from 313 to 284 per year. This drop was due to consumer fretting about the cholesterol content of the egg's yolk—based on research that had been financed by a vegetarian organization.

Specialization also encouraged centralized production. The number of egg farmers dropped from more than 1 million in 1964 to approximately 200,000 in 1980. Ninety percent of the current production comes from fifty or sixty plants, each housing more than 1 million chickens. (Several of these plants are controlled by supermarkets.) California, Georgia, Pennsylvania, and Arkansas are the country's leading egg producers. Arkansas, Georgia, Alabama, and North Carolina lead in broiler production.

The year-round availability of "farm fresh" eggs did not, however, change the urban myth that brown eggs are a lot better for you than white ones. Chain stores still charge a nickel or dime more per dozen for brown shells than for white ones even though laboratory tests certify that yolks and whites have identical food value, irrespective of shell color.

The turkey industry trotted, too. An American native, it was first domesticated by Pueblo tribes in the Southwest. Benjamin Franklin nominated it as the national bird of the new republic; but ever since Centaur invaders declared the eagles on Mount Olympus to be the messengers of Zeus, this haughty predator had been a favorite symbol of nations. Congress rejected Franklin's idea and meekly copied the Romans, the Holy Roman Empire, and the Russian czars by making the eagle our national bird.

Various diseases, and its twenty- to thirty-pound weight at maturity, long limited turkey to its role as an entree for the holidays. Soon after Henry Wallace became Secretary of Agriculture, however, zoologists at the USDA Research Center in Beltsville, Maryland, were ordered to begin crossbreeding experiments for the development of a smaller turkey that would have a preponderance of breast meat. The experiments lasted seven years. In 1941, Beltsville introduced the Beltsville White, a breed that resulted in nine-pound hens and fifteen-pound toms. Subsequent crossbreeding evolved types maturing at five and six pounds.

Raising turkeys became profitable for Mormons and their "gentile" neighbors in Utah, Idaho, and Nevada. During the 1940s and 1950s, David W. Evans, the premier publicist of Salt Lake City, visualized larger markets for the bird by packaging turkey legs, turkey breast meat, smoked turkey, and turkey pies separately, and developing recipes to popularize them. He convinced processors and chain stores to offer frozen packets that could be tucked into corners of a family's deep-freeze.

Retailers stressed the fact that cold cuts blended from turkey meat have lower fat and cholesterol content than cold cuts made from red meats. Sanitary housing and strict feeding routines permitted the turkey to retail at half and sometimes one-third the prices for pork, lamb, or beef. The per capita appetite for turkey rose from four pounds a year in 1950 to more than ten pounds a year in 1980. National production now totals 3 billion pounds a year, with Minnesota, North Carolina, California, Arkansas, and Missouri as the leading producers.

In our 1945–80 transition to the pizza and other fast foods, the most dangerous factor has been the furtive addition of varieties of sugar and salt to processors' recipes. The Mormon experiments with sugar beets in the nineteenth century developed into an annual American harvest of 22 million tons, with California, Minnesota, North Dakota, and Idaho as leading producers. Subsequently, chemists discovered ways to process edible sugar syrup from corn, and more than 850 million gallons of it are now manufactured annually. The result was a sugar surplus. Food processors succumbed to the temptation to add more and more sugar and salt to canned vegetables, canned fruits, bread, ice cream, chewing gum, catsup, soy sauce, gelatine desserts, and electronically cured meats.

As the cereal manufacturers raced for larger profits, new breakfast "goodies" were introduced that had a 25 percent sugar content. During the 1960s and '70s, the sugar proportion climbed to 30 and 40 percent. According to an analysis made by USDA in 1979, two popular brands of ready-to-eat cereal were 50 percent sugar. (A recent analysis of 14 types of granola, a "natural food," showed that the sugar content ranged from 22 to 32 percent by weight.)

Processor additions of salt to bread, puddings, canned soups, pancakes, apple pie, and fried chicken, plus the historic use of salt in curing meats, cheeses, pickles, and sauerkraut, have made the condiment a major contributor to high blood pressure, heart disease, and arthritis. Fast-food restaurants became big offenders. A McDonald's "Big Mac" contains 1,510 milligrams of sodium; a Kentucky Fried Chicken dinner contains 2,285 milligrams of sodium; a Dairy Queen "Brazier Dog" averages 868 milligrams of sodium. Salt consumption by American adults rose to an average of two to three teaspoonsful per day (approximately 15 pounds per year), a terrifying excess of 2,000 to 3,000 percent beyond the body's actual need of one-tenth of a teaspoonful per day.

USDA finally managed to overcome lobbyist opposition and secure legislation ordering food processors to list all of the contents on the container of a retail food product. But the percentage of each additive was not included in the law. Also, processors could use syrup, glucose, dextrose, and other scientific terms for "sugar" and the wide range of sodiums for "salt."

While the fast-food and processor industries prospered and retail prices soared, the majority of agricultural producers sank into poverty because of high production costs and lower and lower payments for harvests. Much of the farmers' plight could be traced to the policies and non-policies of USDA.

On one floor of USDA's South Building, hundreds of clerks, managers, statisticians, and bureau chiefs handled the thousands of tons of forms and filing cards of farmers who received subsidy payments for allegedly *reducing* their acreage production of tobacco, milk, and grains. On an adjoining floor, however, hundreds of secretaries, consultants, specialists, and bureau chiefs supervised the research of biochemists, geneticists, botanists, and zoologists who were enabling these producers to produce *more* tobacco, grains, and milk on reduced acreages and with smaller herds. Thus, for a half century, USDA eagerly persisted in "hoisting itself on its own petard," with taxpayers footing the bill.

By means of hybrids, deadlier pesticides, and more potent fertilizers, scientists doubled the average acreage yield of corn between 1935 and 1960. The 50 new varieties of wheat developed between 1935 and 1945 pushed production per acre from 25 bushels to a peak of 76 bushels. Tobacco production was boosted to an average of 2,611 pounds per acre. Milk production per cow doubled to a national average of 11,218 pounds per year.

By 1959, USDA was paying more than $2 billion annually for crop-reduction subsidies and farm price "stabilization." The federal bill for handling and storing farm crops held "in hock" on government loans that year was $482 million. At the same time, political pressures prevented USDA from improving the condition of agriculture by developing home-grown fuels and economical machines that would enable technologized self-sufficiency on farms and ranches. Similarly, little effort was made to ensure that more than a third of retail prices went to our growers of foods and fibers.

In 1955, a Harvard professor proposed a reorganization of USDA and invented a new word—*agribusiness.*

CHAPTER TWELVE

The Agrivores

After booze and fast women put the prodigal son in the gutter, he repented and went back to the old folks, according to a parable reported in St. Luke. Promptly, the parable continues, his father called in the hired man and ordered "the fatted calf" to be readied for a banquet.

The routine must have been simple. The calf was probably an unessential young bull. The hired man did the butchering. The cook received enough meat for a large roast or fricassee, with leftovers for a week of stews, pot pies, goulash, and meat loaf. The calf's hide went off to the barn to be cured and later made into a cloak or blanket. The feet yielded excellent jelly. Meat from the head could be chopped, spiced, and smoked into a kind of salami. There were no middlemen.

A radically different system confronted the American dad in the 1950s when Dancing Dan renounced his beatnik pad—and assuming he would deign to eat veal. The population odds in the United States made it twenty-to-one that dad would not be a farmer. Consequently, a gauntlet of twelve profit-seekers stood between any "fatted calf" and the banquet table.

In order to breed the cow that produced the calf, a farmer had to pay a veterinarian to inject an expensive needleful of bull semen. Feed for both cow and calf necessitated payments to machinery dealers, gasoline truckers, feed manufacturers, fertilizer manufacturers, and tax collectors, as well as the bank or credit union that held the farm's mortgage. When the calf was plump enough to yield a roast, a trucker who charged $25 an hour hauled it off to a stockyard. The stockyard sold the animal to a packer for $60, and deducted a 10 percent commission from the farmer's check.

The packer who bought the calf stabbed, sawed, and ground it into a score of industrial products. The excess bones were powdered into a "vitamin-rich" bone-meal fertilizer. The blood was dehydrated into a purplish powder, "excellent for your garden." Glands became pharmaceutical supplies and expensive sweetbreads. Viscera were processed into "balanced" pet and poultry foods. The hide went off to a tannery to become a swank $300 coat with a French label stitched into its sateen lining. The carcass was sawed in half and trucked off to a jobber. The jobber re-trucked it to a retailer.

The retailer's electric saws and grinders turned each half-carcass into roasts, filets, patties, and soup bones. Each portion was then placed on a cardboard tray, with chunks of bone and suet carefully concealed, then multi-wrapped in layers of plastic. Finally, a machine affixed a Xeroxed label giving the weight and price and the allegation of "choice, milk-fed veal." (Since all calves nurse throughout infancy, it is all but impossible to produce veal that has not been milk-fed!)

If the modern prodigal son relished roast veal, wiener schnitzel, or timbales, Mom could pick up a plastic wedge of meat at the supermarket for four dollars a pound—and mumble about "the horrid farm profiteers" all the way home.

The array of profit-seekers in the processing and distribution of agricultural products by the 1950s collected two-thirds of the retail price. From February's huge but sour strawberries to January's tasteless pink tomatoes, twelve types of industry came to dominate the nation's agriculture. They were, and are: machinery manufacturers; petroleum pedlars; processors of "balanced" livestock, poultry, and pet foods; the makers of synthetic fertilizers and pesticides; the collectors of federal, state, and local taxes; the banker lending operating funds at 18 to 25 percent interest; the railroad, truck, and airplane transporters; the makers of cans and packaging materials; the food processors; the jobbers; commission men; and, finally, the retailers. Six of these groups had appeared on the agricultural scene since the 1870s because of the hapless dependence of cities on sources of foods. All of these "service" industries were developed, their publicists insisted, to improve efficiency and sanitation. Each "service" was accepted by the consumer as essential, hence became as firmly seated in agriculture as the cowboy, tractor jockey, orchardist, and milk cow. But middleman economic demands caused farmers and ranchers to overcrop land, increase the erosion of topsoils, waste precious water reserves, and raise the spectre of desert from Maine to Oregon. Actually, these service industries were *agrivores*. Their profit urge devoured the greatest American heritage—the land.

Some of the agrivores behaved like kindergarteners with runny ice-cream cones; they slurped at both ends. Chain stores operated massive egg and broiler farms. Meat packers controlled livestock ranches by means of "dummy" corporations. Millers became the absentee landlords of grain farms. Canners leased thousands of acres of rich bottomland, then sent in crews to grow crops from seeds that had been bred for "shipping toughness" by university geneticists. Soup makers became vegetable growers. Railroads operated potato farms and fruit orchards.

The farm magazines didn't object. They had discovered, decades before, that subscription fees weren't really necessary and could be used for promotional advertising and circulation campaigns. The big money was in advertising. Consequently, the publisher was frequently a veteran advertising solicitor who had been the college roommate of the oil millionaire, banker, or politician who owned a majority of the publication's stock.

This situation promoted a news policy that focused on the wonders of mechanical science, insecticides, and cure-all drugs, plus a page of Washington gossip and three pages of kitchen recipes. A nimble editor could keep the magazine's owner more or less pacified by giving his political whimsies bull-roar space in "The Editor's Corner."

The land-grant colleges flopped and gasped in the same net. The wartime baby-boom was reaching high school age and would soon be taking college entrance examinations. Trustees, alumni, politicians, building contractors nagged to expand the colleges to state universities with gargantuan campuses, better football and basketball teams, and all the intramural dignities of the Ivy League. The revered scholar was eliminated as chancellor. The post now required an ambivert who could switch on extroversion at a fund-raising reception, flick back to scholarly concern at a meeting of deans, and charm five-figure bequests out of lonely widows as well as industries seeking a tax shelter. Many of the trust funds thus accumulated were invested in gilt-edged industrial stocks that made the university part-owner of Glibowitz Potato Chips, Coltson's Tractor, Amalgamated Plow, and Jim-dandy Mills.

Faculty members had to learn how to survive in the polysyllabic arena of "publish or perish." The rare ability to mesmerize a hundred and fifty freshmen, stuffed into uncomfortable chairs in a forty-foot room, with a lecture on Poultry Management could no longer be accepted as reason for promoting the instructor up the prestige ladder to Assistant Professor to Associate Professor to full Professor. Merit badges of promotion would be pinned only on those who published articles in "scholarly journals" or who wheedled a grant out of an industry or some branch of the federal government. The editors of the scholarly journals knew all about "publish or perish," so they rarely paid an honorarium for the articles they accepted. Indeed, many of them charged the author $50 or more for the privilege of seeing his or her name on the title page.

Thus, academic promotion through brainstorming an idea into

a project grant from a foundation or from USDA's Agricultural Marketing Service was particularly appealing, especially when there were two youngsters at home, the wife was pregnant again, and payment was overdue on the bank loan that had enabled the struggling young academic to eke out those two quonset-hut years while he earned his M.S.

Some of the projects were so simple that it seemed shameful to accept the $5,000 grant. For example, the fruit company that owned and financed the foundation merely wanted a quicker system for sorting the honeydew, casaba, and Cranshaw melons it bought from California growers and then trucked East. The fruit had to be shipped in wooden crates; the fruit wouldn't cooperate with the crate makers. Some melons were too small; some were too large.

Two instructors of the Farm Machinery II course at a Midwestern state university built four chrome hoops, graduated in size from six-inch diameter to nine-inch diameter and welded on a tubular frame. The fruit company built this gadget into a gate at its unloading platforms. The melons that slithered through the holes would fit the packing crates. The rest of the fruit went back to the farm to be sold for pig food or tossed on a compost pile. Of course, the gadget meant that 50 percent of the melons grown went to pigs or compost, and higher prices could be posted at chain stores and "fancy fruit" markets for the ones that fitted the hoops. Efficiency!

A dedicated vegetarian might devote years of study to the proportion of cholesterol in animal fats. These efforts perhaps resulted in a foundation grant to study the incidence of heart disease and arterial clogging among meat eaters. The publicity this generated ricocheted through medical and health journals for decades; popularized hot dogs and bolognas made from chicken and turkey flesh; launched imitation, no-fat bacon made by grain processors; and enriched pill makers as well as the authors of hundreds of books about diet. It also intensified ancient religious prejudices against the pig—who, if left to his/her own browsing, wouldn't have put on all that fat.

A cheese corporation (that shall be nameless) underwrote research by another state university to devise a process for making mozzarella cheese in five and a half minutes instead of the normal four hours; the results were not very tasty, but good enough.

A meat firm gave funds to a state agricultural college to fiddle around with spices and dyes so that more soybean meal could be mixed into bolognas and frankfurters.

A chain-store conglomerate might send a check to a state college for a three-year project to hybridize varieties of snap beans, lima beans, cauliflower, etc., that would be tough enough to hold up during long truck rides plus a week or two in a warehouse; no need to worry about flavor. And how about a square tomato? It would be a lot easier to ship and would save money on crates!

Or any oil company might—with attached check—beseech an agricultural college to test its new petroleum spray for quicker ripening of fruits and tomatoes—both while growing and in storage. It worked very well as far as the color went, but lowered the vitamin content "considerably."

USDA smiled beneficently. It was all science and science was wonderful. The wave of the future. Perhaps the bye-bye wave, but a wave nevertheless. Anyway, the department was having growing pains. The number of employees was skittering past 100,000—more than State, Labor, and Commerce combined. Food stamps and the national school lunch had been added to its chores. The Secretary had a dozen Assistant Secretaries who in turn had Deputy and Assistant Deputy Secretaries and Administrators, Associate Administrators, Directors, Associate Directors, and Deputy Directors. There was a Farmers' Home Administration that approved fifteen varieties of farm loans, a Rural Electrification Administration, a Rural Telephone Bank, the Agricultural Marketing Service, the Animal and Plant Health Inspection Service, the Federal Grain Inspection Service, the Food and Nutrition Service, the Food Safety and Quality Service, the Agricultural Stabilization and Conservation Service, the Commodity Credit Corporation, the Federal Crop Insurance Corporation, the Foreign Agricultural Service (which arranges to ship farm editors and university professors off to be Agricultural Attachés at foreign embassies), the Office of International Cooperation and Development, the Science and Education Administration, the Forest Service (captured after a long and noisy struggle with the Department of the Interior), the Soil Conservation Service, the Economics and Statistics Service, the World Food and Agricultural Outlook and Situation Board, the Office of Budget, Planning and Evaluation—plus a regiment of publicists, ghost writers, photographers, film makers, and librarians.

Of the thousands of leaflets, magazines, brochures, and press-release handouts issued annually by the department, its most distinguished publication was the *Yearbook of Agriculture*. Since 1946, this volume had been edited by Alfred Stefferud, a quiet Minnesotan who had been an Associated Press correspondent in Mussolini's Italy and Hitler's Germany. Stefferud brought a new lustre to the venerable publication by focusing each *Yearbook* on an aspect of farming, such as *Soils* and *Consumers All*. This task necessitated the horrendous chore of assembling fifty to a hundred specialists in economics, conservation, engineering, chemistry, genetics, then soothing their vanities and extracting two- to five-thousand-word essays that would be more or less comprehensible to a lay reader. Stefferud achieved this each year—with one secretary. His volumes routinely won professional awards of merit for content, typography, and skillful choices of art.

But the *Yearbook* was essentially a monopoly of Congress. Each Congressman received several hundred copies gratis to be shipped out, at government expense, to the Congressman's campaign-fund contributors and most influential supporters. The leftovers could be purchased through the Government Printing Office—if you knew about its catalogue of available publications and were willing to wait six or seven weeks for a secretary to slither your check over to the cashier's office that, eventually, would notify the mailing room. Consequently, the *Yearbook*'s influence on consumer awareness of agriculture's problems was minimal, as were most of USDA's publications.

As USDA grew, farming shrank. The pressures exerted by the

demands of the agrivores, the excessive prices of machinery, fertilizers, feeds, and fuel, soaring taxes—all these generated a massive struggle for survival of the shrewdest. The simplest way to avoid the deputy sheriff with the foreclosure papers, it seemed, was to add acreage. But acreage didn't grow on trees. You could rip open land that should stay in pasture or woodlot, fertilize the hell out of it, and plant it to soybeans. Soybeans was a good cash crop that made its own nitrogen, even if the shallow roots did invite a lot of topsoil erosion. The other available method was to borrow enough from a bank or one of the government loan agencies to buy out a neighbor's property.

Technologic forces also shrank both the farm population and its productive acreage. The automobile and the airplane repeated the land grab that the railroads fattened on after the Civil War. Automakers, gas peddlers, and highway contractors lobbied for more throughways, more side roads, more parking lots. Airplane manufacturers and the scores of airlines lobbied as recklessly for airports at every county seat. Highways are concrete and macadam slabs atop tillable soil, middlin' good pasture, or potential woodlot; an airport must have hundreds of acres of level land that could otherwise nourish a lot of vegetables, grain, fruit, and livestock. All of these highways and airports were built with public funds (which is the lawyers' way of pronouncing "taxes").

This plethora of crushed rock, tar, and multicolored paint persuaded millions of urbanites to leave the smog and noise and muggings of the cities and acquire mortgages on suburban homes. Realtors borrowed funds to buy nearby farms, bulldoze them into fifty- to seventy-five-foot lots, trickle tar or gravel roads in from the "public funds" highway, and dicker with building contractors for identical rows of Dutch Colonial, French Primitive, Swiss Chalet, or Beerbarrel Bauhaus homes.

Enough topsoil and peat was usually trucked in to support a skimpy growth of grass, with four spruce seedlings and a lilac bush beneath the bay windows of the fourteen-by-sixteen-foot living room. Suburban decor dictated that the presence of those old edibles, the dandelion and crab grass, denoted peasant heritage and should be dug out before the neighbors spotted them. A similar snobbery grew against growing vegetables or fruit in the yard. After a few more payments on the mortgage, a second mortgage would yield enough capital to build a swimming pool, instead.

These suburbias, of course, also lured chain stores, department stores, fast-food palazzos, boutiques, and drugstores in from midcity to become neighbors on vast tar and crushed-stone aprons called shopping centers. Beneath these, too, rested reasonably good farmland. From the 1950s on, highways, airports, suburbias, shopping plazas destroyed more than 3 million acres of farmland each year.

In 1955, Dr. John H. Davis was directing the program in agriculture and business at Harvard's prestigious graduate school of business administration. Born on a Missouri farm and trained to be a teacher, Davis had had a distinguished career as head of the National Council of Farmer Cooperatives, and then as Assistant Secretary of USDA. These experiences, coupled with the pragmatism so essential to farming success, enabled him to detect the flaws in the agriculture-agrivore relationship and the government's inanely expensive efforts to control crop subsidies. In an address before the Boston Conference on Distribution on October 17, 1955, he proposed new correctives for the "income anemia" of farm and ranch.

"The technological revolution," he challenged,

> has brought agricultural production and marketing closer and closer together—actually making them interdependent. Thirty years ago agriculture produced seventy-five to eighty percent of its own production supplies, buying only twenty to twenty-five percent from business. Today agriculture buys from business almost half of its production input items in the form of machinery, tractor fuel, commercial fertilizer, mixed feeds and supplements, building materials, etc. Currently these purchases are running about fifteen billion dollars per year.
>
> Farmers combine these purchases with items from the farm

such as land, management and labor, to produce our food and fiber. This food and fiber they then sell to business for an aggregate sum of about thirty billion dollars farm value. Business firms, in turn, assemble, store, process and package these commodities and distribute the end product to the consumer for an aggregate total of about ninety billion dollars.

This takeover of agriculture's traction power, fertilizer, insecticides, livestock feeds, processing, and distribution by middlemen, Davis stressed, made the food and fiber producers "inseparable from the business firms which manufacture production supplies and market farm products. . . . We are so unaccustomed to looking at farm problems in their broad agriculture-business setting that the American language is wholly lacking in any word to describe such a concept. . . . I am suggesting a new term: *agribusiness.*"

Davis defined agribusiness as "the sum total of all operations involved in the production and distribution of food and fiber." But, he warned, if we are to reduce the role of government on the farm front, responsibility for basic farm income would rely on cooperation between the producers and the middlemen.

The coining of the word *agribusiness* and Davis's concept of astute cooperation between the landsmen and the various advocates of technology was the most logical and timely effort yet made to retrieve some self-sufficiency for agriculture, assure lower food and fiber prices for consumers, and move the socially tattered title of "farmer" back to an "archaic" definition in the dictionary.

The speech was given a modest headline in the Boston papers, plus a brief bulletin on AP and UP teletypes. There was little recognition from farm organizations. Although Ezra Taft Benson, then Secretary of Agriculture, had preceded Davis as head of the National Council of Farmer Cooperatives and also advocated that "farmers must have the cooperation of industry and labor," political pressures seemed to deny any motivation for, or acceptance of, the agribusiness concept at USDA.

In addition to writing *A Concept of Agribusiness* by himself, John Davis teamed with Kenneth Hinshaw, a farm-wise author, to produce the book *Farmer in a Business Suit*. Both books stressed cooperation between producers and industries and urged the appointment of non-political commissions to undertake these eight essential studies:

1. Determine methods that would enable "capable young families" to become agricultural producers.
2. Analyze the "organization, scope and functions of USDA" in order to determine its effectiveness in the new age of technology.
3. Re-examine the "adequacy" of the land-grant colleges and universities.
4. Formulate guidelines for the diversion of farmland to uses other than agricultural.
5. Explore price-stability methods that would eliminate the mounting subsidy and surplus storage payments of USDA.
6. Explore the antitrust laws for legal methods to curtail the monopolistic control methods of "commodity organizations."
7. Devise methods to control the price juggling of farm exports.
8. Study the potential of "the multinational corporation as a vehicle for bringing about economic development across political boundaries."

Both books received good reviews; *Farmer in a Business Suit* sold out several printings. There were criticisms from land-grant professors and economists, but, overall, the net result was finger-pointing. The land-grant colleges, like USDA, were deemed as righteous as a Puritan preacher. Farm organizations admitted an inferiority complex by grumbling that the middleman's lawyers and lobbyists would outfox them in any effort at equal rights in the marketplace.

But the deadliest blow to Davis's realism came from the deliberate distortion of the word *agribusiness* by journalists, who popularized it as a name for the agrivores and bigness. General Foods, Ralston Purina, Armour, Swift, General Mills, ten-thousand-acre farms, chain-store poultry and egg factories, thousands of Herefords and Angus crammed into a mucky Colorado feedlot, hundreds of Mexican "wetbacks" whacking Iceberg lettuce out of a five-hundred-acre field in the Imperial Valley were suddenly "agribusiness." The imagery of agriculture became distorted by glib journalese. The millions of families still struggling to break even on traditional family farms didn't matter anymore. The Davis books were abandoned, relegated to reference shelves as the interesting concept of an intellectual idealist.

Technology lurched on. By 1970, our agricultural areas had dwindled to 1,063 million acres operated by slightly more than 2 million families. Only 35 percent of the operators were full owners of the land they managed; only 11 percent were 35 years of age or younger. Yet crop and livestock production rose steadily. Between 1945 and 1970, beef production rose 75 percent, turkey flocks increased by 500 percent and soybean plantings by 700 percent. Rice, corn, and wheat responded to biochemistry, fertilizers, and insecticides.

And farm costs outpaced the crop incomes. By 1976, agriculture's expenditures for machines and other middleman supplies totaled $81 billion, yet the farmers received less than 30 percent of the retail prices for the foods and fibers they grew. Because of farmers' struggles to regain solvency, topsoils eroded while water reserves dwindled, and family members commuted to salaried jobs in towns.

As the final decades of the twentieth century approached, neither the government nor the designers of school curriculums bothered to consider the historical perspective that had persuaded Davis toward his program of re-examination of the American land's decline. Yet the pattern of transition from self-sufficiency to techno-serfdom was sharp and clear.

Self-sufficiency came about when the agriculture of the American Indian and the mores of the European immigrants merged during the seventeenth century. For the first time ever, the agriculturist achieved freedom of horsepower. Variants of the energy-independent farm appeared in different regions of colonial America: the ranch developed in New Mexico; the plantation's one crop and slave-based economy matured in Virginia; the communal farm evolved in New England.

During the eighteenth century, Germans and Quakers introduced the buildings, land-care techniques, and self-sufficiency that became the framework of the family farm. Irish and Scotch immigration led to the eminence of the cowboy. Misuse of land in New England and the South meant that topsoil erosion and the abandonment of needlessly worn out land would be a paramount problem.

The nineteenth century began with the rainbow promise of the American Philosophical Society's research, Thomas Jefferson's dedication to agricultural improvement through botanical experiments, and George Washington's introduction of the durable mule. But technology made it the Century of the Big Land Rape. Whitney's cotton engine caused more tragedy to the land and the people of the South by slavery and sharecropping than the four-year savagery of the Civil War. The vast burn-off of Appalachian forests influenced the growth of cities via canals and railroads, thus initiating transformation of the agricultural economy from barter to cash-and-credit. As machines, barbed wire, and irrigation ditches conquered the prairie and parched the high plains of the West, erosion and loss of water reserves tripled and quadrupled. Farm cooperatives failed to slow the takeover of the marketplace by middleman industries. The sneer terms of "rube," "hick," "redneck," and "clodhopper" were popularized among the urban majority. The family-farm pattern of self-sufficiency began to collapse.

Introduction of the automobile, tractor, and other mobile machinery early in the twentieth century completed the middleman's conquest of agriculture. The self-sufficient power furnished by the horse, mule, and ox was abandoned. Costly machines and fuels forced excessive use of fertilizers and insecticides, excessive erosion, excessive use of water, larger farms, surplus production—and led to lower market prices for crops. Federal funds plus industrial gifts to universities financed the research that made possible the consistent crop increases and the resultant toughness and tastelessness of mass-produced fruits and vegetables. Yet, at the same time, federal subsidy payments for reduction of crop acreages not only mesmerized farm organizations into intensive lobbying for more handouts, but encouraged the super-expensive storage program for surplus grains, beans, cotton, tobacco, and dairy products. The chain stores' plastic curtain, plus blatant advertising campaigns by processors and agricultural suppliers, intervened and completely shut off communication between producer and consumer.

When our so-called statesmen orated about our "highest standard of living on earth" and "feeding the world's hungry," farmers and ranchers muttered, "Is going into bankruptcy our only reward for this?" Another question, as frightening for consumer as for producer, loomed over the issue of food and farms: "Is technology going to serve mankind, or is mankind going to serve technology?"

Official Washington didn't seem to hear the question.

CHAPTER THIRTEEN

"It's Easier to Go Downhill!"

Throughout 1982, conservationists, nutritionists, sociologists, and geneticists agreed with a majority of farmers and ranchers that "It's Easier to Go Downhill!" was the appropriate motto for USDA's 120th birthday. Of the 4,800 lobbyist organizations registered in the District of Columbia, hundreds represented middleman processors and suppliers of agriculture. Retail food prices continued to rise while farm prices for crops declined and farm bankruptcies increased. Deliberate "meddling" with inspection standards put quality labels on inferior grades of meat. USDA timidity about the ravages of acid rain persisted. Despite 12.5 million unemployed, USDA continued to pay a million dollars a day storage fees on its mountains of surplus foods. Research for farm-grown motor fuels was again put off into the future. All of these factors, plus the department's traditional naiveté about public relations with the urban majority, contributed to USDA's resemblance to an old gray mare who "ain't what she used to be."

The USDA had been created in 1862 for the sole purpose of

helping agriculturists achieve and retain a living standard of democratic equality. The implied aim of the agency was perpetuation of the family farm, owned in fee simple, and assured equality of opportunity in the marketplace. But by 1982 our agricultural population had dwindled to 2 percent of the national total. Farm purchasing power from crop sales was one-half of the 1950 purchasing power. While retail food prices tripled, agriculture's net income per crop-acre collapsed from $11 to $4. More than half of all agricultural income was being earned by off-the-farm employment of wives, children, and "moonlighting" fathers. Thousands of farms and ranches were forced into bankruptcy; many of the eviction notices served on the impoverished families were the result of a USDA edict to "get tough" with delinquents of payments on government loans.

While agriculture grew gaunt, financially and socially, USDA fattened. On its 120th birthday, the agency's roster of 135,880 employees was four times as large as the personnel of the State Department, seven times as large as the Labor Department's, and three times as large as the Commerce Department's. The annual budget averaged $30 billion, of which roughly half was allocated to food stamps and the school lunch program.

Apathy about development of farm-grown motor fuel had long been typical of the agency's inability to adjust to technologic change. By 1980, an advertisement by Mobil Oil Corporation bragged, "American farmers use the equivalent of ninety-five gallons of gasoline on each of the over sixty-five million acres of corn under cultivation." Similar fuel usage was necessary to "make a crop" for 13 million acres of cotton, 3 million acres of rice, 72 million acres of wheat, 1¼ million acres of potatoes, etc.

The petroleum fuel bill of a 230-acre livestock and grain farm in northern Illinois averaged $6,000 a year during 1980–83. Evidence from other states indicated that the national petroleum fuel bill of our farms and ranches exceeds $15 billion annually.

In 1960, a medium-size tractor cost $10,000; by 1983, the cost was up to $35,000. Farmers used to be able to make their own repairs. Today's tractors, however, are so complex that they have to be taken to repair shops where the mechanic's fee is $28 an hour, and repair bills may cost $1,000. In fact, there is a much brisker market for old, fix-it-yourself tractors than there is for the fancy new ones.

Petroleum, like coal, is a subterranean secretion from prehistoric plants and weeds. Commendable motor fuel can be processed, like alcohol, from most agricultural crops. It would have been a brief technologic step to distill motor fuel from the colonials' beloved hard cider! The fuel used in the 1860s by the inventors of the reciprocal engine was alcohol made from grain. Henry Ford used grain alcohol to power the first models of his flivver. Efforts to market motor fuel distilled from farm products were made during the 1930s, but without USDA support or encouragement; all were bankrupted by various schemes devised by petroleum pedlars. (Hitler's Reich powered its machines with a mixture of petroleum with one-quarter alcohol throughout World War II. The United States stayed with all-petroleum.)

Farm-grown fuel was again marketed in the Midwest during the late 1960s under the name of gasohol. Advocates of the alcohol fuel, whose chemical name is ethanol, demonstrated that it could be produced in a backyard still by mixing corn, potato peel, even rotten garbage in a brewer's vat with enzymes and some baker's yeast. After a week of fermentation, the alcohol could be steamed off. The technique has been used by moonshiners ever since the Greeks discovered, in 1000 B.C., how to steam fiery *raki* out of the purple mush left from their wine making. Demonstrations in New York, Boston, and other cities indicated that, after a few carburetor adjustments, automobiles would operate on all-ethanol fuel without knocks or stalling.

The *Washington Post* echoed the views of lobbyists, as well as USDA's "official" attitude, in a June, 1979, editorial that alleged: "To divert good grain from the food markets to make motor oil would be wanton waste. It would attempt to mitigate the shortages of gasoline here by aggravating food shortages around the world." A well-publicized agricultural economist parroted the same assumption in the 1980 USDA *Yearbook*. On December

10, 1982, in an editorial about the gasoline tax and highway-repair bill then before Congress, the *Post* again recited that "it is hard to imagine a more wanton misuse of food, or a more foolish way to raise grain prices" than to exempt gasohol from the proposed federal tax on motor fuel.

This touching concern about wanton waste avoided the fact that fuel made from corn or any other farm crop consumes only the crop's sugar but leaves the protein and fiber. As the pre-Borden brewers of New York City knew, livestock enjoy the slops that are the residue from alcoholic-drink processing. Whiskey distillers fatten herds of beef cattle from the runoff of their plants.

"Beef especially fattens real good on distillery slops," veteran stockmen agreed. "About all you need to add is a little vitamin A. The really big problem is transportation of the stuff. Slops are liquids. Dehydration into a dry or semi-dry feed would cost a lot. But then, neither USDA nor anybody else has paid attention to a dehydration process at a competitive cost. While they're about it, the odds are they'd discover that proteins and fibers from slops could make a pretty good food supplement for humans, too!"

Two-thirds of our corn crop goes into livestock feed. The potential exists, then, for the development of compact distilleries on farms that would provide engine fuel from the corn cribs and livestock feed from the protein-rich refuse.

Another potential source for farm-grown engine fuel is euphorbia, a relative of the poinsettia that grows wild on the Pacific slope. The leaves produce a latex that, when mixed with acetone, produces a black oil with the properties of crude petroleum. Melvin Calvin, a Nobel laureate in chemistry, claims that motor fuel can be made from euphorbia and acetone for twenty dollars a barrel.

A third latent source for agriculture's self-sufficiency in fuel is the sunflower acreage that has brought overdue prosperity to the Dakotas, Minnesota, and sections of Texas. The sunflower has long been a favorite food source in northern and central Europe.

Its cholesterol-free oil makes commendable margarine, salad dressing, and cooking oil. The seeds are a favorite snack, either whole or ground into "sun butter." More than 3 million acres of sunflowers now grow along the upper Missouri and in Texas.

Sunflower seeds have an oil content of more than 50 percent. Treated with acids and heated to 104°F, the oil becomes an excellent diesel fuel—and the residue of solids left from the pressing is still an edible "spread."

But until research into sunflower oil, euphorbia, farmyard distilleries, and protein food from slops is encouraged by USDA approval, agriculture's motive power will continue in serfdom to OPEC and the gasoline peddlers.

Although it admits that "the energy crisis of the 1970s will take a back seat to the water crisis of the 1980s and 1990s," USDA has similarly dallied on long-range programs of water conservation. Agriculture is responsible for half of the nation's annual water consumption and contaminates the runoffs with herbicides and pesticides. It takes 130 gallons of water to grow 2¼ pounds of wheat, and 14 gallons of water to make one egg available at a retail counter. Much of the West's production of fruit, vegetables, grain, and meat depends on irrigation.

But in recent decades, the subterranean lake extending from South Dakota to Texas—called the Ogalalla Aquifer by geologists—has been depleted by irrigation projects twice as fast as it has been replenished by rains and runoffs. If the depletion continues, the Ogalalla is expected to dry up by 2000 A.D. By 1982, it was a felony in Arizona to dig a well. Some California crops will parch after 1985 when the state is scheduled to obey a court decision and surrender its diversion of water from the Colorado River.

In the East, drought and pollution forced New York and New Jersey to take drastic water-rationing measures. Huge reservoirs built to assure city water supplies never filled.

The mysterious changes in ocean currents and jet streams that were assumed to be the cause of excessive snowfalls and rains during early 1983 brought temporary relief for water supplies.

But the resulting floods in spring and early summer indicated that only modest amounts seeped into our subterranean reserves, and the erosion of topsoils increased. The June–October drought that stunted food crops from the Rockies to the Atlantic re-emphasized our national peril of not enough water and inefficient conservation measures.

Water-conservation techniques in Japan and Israel are twice as efficient as the ones used by our agriculture and industry. Little publicity has been given them in USDA literature. (A meager five paragraphs were devoted to "water management" in the 373 pages of the 1982 USDA *Yearbook*.) For instance, types of synthetic membrane have already been developed that will withstand 600 pounds of pressure and will enable removal of 99.8 percent of the salt from ocean water, at an energy cost of 12 kilowatt-hours to desalinate a thousand gallons. Use of the membrane to provide irrigation water for the Southwest and California was still "under investigation" at USDA in the spring of 1983.

As the blizzards, tornadoes, and torrential rains swept in a U-shaped arc across the continent, USDA faced an agricultural price support and surplus program that might cost $18 billion for 1984. Owing to our scientists' skills, although our dairy herds had been reduced from 15 million to 11 million cows since 1965, milk production per cow had increased from 8,305 pounds to 12,400 pounds per year.

The surplus foods held in storage in caves and warehouses on January 1, 1983, included more than 1.8 billion pounds of dried milk, 1.1 billion pounds of cheese (though a USDA supervisor testified that 44 million pounds of the cheese was moldy), 715 million pounds of butter, 431 million bushels of corn, 185 million bushels of wheat, 46 million bushels of grain sorghum, 7.5 million bushels of soybeans, 39 million pounds of honey, 73,000 bales of cotton, and 2 billion pounds of rice. The 1983 storage costs for these foods exceeded $2.8 billion.

Political pressures have prevented USDA from an edict of "take it easy!" to the scientists. Instead, a program called

Payment-in-Kind (PIK) was devised to reduce plantings of grains and cotton. Producers who cooperated with PIK would be paid USDA surplus food in return for reducing their plantings of corn, wheat, rice, and cotton. The raw materials could then be marketed, or used, by the producers.

Farm prices were so low, and operating costs so high, that producers quickly pledged to take 82 million acres of cropland out of production. Meanwhile, in an effort to increase grain exports and to pressure the European Economic Community to lower subsidies to its farmers, USDA negotiated a "cut rate" sale of 44 million bushels of wheat to Egypt. This sale, plus an inept use of its computers, brought from the agency the admission that they would have to purchase millions of tons of grain and multi-thousands of bales of cotton on the open market in order to fulfill the 1983 payments to producers who had signed up for PIK. By spring of 1983, the PIK program was still in a state of confusion, but it looked as though it would be twice as expensive to the taxpayer as the hoary crop-subsidy system.

As PIK moved toward fiasco in the summer of 1983, the U.S. Conference of Mayors met in Denver and blamed USDA "mismanagement and inefficiency" for not distributing more of its huge supplies of dairy products, honey, and grains to the urban needy. "We have tens of billions of dollars worth of surplus commodities. We have hungry people in our urban areas. And somehow we aren't able to get them together," Senator Mark Andrews, a North Dakota Republican, told the convention. Allegations that their USDA allotments of surplus cheese and butter for the needy had been cut "because of heavy lobbying by the grocery industry" came from Dianne Feinstein of San Francisco and other mayors of large cities.

The mayors' complaints came only weeks after a study revealed that of the $13-billion increase in retail food costs during 1982, more than $12 billion went to processors and retailers, but less than $1 billion to agricultural producers. Of the nation's $298 billion food bill for 1982, labor received $95.5 billion, agriculture received $83.5 billion, advertising and "other costs" totaled $70 billion, packaging cost $24 billion, transportation costs exceeded $15 billion, and corporate profits (before taxes) reached $13 billion. This array of costs brought farm and ranch returns down to 28 cents of the retail dollar. USDA acknowledged the veracity of the statistics but, again, remained silent about the increases in food distribution costs as well as the ominous growth of conglomerates in the processing and distribution industries.

The monopolist is as old as the republic. "Robber barons," "railroad trusts," "oil cartels," "the meat trust"—these phrases appear regularly in history texts. Theodore Roosevelt grinned approval of his "trust buster" nickname, but—perhaps because of skilled lobbying on an international scale—no agitation for trust busting was generated during the decades when the Bunge Company, the Fribourgs of Continental Grain, the Cargills and MacMillans of Cargill, as well as the Louis-Dreyfus and André holdings achieved control of approximately 80 percent of the world's grain trade. The situation remained "classified information" throughout the federal government's strident campaign to increase export sales of American grains.

It was no surprise when other industrialists decided to build conglomerates in the food processing and distribution fields. Procter & Gamble, assured that Ivory would always float, acquired control of Duncan Hines Foods, moved on to soft drinks, and in 1983 announced plans to enter the cookies and snacks arena. Greyhound, the bus and trucking giant, acquired Armour. Campbell Soup Company gained control of Swanson, Pepperidge Farm, Godiva Chocolates, and, along the Atlantic seaboard, began a commendable job of marketing plastic-sealed fresh mushrooms. San Giorgio Macaroni Company became a subsidiary of Hershey Chocolate. Nestlé's, initially a Swiss chocolate maker, took over Libby and Stouffer. Pillsbury acquired Green Giant. Beatrice Foods took over Oscar Mayer meats, Meadow Gold dairy products, LaChoy Chinese foods, Sunbeam breads, Clark candy bars, Eckrich meats, Samsonite luggage, Airstream trailers, and Hart sports equipment. Occidental Oil bought Iowa Beef, the nation's largest meat packer. The University of California owned one-fifth of DelMonte Packing Company's stock, but R.J. Reynolds, the cigarette maker, decided to diversify and became DelMonte's principal owner.

Conglomerate fever moved on to the seed and garden-supply field. International Telephone & Telegraph took over W. Atlee Burpee Company, the veteran gardening specialists. Celanese Corporation bought Joseph Harris Company, a fourth-generation supplier of garden seeds, bulbs, and supplies. Jackson & Perkins, long a favorite supplier for rose gardeners, was uprooted from New York State to Oregon and combined with Harry & David, a mail-order supplier of fruits. Gurney Seed & Nursery Company and Henry Field Seed & Nursery Company, both Midwest veterans, were purchased by AMFAC, a Hawaiian conglomerate specializing in foods and hotels. Northrup King and Ferry Morse, other gardener favorites, were absorbed by conglomerates. (In 1983, many of the seed packets contained fewer seeds, but cost more; in addition, the seeds were coated with pesticide and fertilizer compounds.) "When I look around at my friends in the business," commented the president of the 114-year-old George W. Park Seed Company, "I realize we are the last of the privately owned major gardening seed companies."

Four companies produced 90 percent of soft drinks sold in the United States; four processors marketed 80 percent of the ready-to-eat cereals; three companies made, or controlled, 90 percent of all cake mixes.

"Considerable research tells us that when relatively few firms hold most of the sales in a market or industry, [retail] prices tend to rise, competition deteriorates, and efficiency and progressiveness fall off," food marketing specialists at the University of Wisconsin wrote in the article, "Marketing's Frailties, Faults and Frustrations," included in the 1981 USDA *Yearbook*. "Opportunities for small companies have declined, small farmers have difficulty finding buyers for their products, and small food manufacturers cannot meet the supply demands of chain stores that operate hundreds of retail outlets."

Decreased competition in food processing and retailing, it was estimated, was already costing consumers $14 billion per year, or about $200 per family. Some economists predicted that 90 percent of food processing and retailing would "be controlled by a half dozen huge conglomerates before 2000 A.D."

"The corporate organization has a tendency to clone itself," the economist/diplomat John K. Galbraith wrote. "People are promoted who most closely resemble the people who are already there. In consequence, investment becomes cautious; analysis becomes a surrogate for action; innovation has an aspect of danger; the ability to adapt to changing circumstances dwindles; the future is sacrificed to the near present. Performance becomes increasingly mediocre—or less."

But the conglomerate and its dire potential for the American land continued to be "off limits" for USDA's administrators. The department also chose to ignore the impressive evidence from European, Canadian, and American scientists that the acid rain caused by environmental pollution poisoned waterways, killed forests, and might be doing irreplaceable harm to soils. One probable effect of acid rain was that, from Maine to Georgia, sugar maple, spruce, and pine trees mysteriously shriveled and died. Other trees showed a narrowing of annual growth rings. In 1983, the USDA's Forest Service rejected an application by the University of Vermont for grant funds to continue its research on acid rain damage in the Green Mountains. Similarly, the National Academy of Sciences was denied government funds to research the causes of acid rain damage. Consequently, the Academy dipped into reserve funds, made the study, and released its conclusions on June 29, 1983. The report placed the blame for acid rain on sulphur dioxide emissions from industrial smokestacks and on nitrogen dioxide emissions from motor vehicles. Lobbyists promptly attacked the report. The Environmental Protection Agency, still entangled by a political scandal, announced that it would "study the problem." A Clean Air Act remained "under study" in Congress. Throughout all of the meowing, USDA maintained a discreetly low profile.

On March 10, 1984, EPA finally announced a plan that "might" reduce "airborne particles most dangerous to public health," but added that its new standard is more than a year from adoption, and that it would then require another three years, at least, to install $4 billion worth of monitoring equipment and win Congressional approval for an operating budget of $740 million. Thus, factories and motor vehicles and airplanes and agriculturists could continue to vomit air pollutants willy-nilly for at least another five years!

Meanwhile, both USDA and the Food and Drug Administration became involved in a scandal caused by "continued approval" to use ethylene dibromide (EDB) both as an agricultural pesticide and as an ingredient of leaded gasoline. Permission to use EDB as a chemical fumigant on grains, fruits, and vegetables was granted in 1956 by FDA. It was assumed that EDB would not leave any residue on the crops sprayed. But by 1965, researchers had conclusive evidence that traces of EDB persisted "at high levels" in whole-grain breads and citrus fruits. Coincidentally, medical research indicated that human ingestion of EDB could cause or contribute to cancer, kidney disease, and other malignancies.

Allegations that both USDA and FDA had failed to notify the Environmental Protection Agency of EDB's health hazards were made at committee hearings in Congress during March, 1984. "Unfortunately," charged Congressman Mike Synar of Oklahoma, "USDA expended more of its energies and resources in joining with industry to defend the continued use of EDB . . . than on searching to find suitable substitutes for EDB." In evidence, he cited a "cooperative agreement" signed by USDA officials and a group of fruit and vegetable marketers during August, 1983, under which USDA agreed to pay most of the costs for research that could "maintain the registered use of EDB."

In recent years, the ghost of meat scandal again wandered the halls of USDA. Ever since Upton Sinclair wrote *The Jungle* in 1906, meat processors have been favorite whipping boys for Humane Societies, vegetarians, the antitrust division of the Department of Justice, and federal inspectors. Soon after publication of Sinclair's book, USDA was empowered to initiate an inspection service for every carcass swaying through meat packing plants. The inspectors' efficiency over the decades gave them the reputation of "best in the world."

But substantial evidence of deterioration in the inspection routine followed the post-war popularity of hamburgers. Inspectors have been accused of accepting bribes to place their stamps of approval on carcasses that contain "drugs, pesticides and other contaminants." Bits of metal, mangled bugs and cow hair have again been found in ground beef.

The hamburger zest, four or five competitive nationwide chains, encouraged imports of fresh and frozen beef from Australia, New Zealand, and Central America; by 1979, these imports totaled 713,353 metric tons at prices that American ranchers could not match. During 1981, Customs inspectors found horse and kangaroo meat in some of these low-price "beef" shipments.

Early in 1982, USDA had proposed legislation that would reduce the meat-inspector force by half. At the same time, feedlot lobbyists, meat packers, hamburger chains, restaurants, and chain stores clamored for legislation that would upgrade beef carcasses. Scrawny cuts now stamped "U.S. Good," they argued, should be stamped "U.S. Choice"; cuts with moderate marbling should be upgraded from "U.S. Choice" to "U.S. Prime."

By not-so-odd coincidence, the undersecretary of USDA was a former president of the American Meat Institute, a meat packers' trade association long noted for its lobbying acumen, and the assistant secretary in charge of USDA's Marketing and Inspection Services was a former employee of Swift and Company. During February, 1982, a coalition of consumer-interest lobbyists gave USDA its "Consumer Casualty of the Month" award because, they claimed, the reduction in meat inspectors and the upgrading plan "will give a blank check to individual meat processors to cheat." So much for USDA's role of retaining the family farm with its individualism and self-sufficiency and freedom of the marketplace. The agency has failed to keep the promises it made in 1862.

USDA has also been indolent about developing cooperative

understanding between the farm/ranch minority and the urban majority.

Despite the rapid increase in home and community gardens, the agency paid little attention to gardening techniques until it issued *Gardening for Food and Fun* as its 1977 *Yearbook*. By that time, bookstores and newsstands were already glutted with garden books and television networks were programming scores of "garden chats" in color. Despite the growing popularity of organic gardening, USDA administrators permitted only five pages on organic gardening in the volume's 392 pages. As usual, the book was a congressman's handout; sales were modest.

Some of USDA's failures may be explained by the burden of non-agricultural tasks that have been imposed on it by Congress and the executive branch since World War II. These tasks range from the distribution of food stamps and decisions on the contents of school lunches to brochures, speeches, and press releases about "proper diet." Both the food stamp and school lunch programs should logically come under the jurisdiction of the Health & Human Services and Education departments. But, as a senior executive of USDA explained, "Once we were stuck with the jobs, we discovered that we needed them. There are so many city-minded representatives in Congress who don't give a damn about farms and ranches that we realized the food stamps and the school lunch were the only items in our budget they cared about and would vote for. That's how we manage to get our budgets approved!"

"I've looked up some of the legislation which brought the United States Department of Agriculture into being through the action of President Lincoln," Ezra Taft Benson, 1953–61 Secretary of Agriculture, wrote me from Salt Lake City. "I've often wondered if it would not be well to have a Blue Ribbon Commission study the whole question of the objectives and purposes of USDA in the years of Abraham Lincoln, then trace the history of more recent developments and determine the future possibilities of USDA."

Benson's suggestion was so similar to John Davis's 1955 recommendation that I asked Davis for an updating of his views about USDA during the twenty-eight years since he coined the word *agribusiness*. Davis told me:

> We ought to have four or five agribusiness research regions, each with facilities. Then set up a policy board for each region. These boards would include farmers, processors, consumers, and so forth. Have these organizations carefully select the problems needed for regional research; subjects that would receive comprehensive analysis and multi-discipline research.
>
> When the projects have been chosen, contract for people to work on them, from whatever disciplines needed. You'd get some from USDA, some from land-grant colleges, some from producers, some from private processors and distributors. If you found a better person in France or England or Canada— an exceptionally skilled person—you'd bring him or her into it. Also bring in the managers of the most successful cooperatives.
>
> Let it be an honor, a real honor, to be chosen to do this research. These people would never become permanent employees of the research centers. They'd do the task assigned them, then go back to their regular duties after they have analyzed the problem thoroughly, vertically and horizontally. New directions and directives for our agricultural policy would be drawn from their findings.

Failure to analyze broad policy questions, to keep pace with technologic change, and to educate the consumer "about where food and fiber comes from" are three major shortcomings of USDA cited by Davis.

> With the bulk of our people living in cities and knowing nothing about the problems of the producer or even the food and fiber industries, they are easily motivated by publicity and advertising that is very narrow-based and which further complicates the things that need to be done.
>
> Within our democracy, things of this type do have a bearing

through time on what politicians do; and our democracy is a live organism—it's not something that is inorganic. To preserve the fundamental concepts of the Constitution and the Bill of Rights and the Declaration of Independence and so forth is a very difficult thing to do in times that are rapidly changing. There needs to be somebody concerned about it and somebody looking at it. The danger is that people who look at part of it may pull the wool over the politicians' eyes, or pressure groups that are narrowly based may themselves cause the wrong policies to be established. So I think we're probably in greater danger today than we were when we were more rural. We need education that enables people to understand more about where food and fiber comes from. It hurts me that the Department of Agriculture is doing so little in this field of educating the consumer.

In 1982, the USDA did issue an appeal to state governors and agricultural organizations to support an "Agriculture in the Classroom" project. For more than a decade, the nutritionist, Dr. Jean Mayer, had urged curriculum changes to bring courses about farming and food production into high schools and liberal arts colleges. The USDA's appeal asked for the introduction of "information and ideas about agriculture" into public school curriculums from kindergarten through high school. During April, 1983, a seventy-page brochure by USDA, *Resource Guide to Educational Materials About Agriculture,* was distributed to schools. Approximately half of the resource materials it recommends are booklets, audiovisual kits, and films written by USDA's publicists. The other materials include publications prepared by tractor manufacturers, the Fertilizer Institute, the supermarkets' trade association, DuPont Company, National Agricultural Chemicals Association, farm equipment manufacturers, National Dairy Council, a large life insurance company, the American Egg Board, and the National Livestock & Meat Board. Unfortunately, none of the hundreds of classical histories, social documents, or novels written about the 383 years of intensive cultivation—and deterioration—of the American land were recommended for use by public schools.

The dire problem confronting the United States is the land and its caretakers. This is the subject that should be introduced into the curriculums of our schools. This is the challenge confronting our federal and state governments, our cities, and every American. We no longer need a USDA—a massive and expensive federal agency that seemed unable, or unwilling, to adapt to the socio-economic urgencies, and environmental realities, of our supertechnologized way of life. We desperately need a United States Department of the Land.

"It makes sense to have a Department of the Land," a distinguished botanist told me.

> But this doesn't mean it will happen soon. The present policies are established for political convenience and bureaucratic turf grabbing. But if it is said often enough by enough people, the idea may take hold.
>
> We've been so successful in producing food in this country that we take it for granted. So support for basic research has been minuscule in comparison to what goes into, say, the "firefighting" sort of thing, of pests and fungicides and all the rest.
>
> The basic information that's necessary to support a modern agriculture has been poorly supported. As for research in the basic plant sciences, there wasn't very much, and the USDA never did support any until the Competitive Research Grant was started a few years ago. They've been fighting that. So have the agricultural lobbyists. . . . We're riding on the backs of our grandfathers. But now we've got to look ahead. We have to look for new solutions.

"Something's got to give," rumbled the past president of a national livestock-research organization.

> When you can't produce a bushel of corn for profit, you're in trouble. And that's what's happening right now. The same is

true in producing beef and pork. A lot of our farmers are in
real trouble. They've got a lot of debts, a high rate of interest,
and damned little to look forward to.

One of the smartest moves that could be made right away
would be to fire a few thousand of USDA's economists. . . . I
hark back to that old saying that if all agricultural economists
were laid end to end, that would be jimdandy. Most of them
have been wrong, and they still are. That's another of the
things that's "old gray mare" about USDA—the double-damned
bad predictions and statistics that these characters put out each
year.

The economists perform the tasks assigned to them. The chemists, agronomists, loan evaluators, school-lunch programmers,
food-stamp guardians, overseas-grain salesmen, PIK accoun-
tants, speech writers, home economists—all perform the tasks
assigned to them. Throughout USDA's metropolis of employees,
the vast majority are sincere and competent workers, devoted
to their assigned tasks and as fearful of budget cuts and layoffs
as any worker in industry. The sickness that afflicts USDA is
political control of its functions by lobbyists and not a few elected
officials whose dollar-hunger blinds them to the catastrophe that
threatens the American land.

Consequently, our only hope for a green and abundant future
for the American land relies on individual initiative and research.
Praise be to the gardeners and the geneticists. By 1984, we had
approximately 40 million home gardeners. Every one of them
faced as many challenges from nature and polluted air as the
professional farmers faced.

CHAPTER FOURTEEN

To Make the Gardens Fair

"**N**o occupation is so delightful to me as the culture of the earth and no culture comparable to the garden," Thomas Jefferson wrote in 1811. In 1984, approximately 40 million American families harvested tastier fruits and vegetables, year-long floral bouquets, and new appreciation of the land and its laws. During that same year, a few thousand botanists and geneticists worked to learn more about microscopic forces of the land that may assure a green future for both home gardeners and professional agriculturists. Gardeners and geneticists are our best hope of healthful diets and bucolic serenity for our children and grandchildren.

Nutritional research, the insipidness of trucked-in fruits and vegetables, and a rapid population increase in the number of senior citizens were major causes for the renewed interest in home gardens and community garden plots after 1960.

Until then, appreciation of the garden was overshadowed by a snobbery inherited from feudalism: the manicured grass lawn.

The word *lawn* originally meant "an open place in the forest."

Europe's feudal lords changed this meaning when they realized that open fields around their castles offered a good opportunity for observing enemy forces before hurling rocks, arrows, and hot lard on them. By the time Henry VIII's dalliances caused England to join the Protestant revolt, manor lords were copying this green-grass decor for their mansions; sheep and horses did the grass trimming. Virginia planters and New England merchants imitated the prestige symbol as a setting for their Tudor, Georgian, and Northern Colonial homes. From 1750 on, the grass yard was in front of every village and city home more than five feet from a cart path.

One of the requirements of lawn care was that its dignity must not be sullied by food plants. This, like the taboo against eating horse meat, was another hand-me-down from feudalism. Food plants were, of course, grown by peasants and farmers. It would be socially demeaning to grow them on one's lawn. The British homeowner who enjoyed gardening and its harvests secluded the operation at the rear of his residence. Americans copied this propriety as a status fix.

Exorbitant increases in land values evicted most gardens from American cities before 1850. The wealthy maintained small lawns, cameo'd with flower beds and herbs, behind the walls of their estates. The yardless were appeased by public parks, gazebo bandstands, zoos, and hobby-horse statues of the more adept politicians and generals. (Hotels charged more for a room with a park view than they did for identical rooms across the hall with fire escape and garbage-can views.)

So the family garden became a folkway of the farmer and the villager. The rural male proclaimed that gardening was a chore for women and children—except for springtime plowing and construction of a root cellar. Women and children planted the seeds, fashioned the scarecrows, chopped out the weeds, picked off destructive bugs, watered the growing plants with infusions of animal manures, and—nature permitting—gathered the harvest.

Beans dried pebble-hard on their vines. Herbs could be dried on strings suspended near a fireplace or window. Small fruits, stuffed into stoneware jugs, then covered with rum and loaf sugar, aged to delicious cough syrups and "fever remedies." Salt, sweetening, and patience turned cucumbers, green tomatoes, young string beans, and tiny onions into pickles. Apples could be sliced and dried into "schnitz" as a filling for wintertime pies and pastries. Cabbages, potatoes, beets, turnips, squash—all sustained freshness in the cool dark of the root cellar, as did apples, some pears, and quinces. Green tomatoes, wrapped in paper, would slowly turn to succulent scarlet. Both parsnips and carrots seemed to relish frosts, so could be whacked out of the ground in pristine condition most of the winter.

After glass canning-jars became available at the general store, shelves were hammered into root cellars. On them went rows of processed vegetables, fruits, jams, jellies, and pickles. Barberry jelly and beach-plum jam became Yankee specialties. Watermelon pickle sang "Dixie." In Iowa, corn relish was more popular than the state fair.

Bees, the rural gardeners knew, are as important to a successful garden as fertilizers and a hoe. Buzzing into a blossom to extract nectar for its honeymaking, a bee spreads pollen from plant to plant. Without bees, there would be very little pollenization and very little harvest. A beehive near a garden is a twofold insurance policy. It ensures a better harvest from the garden and luxurious trays of honeycomb from the hive. (After sulphur, arsenic, and DDT were introduced as pesticides, millions of bees died from the sprayings.)

Collecting seeds for the next year's crop was essential before the 1850s. But some seeds were sterile, and others didn't reproduce faithfully. The communes of Shakers in eastern New York are credited with the development and first marketing of "tested seeds." After the Civil War, scores of seed and nursery firms originated. Seedmen, nurserymen, beehives, dedicated wives, youngsters with hoes and bugcatcher jars, animal manures, sunlight, and water—all cooperated to make the countryside's fruit and vegetable gardens a heart-place of good living.

Dedication to the economics of cash and credit has prevented USDA from paying attention to the needs and problems of home gardeners. USDA defines a farm as "a place of agricultural production that sells more than a thousand dollars worth of produce annually." Under this definition, the home gardener was banned from departmental interest.

The bugs, weeds, blights, windstorms, and soil chemicals weren't so selective. They affect gardens as readily as they affect farms. As Thomas Jefferson pointed out in his *Garden Book*, a gardener has to learn as much about nature as a farmer. Soils, seeds, bugs, photosynthesis, water allotment, and weather whimsies are as important to a yardful of tomatoes, onions, swiss chard, parsnips, and peas as they are to a horizonful of corn or wheat. But USDA held to its bias for more than a century.

From 1890 on, the horsecar, the commuter train, the trolley, the bus, and the automobile increasingly beckoned city workers out of tenements and rowhouses into the countryside. Most took the caste symbol of a grass lawn with them; the realtors assured its perpetuation. The new suburbs were developed on farmlands that had been divided into home lots fifty to seventy-five feet wide and a hundred feet deep. The homes hammered up on each plot were identical in design and set in straight lines twenty-five to thirty feet back from the new streets. Building contractors urged that the mortgage be increased to cover the cost of "a nice lawn." This involved trucking in enough black loam for a three-inch cover of the plot's native clay or sand. Slabs of turf were laid on this, like linoleum blocks, from street curbing to basement wall. Further investment in a sprinkler, a truckload of "turf builder," and excessive use of the community's water supply might produce an emerald fuzz that, within a year or two, could be mowed every Sunday afternoon, with beer and pretzels on the redwood lawn table.

Inevitably, the Lawn Care Specialist appeared. He offered "full service" for lawns—including fungicides, insecticides, herbicides, fertilizers, advice from staff horticulturists, and, for an extra fee, "a complete program to maintain the health and beauty of your landscape plantings." In the spring of 1983, professional care for an "average" lawn of 7,500 square feet cost between $250 and $300 a year. (Mowing, snow shoveling, and removal of beer cans and fast-food containers tossed in from the street were not included.) The same investment for a garden could return more than $2,000 worth of fruits, vegetables, and year-round floral bouquets.

In the spring of 1917, Congress approved a declaration of war against Germany, and government publicists coined the phrase "Food will win the war!" Jackhammers ripped up sidewalks to make room for Victory Gardens on New York City's Union Square and Chicago's Michigan Boulevard. Community gardens materialized in city parks. Thousands of suburbanites decided that backyard puttering was not only patriotic but rewarding. Seed and nursery sales flourished.

Although most of these garden projects were abandoned in 1919, interest in gardening lingered in the expanding suburbias because of two social factors: recent migrations from the Mediterranean's shores and the increasing life span of Americans.

Southern Europeans had been solicited, in much the way William Penn solicited Germans for the frontiers of Penn's Sylvania, to undertake the menial tasks of digging ditches for urban sprawlouts and laying tracks for new railroads and interurban trolley lines. Italians, Greeks, and Slavs are dedicated gardeners, with a rich tradition of skills in teasing prime crops out of rocky, clay-slick soils. Many of them scrimped enough savings to escape tenement squalor after a few years and acquired suburban homesteads with room for a truck garden, a vineyard, and a henhouse. The crops they achieved, and retailed at neat roadside stands, won converts to the plum tomato, the paprika pepper, and the amazing zucchini squash.

The other social force is pervasive, too. In 1910, the American life-expectancy averaged 47 years. The average woman—if there is such a being—lived two years longer than the average man. But science was bringing diphtheria, yellow fever, scarlet fever, and other killers under control. Sanitation improved. Homes were more adequately heated. The bath, disdained by our colonials, was conceded to be at least a Saturday-night ritual. Hospitals and health clinics became a way of life; surgeons learned new skills. Snake oil, pink pills for pale people, and Father Mike's Elixir were being replaced by medically sound serums, vitamins, and ointments. By 1930, our average life-expectancy had increased to 59 years, with the ladies still out in front by 3½ years.

One of the most fascinating adventures of middle age is the rediscovery of nature. Often it grows so slyly that it isn't realized until you find yourself installing bird feeders on the balcony and buying flats of pansies and petunias for that bleak spot beside the garage. Residents in urban apartment houses succumb to pots of geraniums on windowsills, African violets in the bedroom, membership in the Audubon Society, subscriptions to garden magazines, and weekend wanderings in the mountains and back-country.

In reality, the phrase "the golden years" is a misnomer; the years after forty-five are "the green years." Wonderment grows about the miracle of the seasons and springtime's life renewal. Soil feels as good to the touch as it did when you were eight years old. A speck of seed germinating into a chartreuse tip, a green leaf, a bud, a flower, becomes as stimulating as a back pat at the office or factory. An hour with a shovel or hoe in the backyard whisks away the fog of job tension, and works off some of that extra weight, too. Pretty soon you learn that a "green thumb" is not a genetic inheritance; it is the reward of patience, of respect for the plant and its needs. Anybody can achieve a greening of the thumb.

Throughout the nine years of the Depression, thousands of parents discovered the rewards of home gardening. Work projects developed by the New Deal's WPA encouraged gardening to supplement the dried beans, salt pork, and sugar given to welfare recipients. Harvard Medical School and other pioneers in health research initiated studies in nutrition and gave their blessing to the vegetarians' avoidance of meat.

World War II was our ugliest yet, and the longest since the

Civil War. Again, the government hauled out the slogan, "Food will win the war!" The Victory Garden became stylish. "The demand for seed of vegetables of all kinds increased enormously," an executive of the Joseph Harris Company recalled. "We were not able to fill a large proportion of the orders we received."

Most Victory Gardens returned to weedpatch in 1946. Chain stores and shopping malls brought the lure of downtown to the suburbs. The blood of World War II fertilized both wages and living standards. Fast freight assured winterlong delivery of Cuban tomatoes, California lettuce, Peruvian grapes, Mexican strawberries, and Hawaiian papaya.

But the war also brought new and deadlier pesticides. Ever since the copper sulfate powder called Bordeaux mixture was first used during the 1890s, chemical pesticides had become increasingly important to farmers. Expensive machinery, freight costs, and the agrivores' control of the marketplace all demanded more pesticides on cropfields. Decade by decade, pesticides became more potent. Decade by decade, bugs and bacteria bred a greater resistance to them.

The year World War II began, a Swiss chemist named Paul Müller found that a hydrocarbon compound called DDT was devastating to bugs. (He was awarded a Nobel Prize in 1948 for his discovery.) But DDT was toxic for humans, too. DDT sediment, lodged in the stem hollows of apples, poisoned the eaters. Since DDT is what chemists call "nonbiodegradable," DDT sprays stayed in soils, washed into streams, and poisoned fish. (The poisoning of bees was so drastic that, before a field was sprayed, worker bees had to be lured back to their hives and the hives covered with wet blankets.)

Before 1950, fear of DDT gave impetus to a movement that would have a profound influence on popularization of the home garden. The originators of the movement called it "organic culture," somehow overlooking the fact that everything in nature is organic. They pledged to grow and eat only foods grown without use of chemical pesticides or chemical fertilizers. This goal of returning to the self-sufficiency pattern of mid-nineteenth-century agriculture seemed hopelessly frustrated by the drastic changes that technology had imposed. Animal manures were scarcer, hence expensive. Cottonseed meal, bone meal, and dried blood were in demand by processors for use in their "balanced blend" of livestock and poultry feeds. More than 6,500 varieties of bugs, bacteria, and other so-called pests had been identified by scientists as agricultural enemies. Many of them had been imported from overseas on plant, bulb, and seed shipments.

The organic devotees responded to the challenge with a series of experiments demonstrating that soils could be enriched by composting kitchen and garden wastes, and that many varieties of pests could be controlled by growing plants that are bug repellents. Also, they loosed ladybugs, praying mantis, and other bug-eaters in their gardens.

Kitchen wastes were causing disposal problems in cities and suburbs. Coffee grounds, potato and carrot peelings, eggshells, meat scraps, chicken bones—all went into garbage cans or sink disposals to be chemicalized into sludge at expensive sanitation plants. Sewage runoffs in rivers killed marine life. Scowloads of garbage dumped in the oceans poisoned shellfish as well as the diatoms that play such a critical role in maintaining an adequate supply of oxygen in the sea. Lawn clippings, and the fall's tumble of leaves, were all raked, stuffed into bags, and hauled to curbside for pickup by tax-financed garbage trucks.

Organic zealots knew there could and should be a life renewal for potato peelings, coffee grounds, brown leaves, grass clippings, and much of the other "trash" that gurgled into sanitation plants. The means? A compost pit! Dig a hole three feet deep and four to five feet square in the back yard. Dump in a six-inch layer of kitchen wastes. Sprinkle on a layer of seaweed, aged cow or horse manure, sawdust and straw. Put back a layer of earth. Dump in another layer of kitchen wastes, faded flowers, leaves, or grass trimmings. Repeat the wastes-and-soil sandwich until the hole is filled. To hasten the resurrection process, go to a bait shop, buy some angleworms and release them into the pit.

Within a few months, the pit's mixture—routinely watered—

will have decomposed enough to be used as a top dressing on
the garden before the spring plowing, or for use throughout the
growing season as a mulch and side-dressing between rows of
vegetables and flowers. And why not? Soil is decayed rock and
vegetation, aged a few millenniums. It can be manufactured, in
a year or two, from kitchen and yard wastes!

Engineers and chemists approved this home adaptation of the
Penn Dutch technique of fertilizing croplands with aged animal
manures. Metal compost bins, machines to chip and grind kitchen
and yard wastes—even newspapers—into mulch readiness, and
chemical compounds to hasten the composting process, all entered the marketplace during the 1960s and are routinely advertised in gardening magazines and seed catalogues.

The pest problem was attacked just as vigorously by the organic
gardeners. Plants, they learned, have a tendency toward segregation. Onions and tomatoes are compatible enough in a salad
but don't get along side by side in a garden. And the odors of
some plants will shoo off some varieties of bugs. The African
marigold has such repellent properties. So does garlic. (Oil of
garlic is a fungicide.) Basil is a good companion plant for tomatoes.
Beets, onions, and dill are buddies. Nasturtiums will cheer up
the rows of peas and turnips and lure most of the aphids and
other leaf-drinkers away from beet and turnip greens.

Some of technology's gadgetry proved to be pest discouragers,
too. Sheets of aluminum foil anchored alongside young plants
discourage cutworms and cucumber beetles. Wilt-producing fungi,
nematodes, and weeds can be "cooked" out of a garden patch by
the simple process of covering it with clear polyethylene plastic
on a warm, sunny day. (Water the patch first, spread the plastic,
tuck it down, and let the sun do the sterilizing.) Black polyethylene plastic laid between rows of plants discourages weed growth
and allows the soil to retain moisture. Soda bottles planted up-
right and cap-end deep at each end of a row of leafy plants will
frustrate a rabbit's yearning to munch off the leaves. (The reason
is that any breeze whispering across the bottle tip creates an
almost subsonic whistle that Ol' Hoppity abhors.)

The most important rule of all, organic gardening's exponents stressed, for a successful garden was *healthy plants*. Sturdy plants are far more resistant to disease and bug nibbles than spindly growths with yellowish leaves and tiny root systems. Therefore, soils must be provided with scientifically sound balances of trace elements and such power-givers as nitrogen, calcium, iron, zinc, and sulphur. All of these would be provided by compost pits, animal manures, fish-oil emulsions, or seaweed solutions. As for the seeds and bulbs, seed dealers and nurseries had already crossbred varieties with strong genetic resistance to bacteria and bugs. The organic house-rule became: "Read the label on the seed packet carefully before purchasing!"

The urbanite flight to new suburbs continued. Hundreds of thousands of these families, disturbed by the potential of pesticides on marketplace produce and the steady deterioration of flavors, became organic gardeners. Auto manufacturers began making garden tractors. Soon the handier rototiller appeared. Health-food shops specialized in "organically grown" dried fruits, nuts, and granola. Community cooperatives were formed to purchase truckloads of organically grown citrus, apples, peaches, and strawberries.

By 1970, so much fear about DDT had been stimulated by the organicists and conservationists that USDA gave grudging approval to a bill to ban the insecticide's use; the bill passed Congress and became a law. Since fruit and vegetable growers considered DDT their easiest protection against bugs and blight, the law intensified USDA's negativism toward organic gardening. Brief mention was given the movement in the 1977 *Yearbook* and—approximately 3,500 years behind the Egyptians and Greeks—the same volume did concede that "garlic . . . serves as a bug repellent in the garden," but official haughtiness persisted. Dismissals of USDA employees who championed organic methods were reported during 1981–82.

But more realistic research stressed the importance of fresh vegetables and fruits and home gardening to sedentary America. Our per-capita consumption of meat, poultry, and fish had risen

50 pounds per year between 1940 and 1980. Breakfast cereals, granola, catsup, pickles, canned goods, cold cuts, and pastries were increasingly saturated with sugars and salts. Nutritional studies revealed that the businessman's martini at lunchtime fueled him with 200 calories, and the basket of rolls and bread on the restaurant table during the drinking hour offered several hundred more. The gravy-bathed meat, french fries, oil-doused salad, and $1.80 sliver of pecan pie that followed challenged digestive tracts with several hundred additional calories. In all, a two-martini lunch gave two-thirds of a day's allotment of calories for a healthy diet. But advertising lures, inflationary wages, and a fascination for "snacking" the 500 calories of a bag of potato chips, or the 300 calories of a carton of popcorn, pushed the majority of diets above 4,000 calories a day.

More heart disease, more diabetes, more cancer enabled undertakers to buy Georgian mansions and fleets of Cadillacs. Body weight, the medical researchers learned, encouraged many of the diseases. If gluttony could not be controlled, diets could at least be developed for those anxious to retrieve the Social Security payments that the New Deal had imposed on their paychecks.

The deeper the researchers probed, the stronger was the evidence that vegetables are much more beneficial to human health than meats, animal fats, and the multi-forms of sugar and salt. Diets in which vegetables predominate have lower calorie content and far less cholesterol-producing fats than the meat and potato diet inherited from the heavy manual labor and twelve-hour workday of previous centuries. Studies conducted throughout the United States and overseas testified to lower incidence of cancer, lower levels of cholesterol in the blood, less heart disease, and trimmer figures for people whose diets were preponderantly vegetarian.

Professional historians had become so obsessed by battles and political bickering that they had neglected research into the dietary habits throughout recorded history. The data they discovered indicated that the American appetite for meat is as modern as the electric light bulb and the flivver. Historically, fruits, nuts, vegetables, and some type of bread had been the normal diet, with meats usually limited to the entree on religious feast days. The Greeks did not snack on hamburgers, french fries, and Twinkies during the siege of Troy. Christ's Last Supper was bread and wine. George Washington did not gobble up a salami sandwich an hour before going to bed. Billy the Kid, the Jesse James Gang, and Buffalo Bill never guzzled three-layer hamburgers and bowls of corn chips in midafternoon.

Further research by nutritionists and psychiatrists revealed the startling "green therapy" offered by the garden. They had the example of a Scotch physician who, early in the nineteenth century, assigned patients who had been pronounced insane to undertake the hard physical labor of operating his farm in the Highlands. After a few months of working with crops and livestock, their emotional stresses vanished and medical examiners found them "relaxed and sane." Intensive American research of the values of garden therapy began during the 1960s. By 1983, some impressive evidence had been collected. Universities now offer courses in "horticultural therapy." Factories provide gardens where executives and workers can "unwind job tenseness" with half-hour work breaks of green thumbing. Hundreds of retirement homes and mental institutions depend on gardens for therapy.

"I want to be on record as believing strongly in this program of training," said Dr. Karl Menninger of the famed Menninger Foundation in Kansas. "It is one type of what we call adjunctive therapy, which brings the individual close to the soil, close to Mother Nature, close to beauty, close to the mystery of growth and development. It is one of the simple ways to make a cooperative deal with nature for a prompt reward."

The Menninger Foundation's 700-acre Kansas headquarters contains a large greenhouse, a nature trail, a wildflower preserve, and landscaped lawns. All of the green thumbing is done by patients as "an integral part" of the therapy program.

"The relationship between plants and people is assuming a

greater role in our lives," reported Dr. Diane Relf, former president of the National Council for Therapy and Rehabilitation Through Horticulture.

> We're learning that plants are a tool to handle the stressful urban environment. For the handicapped, gardening is invaluable, not only for a sense of pride and accomplishment but as a real means to become self-supporting. . . . Caring for plants gives the older person a sense of responsibility and of being needed. This is too often lacking in geriatric programs. It also brings a new sense of excitement about the future as gardeners anxiously await the opening of a flower or the first tomato harvest. . . . Gardening is particularly well suited for people suffering from eye trouble, as it is often one of the few activities which can be encouraged due to the lack of stress on the eyes. Gardening is rewarding to the blind as well as to the sighted.

Soaring store prices, awareness of green therapy, and the continuing flight to the suburbs have made the "backyard putterer" one of the most important, and certainly one of the most hopeful, forces of the American economy. According to a 1980 survey made by Gardens for All, the nonprofit national gardening organization in Burlington, Vermont, the average garden used 663 square feet, cost $19 for seeds and materials, and produced $460 worth of edibles annually, plus a lot of therapy. Since the retail prices for fruits and vegetables rose steadily between 1980 and 1983, the value of returns from a garden has increased. During the late spring and summer of 1983, for example, chain-store prices for leaf lettuce wavered between 99 cents and $1.20 a pound; deterioration during long freight hauls produced an average wastage of 4 ounces to the pound. Consequently, a 75-cent package of lettuce seed yielded between $40 and $50 worth of super-fresh lettuce in a home garden.

The introduction of Oriental and European garden tools and techniques have simplified weeding problems and increased yields.

The raised-bed system, which originated in China centuries ago, consists of shoveling garden soil into a flat-topped oblong six to eight inches above the original soil level and four to five feet wide. Water collects in the deep walkways between the beds. The tops of the beds, where seeds are planted, is several degrees warmer than the original soil level—thus permitting a longer growing season. Soils are enriched with composts and an occasional planting of such "green manure" plants as buckwheat, rye, or mung beans. Tools such as the British swoe, the Dutch hoe, and the Easy-Weeder make gardening chores simpler than the venerable hoe, rake, and spade.

By 1978, the success of home and community gardens was pioneering a movement toward farms of twenty-five to fifty acres, each one specializing in fruit and vegetable crops, plus a fish pond and flocks of such gamebirds as pheasant and quail.

In New York state, the number of farms rose from 44,000 to 49,000 between 1978 and 1981. The state's vegetable crop increased by 38 percent; production of apples, pears, and cherries became so profitable that orchardists bought out dairymen in order to expand their orchards. Equally "bullish" reports came from New England and the Middle Atlantic states. Connecticut encouraged the small-farm movement by publishing a catalogue listing all farms in the state where crops can be purchased, "from a bale of hay to picking your own apples or strawberries."

A small-farm model advocated by Dr. Booker T. Whatley, Professor Emeritus at Alabama's Tuskegee Institute, during a symposium on small farms held by USDA's Agricultural Research Service during November, 1981, claimed a potential "minimum gross income of three thousand dollars per acre per year on a twenty-five acre property." Whatley began experimenting with this type of farm at Tuskegee in 1974. He stresses production of vine fruits, salad greens, strawberries, sweet potatoes, and turnips, plus a fish pond and "a rookery for bobwhite quail." The crops are seasonal and marketed as "a pick-your-own operation." Such a farm, he says, could offer "a clientele membership club, for twenty-five dollars a year, that gives a member the privilege of coming on to the farm and picking products at sixty percent of supermarket prices."

There is need for forty-five to fifty thousand farms of this type in the Northeast, Whatley believes, and thousands more in the peripheries of major cities of the South and Midwest. Sales would focus on roadside stands or the pick-your-own system. Growing consumer weariness with frozen foods and canned goods will, he is convinced, assure profits.

Another intriguing gardening frontier is re-evaluation of the grass lawn. Approximately fifty million gallons of gasoline for lawnmowers, three million tons of fertilizers, and billions of gallons of water are expended annually on lawn care. Total lawn acreage across our strip of North America equals the size of a Midwestern state. Maintenance costs must exceed twenty billion dollars a year.

A significant step toward bringing the American lawn out of the dark ages was taken during 1982 by Rosalind Creasy, a California landscaping consultant. Her book, *Edible Landscaping*, describes 225 edible plants that will blend delightfully with flowers and grass on a lawn. She provides examples of planting and maintenance techniques as well as patio designs. For example, a sidewalk edging of peanut plants with their sheen of cloverlike leaves and yellow blossoms is as pretty as petunias and ageratum. Given enough sand to "nut in," they will grow as far north as Boston. Chives, rosemary, thyme, summer savory, sage, marjoram, lavender, and lovage are both picturesque and useful. The billowing leaves of Swiss chard and beets conceal the yellowing of daffodil and tulip leaves during June and July. One dwarf tree can be grafted to produce a half-dozen varieties of apples, pears, or peaches. Egyptian onions are grotesque enough to be distinctive. Garlic is an excellent bug repellent for a flower bed, and its cloves retain their pungent oil when stored in a freezer. Purple basil is a pretty border plant, a zesty salad ingredient, and as effective for pesto sauce as its green cousin.

For the first time since the invention of diversified agriculture prompted the development of cities, home gardens and specialty farms of twenty-five to fifty acres are opening channels for comprehension about the land's importance by our urbanized majority. Modernization of the all-grass lawn is as effective an education program for improved agriculture-urban communication as the public school programs proposed by USDA.

Recent developments in solar energy can ensure year-round gardening from Wyoming to Maine. One result is that more cities and suburbs are including community garden plots in their master plans. But genetic engineering promises to be our most effective pathfinder to a green future. Experiments underway at state universities in North Carolina, Michigan, California, Minnesota, New Jersey, and Massachusetts indicate that familiar species of plants such as corn, wheat, and tomatoes will be abandoned for clones that can resist disease, manufacture their own fertilizer, grow in semi-desert regions or in sea water, and triple present acreage yields. Already on the horizon are varieties of lettuce and tomatoes that grow in sea water, tobacco produced as a high-protein food supplement, and edible plants that thrive in semi-desert conditions.

Synthetic roasts, chops, and patties will be substituted for beef, pork, and lamb. Amaranth salami-on-barley with a side of garlic-buttered grasshoppers are potential replacements for hamburgers-and-fries. So are cutlets made from tobacco protein. In the twenty-first century, appropriate lyrics for the beloved Old West song could be:

> Clone, clone on the range,
> Where the genes and the nitrogen play,
> Where seldom is heard a bellowing herd
> Because hamburg is made from green hay!

In August, 1981, the Smithsonian's Museum of Natural History took a pragmatic look at diet during an anniversary party for its Insect Zoo by serving chocolate chip cookies made with mealworms. "You eat them every day," the director of the zoo explained. Under the "allowable limits" of canned food production, "for every one hundred grams of tomato paste, there can be thirty fruit flies or one maggot. For every ounce of golden raisins there can be ten whole insects, plus thirty-five fly eggs." Grasshoppers are 60 percent protein, house flies are 63 percent protein, and ants are high in riboflavin and thiamine. French-fried termites, caterpillars, and grubs are standard fare in parts of Africa and South America; fried cactus worms have long been a cocktail snack in Mexico.

"The rate of growth of population is outstripping the rate of our ability to grow, harvest, store, and distribute food where it is needed," specialists at the Charles F. Kettering Research Laboratories, the center for photosynthetic research, reported in a special "Our Hungry World" edition of the *Antioch Review* for fall of 1980.

> Current estimates suggest that one billion people are undernourished. The world grain reserve is small; adequate food for the poor is very much dependent upon the weather. Not more than a dozen plant species provide most of the food for seventy percent of the world's people, and the three most important seed grain plants—rice, wheat and maize—require large quantities of chemical fertilizer and water for maximal, dependable yield. . . . Pest problems are becoming severe as the land is intensively farmed all year without a fallowing period or traditional crop rotation. . . . We are running out of fossil fuels, the feedstock for industrially produced nitrogen fertilizer, and most pesticides and herbicides. . . . The National Academy of Science has identified twenty-two critical, high priority areas of research where fundamental information is needed in order to establish and sustain long-term increases in productivity.
>
> Recent progress has been encouraging, but it cannot be maintained at its current level of government funding. In 1980 the federal budget for research and development in the National Institutes of Health, the National Science Foundation, the Department of Agriculture and the Department of Defense totalled twenty billion dollars. Of these funds, seventy-two

percent were allocated for Department of Defense research, eighteen percent for health-related research, and five percent for agricultural-related research.

Although molecular biology may never become as hypnotic to headline writers and editorialists as the latest marriage of Elizabeth Taylor or the call girls on Washington's Capitol Hill, it is far more important to Bronx, Back Bay, Skokie, and Walnut Creek families; all of the life on earth depends on its efficiencies. Molecules, atoms, and subatomic particles became available for study by scientists only a half century ago. Genetic engineering investigates the methods for changing the biologic processes in plants by manipulating these building blocks of life. The insulin so essential to diabetics, for instance, is a product of genetic-engineering success in modifying the pancreas glands of cattle and pigs.

"The word *clone* was popularized by humorists and columnists a few years ago, but its importance to us should be more widely appreciated," explained Dr. G. Ray Noggle of North Carolina State University's genetic laboratories.

A clone is a collection of individuals with identical genetic makeup. . . . Recent advances in plant tissue culture enable botanists to grow isolated parts of plants in such a manner that individual cells can be cultured and intact plants grown. Thus from a single mass of tissue, thousands of mature plants can eventually be grown. All—99.9 percent—of these plants will have identical genetic backgrounds; they are clones.

But there is danger in using cloned plants for large-scale agricultural operations. Since all of the plants would have identical genetic material, a new disease could overwhelm the entire population. Fungi mutate, too, and a new race would find the uniform plant material perfect for feeding purposes. Plant breeders must develop new strains of disease-resistant plants. That requires time and large supplies of germ plasm.

Genetic engineers have learned how to identify genes on chromosomes and move them from one organism to another.

There's no reason why the higher organisms, such as plants, should not be able to take advantage of these techniques. Most of the nitrogen fertilizer used today is made from petroleum. The air around us is eighty percent nitrogen, but most of the green plants can't use it. So it is important to see if you can expand the number of plants that can take advantage of that eighty percent of nitrogen in the air and fix their own nitrogen. Soybeans, indeed the whole leguminous family, fix their own nitrogen from the air. They are able to, because they have a symbiotic relationship with a bacterium in their root via a nodule. In that root nodule the bacteria can grow and fix nitrogen and make it available to the plant.

Well, it's been found that those bacteria can be grown outside of a nodule. They can be grown in a test tube and will fix nitrogen. Now the next step is to identify in that bacterium the particular segment of its chromosome complement that specifies the nitrogen fixation ability. Identify it. Excise it. Take it out and put it into another organism that doesn't have the ability to fix nitrogen. They have done this with bacteria. There are bacteria that will fix nitrogen, and there are bacteria that will not fix nitrogen. They've been able to transpose one to the other—make it a nitrogen fixer. The next step then would be to take that nitrogen fixation complex—they call it a gene—and put it into a green plant. Put it into a corn plant that cannot fix nitrogen and make it into a nitrogen fixer.

Look for the genetic basis of difference in plants, the geneticists say, then combine the characteristics. They want to know what makes an apple, what makes an orange, and why do peanuts grow that way. "It's like this business of screening melons so they'll fit the packaging case," a veteran researcher told me. "If they don't fall through the hole, the growers are forced to throw them away. Genetic engineering wants to make changes without the throw-away. There's no reason, either, why the old flavorable styles of fruit and other things we remember from childhood as enjoyable eating can't be restored to tomorrow's foods. Their characteristics are still present somewhere in the germ plasm.

But you've got to have a broad base of germ plasm available, and develop resistance to fungi and pests."

Scientists disagree on how soon genetic engineering will be able to develop crops that can manufacture their own nitrogen, flourish in semi-deserts, and be less susceptible to disease. Some Californians are convinced that clones of corn, wheat, rice, soybeans, tomatoes, sugar cane, and cotton will be on the market during the 1990s. The consensus of guess elsewhere is that such wonderplants will be developed during the first half of the twenty-first century.

Either way, successful cloning will probably mean an end for the storied mom-and-pop family farm. The technology of the twenty-first-century farms now envisioned calls for underground moisture sensors, electronically controlled irrigation pumps, infrared aerial photography, computerized harvesting machines, bulldozers directed by lasers, and "spreads" of 50,000 to 500,000 acres. Consequently, farming, like food processing, could be dominated by a small number of conglomerates, controlled by executives in city skyscrapers. If this pattern of "California bigness" prevails, most of our fruits and vegetables would continue to be exposed to the deteriorating effects of the three-thousand-mile jounce across the continent.

"We will almost certainly have to renounce meat in tomorrow's menus," Giuliano Ferrieri, science editor of the newsmagazine *Europeo* of Milan, concluded in an article published during 1980. "Meat is a most inefficient supplier of protein. Beef, for example, has only a sixteen percent protein content. Furthermore, a high expenditure of space and energy are necessary for the production of grain fed to animals destined for slaughter.

"Meat will eventually have to be replaced by meat-flavored vegetable protein, or by 'sea beef' now being produced in Japan by the Niigate Company. This is a fish flour processed into a fibrous form that is similar to veal. Proteins extracted from mushrooms may provide another form of meat substitute. A British company already holds a patent for 'mushroom meat.' "

The continuing loss of farmlands, our refusal to practice birth control, and livestock's ability to convert only 10 percent of the grains consumed are all cited by nutritionists as reasons for a world decline in meat production. Calories, fats, proteins, carbohydrates, and other essentials of human diet are just as available from plants as from animals (although there may be a basic need for some unsaturated fat). Some of the more ardent vegetarians have gone to the trouble of dusting off a quotation from the Greek historian Polybius complaining that "Tyrants introduced meat into our diet so that they could have violent men at their disposal."

Genetic engineering, however, may also influence meat production. Hundreds of experiments are under way throughout the United States and Europe to develop breeds of cattle, pigs, and sheep that will have more "red meat" and less fat. One of the most intriguing achievements is crossbreeding the bison with familiar British, French, and Asian breeds of beef cattle. After three decades of experimentation, Art Jones of Portales, New Mexico, succeeded in crossing bison with domestic breeds. His American Breed cross, listed in the National Breed Registry for livestock, is one-eighth bison, one-sixteenth Hereford, one-sixteenth Shorthorn, one-quarter Charolais, and one-half Brahman. The American Breed, Jones claims, has a digestive system that enables it to eat a greater variety of range forage without laying on fatty layers of "marbling." The breed also shows greater resistance to pinkeye, cancer, and other cattle diseases.

A second crossbreed with the bison, called the Beefalo, is being promoted by the American Beefalo Association in Louisville, Kentucky. Breeder herds are developing all along the Atlantic seaboard, especially in Virginia, Pennsylvania, and New York. Beefaloburgers as tasty as "prime ground round" were on sale in New York City's suburbs in 1982. Producers claim that the meat has higher protein content, fewer calories, and less cholesterol than other beef breeds, and that the animals can be readied for market on an all-grass diet. Beefalo and American Breed advocates are convinced that these crossbreeds will be roaming nationally before 2000 A.D. (The switch to American

Breed and Beefalo by beef producers would be simplified by the new technique of impregnating heifers with speck-sized embryos taken from pregnant cows.)

Nevertheless, most animals will have more and more competition from plants as scientific research continues. One of their most surprising competitors could be tobacco. Throughout the decades when tobacco smoke became a favorite whipping boy of medical researchers, only a few botanists remembered that the tobacco leaf is one of the most prolific producers of protein in the realm of domesticated plants. One acre of tobacco will yield more than 2,500 pounds of nicotine-free protein per year that could be used for human or animal food. Of this amount, 286 pounds of pure, crystalline protein—called Fraction-One by researchers—exceeds soybean protein in purity and has potential uses as a liquid diet for patients suffering from kidney disease and digestive disorders. Research in tobacco protein began in California in 1947 and has continued at North Carolina State and the USDA laboratory at Oxford, North Carolina.

The protein content of a tobacco leaf reaches its peak when the plant is six weeks old. The crop can then be cut with a mowing machine. The plant stumps promptly grow new stalks and leaves, and will repeat the effort to mature until killed by frosts in late fall. Consequently, five or six harvests each growing season can be taken from a field. This generosity makes "leaf-for-protein" an appealing cash crop for owners of small farms or for any rural home that has "an acre or two out back." (Equally appealing to physicians and persistent smokers is the prospect of producing cigarettes with lower nicotine content from the green paste left after the protein extraction process.)

But economic timidity still blocked tobacco-for-protein production in 1983. Leaders of farm organizations worry that so radical a change in the flue-cured and burley tobacco processes first developed in Virginia more than three and a half centuries ago would upset the existing industry. The U.S. Food and Drug Administration demands "years of testing with both animals and humans" in order to win its approval for food and medical uses.

Experiments with tobacco protein in France and Italy were reported to be at the test-marketing stage in 1982, thanks to stronger government and industry support. Perhaps, as with many other products in recent years, overseas success will hasten American development.

Puritan farmers mumbled and shook their heads in 1749 when Jared Eliot urged greater consideration for the land in his *Essay on Field Husbandry*. When the King of Spain sent President Washington two jacks and a jenny, crowds guffawed at the zany idea that a mule would be useful on an American farm. The crowd that gathered at New Jersey's Salem Courthouse on September 26, 1820, confidently expected that Colonel Robert R. Gibbon would drop dead after fulfilling his promise to eat an entire tomato, without purgatives or medical help. During the 1920s, Midwesterners guffawed at "those crazy guys going for broke" while trying to perfect hybrid corn.

Doubters have served as a hand-brake on social and economic change throughout history; our dedication to freedom of speech often gives them more notoriety than their ultra-conservatism justifies. Genetic engineering, too, has many sincere doubters. Fears tend to focus on the potential of genetic cloning of human beings and a subsequent distortion of family life and religious beliefs. Such fears are easily magnified because of the chasm that has grown between "pure" science and the humanities. After all, a few scientists developed the atomic bomb to the terrifying stage where clusters of it can destroy all forms of life on every continent, and perhaps explode our planet out of its orbit around the life-giving sun.

But some scientists have become deeply concerned about their social responsibilities. "It is shocking that nobody studied the social consequences of the steam engine invented in the late eighteenth century, or of developments in the nineteenth century when science was ascendant," John Maddox, editor of England's 114-year-old science weekly, *Nature*, reflected in a 1983 interview with *World Press Review*. "History has caught up with us. Pressure from the community is something scientists must learn to live with. It will increase."

Genetic research to halt the catastrophe of our vanishing land is humanitarian, just as the home garden and the small specialty farm are humanitarian. Social awareness and cooperative effort can provide the pressure to keep them that way.

The United States began with individual decisions and group cooperation. The greatest virtue of liberty is providing the opportunity to work for perpetuation of that liberty. But we cannot keep liberty without rich topsoil, clean water, clean air, forests, and adequate incomes for the producers of our foods and fibers.

There is still time to assure all of these. The correctives must begin at home and on "our street" with family decisions.

CHAPTER FIFTEEN

Tomorrows Are Built Today

Adequate diet and the serenity instilled by country landscapes are essential to the continuation of American democracy in the twenty-first century and beyond. Preparation for tomorrow's "life, liberty and the pursuit of happiness" can and should begin today in our homes.

"Mankind's continuous tapping of natural resources is the most important long-run element of mankind's fate," the eminent economist Nicholas Georgescu-Roegen warned in 1970.

> The unprecedented achievements of the Industrial Revolution so amazed everyone with what man might do with the aid of machines that the general attention became confined to the factory. . . . It induced the literati to overestimate and ultimately to oversell to their audiences the power of science. Naturally, from such a pedestal, one could not even conceive that there is any real obstacle inherent in the human condition.
>
> The sober truth is different. Even the lifespan of the human species represents just a blink when compared with that of a galaxy. So, even with space travel, mankind will remain con-

fined to a speck in space. Man's biological nature sets other limitations as to what he can do. Too high or too low a temperature is incompatible with his existence. And so are many radiations.

The fallacy of machine technology, Georgescu-Roegen went on to stress, has been industry's almost total dependence on petroleum, iron, aluminum, copper, and other *non-renewable* minerals and chemicals from the earth's interior.

Perilous depletion of American petroleum deposits was responsible for the current dependence on OPEC imports and the 500 percent increase in gasoline prices between 1970 and 1984. Exhaustion of Minnesota's treasure trove of iron ore in the Mesabi and of other important ore sources in the South and West has created ghost towns, forced hundreds of thousands of miners and mill workers out of jobs, and added to our export deficit.

By 2000 A.D., world demand for petroleum will exceed available supplies "by as much as nine million to twenty-one million barrels per day," Elfe Lantze, executive director of the International Energy Agency, predicted in a speech at the National Press Club in Washington on October 12, 1982. He also warned that "dependence of the industrialized countries on imported natural gas is also bound to increase."

None of these natural resources is renewable. Inevitably, we must learn how to produce machinery parts from agricultural products and how to derive the power to run them from two forms of sunlight: the direct rays or compressed energy obtained by means of photosynthesis.

This techno goal for our futures in green can be achieved only with an atmospheric balance of carbon dioxide, an abundance of potable water, and a healthy topsoil, along with greater economic opportunity for the agricultural producer. Consequently, achievement of the goal is everyone's challenge. We are again confronted by the same warning that Ben Franklin gave to the Continental Congress: "We must hang together or we shall all hang separately."

The legal and bureaucratic intricacies of government agencies, the power of conglomerates and their lobbyists, the hypnotic blandishments of advertising campaigns and "coupon offers" may seem to be insurmountable barriers to individual and family action in correcting our land problems.

They are not.

The American Revolution began with local committees of safety and volunteer squads of Minute Men. Individual action in the 1980s and 1990s can generate a peaceful revolution that will assure a "future in green" for the United States and pioneer a pattern of self-sufficiency for the underprivileged nations of the world. Suggestions follow for "building tomorrows" that can be undertaken at home or in community meetings.

Start a Garden! The most important first step anyone can take to assure an ample food supply, healthful air and water, and the serenities of countryside for our children and grandchildren is to discover the challenges and values of a garden. Gardening experiences are more educational—and far more rewarding—about the intricacies of nature and our abject dependence on the varieties of soil, palatable water, and sunlight than any set of how-to books.

Engineers and scientists have made some type of garden possible for every American. A kitchen window can be expanded into a greenhouse large enough for pots of herbs and salad greens and flowers. Also, architects have designed greenhouse extensions at the rear of townhouses in the "clusters" of new suburbias.

Many cities and planned suburbias have set aside tracts for use as community gardens. Annual fees for a 25-by-30-foot plot range from $25–$50, depending on the local government's whim. The services usually provided are water taps, an occasional mowing of pathways between the plots, and a truckful of horse-stable refuse each spring. The challenges offered by weather, bugs, and weeds nourish gardener cooperation. Seeds and produce are exchanged; friendships develop. Crop surpluses can be given to charity organizations or homes for the aged.

Wherever the garden, and whatever its size, challenges are

constant from planting time through harvest. Sudden death leers
from every one of these plots. The soil mixture must be properly
balanced in nitrogen, potassium, phosphorus, lime, and other
vital elements. Too much water will cause seeds to rot; not enough
water will cause them to dehydrate to death. After the first pale-
green sprouts appear, bacteria and bugs arrive. There can be
blights, cutworms, leaf-eaters, borers, grubs, slugs, and fungi.
Rabbits and woodchucks are avid admirers of young leaves. A
squirrel will scamper a mile for a bulb, peanut, tomato, squash,
ripening sunflower, or any other growth containing protein. A
raccoon will nibble through a row of sweet corn in one midnight
visit. Birds adore cherries and bush fruits.

"Daily planting and weeding will make a philosopher out of
him who never was one before," John Erskine wrote. "I mean
philosopher in the true sense, not simply a placid soul who can
accept life without protest, but a mind awakened, fertile and
discriminating."

With garden awareness throughout our fifty states, the political
and economic tasks of assuring our future in green will be greatly
simplified.

Make Yourself Heard!   The zoning decisions that
determine the fate of farmlands are generally made by the county's board of supervisors. In urban areas, the city council holds
the same power over parks, community gardens, and other potentially tillable or beautification areas within the corporate limits. Attend the meetings where these decisions are made, and
give out with your opinions!

Between 1967 and 1977, more than sixty million acres of land—
an area equal to all of Ohio—were allocated to real estate developers for rip-up into new airports, new throughways, factories,
strip mines, and rowhouse suburbias. This loss of potentially
productive cropland bulldozes on at a rate of three million acres
a year.

Throughways have made it commonplace for city workers to
commute as much as forty and fifty miles each workday morning

and afternoon between homes and offices. Their homes are in suburbs built on appropriated dairy farms, grain fields, or truck gardens because of a county's zoning decision. In 1983, farmers and villagers in Virginia successfully negotiated against the harangues of realty attorneys by winning their county board of supervisors' approval of a zoning law that limited suburban and factory developments to land of inferior quality, and banned "prime land" from transformation into housing or industrial sites. The victory was won only because voters asserted their right to be "heard in meeting."

Suburban and rural programs of environmentally sane zoning ordinances are desperately needed coast to coast. They cannot be achieved until consumers make themselves heard at county board and city council meetings.

Start with the Kids!   Studies about the land and the environment must become important subjects in our public schools, kindergarten through high school. But, as with reading and writing, awareness of nature and our dependence on it should begin at home. Babies are born with inquisitiveness "on automatic pilot." A lettuce leaf, a nosegay of flowers, a dandelion's lion-tooth leaves and footlong taproot can become a stage set for introducing a toddler to the awesomeness of nature and our obligations to a future in green.

All of my own children have become skilled gardeners; one has won a reputation throughout New England as an authority on gardening history and herbariums. Their earth-song awareness began with garden weed-pulls, botanical seminars on the moors, and the adventures of collecting wild berries and leaves for jams and vegetable dishes when they were kindergarteners.

The home-learning process is as available in a metropolitan apartment as it is on a Wyoming ranch. Moreover, it will stimulate parents' interest in "the goings on" at Parent-Teacher Association meetings and the drone of school board sessions.

Raise questions and initiate discussions about the need for greater emphasis in the school curriculum on the reasons for our vanishing land resources and the environmental perils of pollution, acid rain, toxic-waste dumps, and topsoil erosion. Textbooks that deal with these doomsday potentials should be adopted by school boards. Similar pressures must be applied to state departments of education and the trustees of universities to set up teacher-training programs that will make both undergraduate and graduate students aware of the land and end the insularism too often found among university deans and professors.

Vacation on a Farm! Try an exchange visit with a farm family. International exchange visits for high school and college students have been modish, and socially valuable, since World War II. But the myth that "the farm problem is a government matter," plus the label-emblazoned plastic curtain at the grocery store, has segregated agricultural producers from our urban majority as thoroughly as the folkways of our geographic regions are segregated from the folkways of Somalia or Peru. Exchange visits between urban families and the families of agricultural producers, as well as between rural high-school students and city high-school students, would have far greater worth in achieving understanding of the land and its problems than the current practice of slide shows at service-club luncheons and Arbor Day speeches on the school lawns.

Realistic "live-ins," without the dude ranch niceties, could become a stellar program for establishing producer-consumer understanding and cooperation. During the 1830s, a Washburn family son migrated from Maine to Minnesota and became one of the founders of General Mills. His earth song continued to be the seasonal glories of Maine, so he and his brothers expanded the family farm into a 400-acre estate and used it for summer vacations and holiday reunions. In 1973, Washburn heirs turned the estate into a nonprofit corporation. From February through November each year, it is open to school groups and urban families as a live-in experience of Maine's farm life in the mid-nineteenth century. Guests must wear farm clothes, sleep on corn-husk mattresses, use outdoor privies and chamber pots, eat typical farm fare on plank and sawhorse tables covered with oilcloth, and become hired hands for the dawn-to-dusk routine in barns and fields. It is impossible to come away from a weekend of this without a real sense of what rural life was like a century ago, participants insist. Similar programs for participation in the routine of the agriculturist during these final decades of the twentieth century would do much to strengthen producer-consumer understanding.

In 1983, on-the-farm vacations were also being pioneered for the countryside where the family farm developed almost three centuries ago. The Pennsylvania Dutch Visitors Bureau in Lancaster offers brochures about guest facilities available on farms in the storied Penn Dutch region. In addition, the Pennsylvania Department of Agriculture's Bureau of Agricultural Development offers a free directory of twenty-five working farms—dairy, hog, poultry, diversified crops—that take paying guests.

Watch Out for la Calorie Cuisine!   By late 1982, despite the highest unemployment rate in a half century, between 35 and 40 percent of all American meals were eaten in restaurants. Obviously, our restaurants and fast-food shops have become critical factors to both our nutritional well-being and the family budget.

"Learn how to make sensible choices and watch for the booby traps on menus," advises the personal-health columnist of the *New York Times* in her splendid *Jane Brody's Nutrition Book*. Brody cites the recommendations of the Institute of Human Nutrition at Columbia University in urging caution about fried foods, cream sauces, batter-dipped meats or vegetables, as well as biscuits, croissants, muffins, butter rolls, and rich desserts.

Most eateries are guilty of serving too much fat, too much starch, too much salt, too much sugar—and all of it at excessive prices. Consequently, the restaurant contributes to our perils of overweight, heart disease, arteries clogged by excessive cholesterol, diabetes, acne, nervous tension, and even some forms of cancer.

Restaurant purchases of millions of tons of fatty meats, cooking oils, "enriched" flours, and various forms of sugar and salt influence the land erosion caused by repeated plantings of grains and sugar beets on marginal soils, the "fattening out" of meat animals by feeding them diethylstilbestrol and other dangerous synthetic hormones, and the packer practice of enhancing meat color with nitrite or nitrate.

The health of both the land and the diner would be helped if restaurants would abandon the practice of placing a basketful of cholesterol-rich muffins or rolls on the table before the first course is served. Also, little effort is made, either at the fast-food emporium or the table d'hôte hostelry, to provide diners with information about the calories, cholesterol, fat, sugar, and salt content of the foods being served. In a sedentary society, dietary information on the menu would be stronger evidence of a gracious host than a wicker basketful of hot cornbread and Parker House rolls.

During the early summer of 1983, Joe Theismann, quarterback of the Washington Redskins, announced that the restaurant he owns in suburban Virginia would list the calorie count, sugar and salt content of all foods offered on its menu. About the same time, the Marriott hotel chain introduced a "Good for You" menu for all its restaurants. Developed under guidelines of the American Heart Association, the menus feature low-fat and low-cholesterol selections.

The need for smaller servings and dietary balance in restaurant meals is particularly vital to the senior citizen, who is everlastingly plagued by the dangers of overweight, osteoporosis, diabetes, and cholesterol-clogged arteries. In 1983, more than 25,540,000 Americans were 65 years of age or over. Barring such catastrophes as nuclear war or new forms of bacterial disease, 67 million Americans—21.7 percent of the population—will be senior citizens by 2050 A.D.

Morrison, Inc., operators of a large chain of cafeterias in the South, has researched the potential of a "Senior Menu." "As you know, we operate many restaurants in the state of Florida and most of these are in areas where retired citizens make up the base of our customers," E.E. Bishop, president of Morrison, Inc., wrote me. "We are offering special consideration to menus and prices in some of these areas. We are well aware of this growing market and are trying to position ourselves so that we can take advantage and also be of service."

Buy from Farmers! During my childhood, the open-air markets of big cities were wonderlands. I learned more about geography, botany, zoology, cuisine, and the intricacies of nature at lower Manhattan's Washington Market and Boston's Faneuil Hall stalls than I learned in school. The ribbed gold of a casaba melon evoked a North Africa never hinted at in the *Beau Geste* movies shot on a Hollywood sandlot. Navaho shepherds, Apache warriors, the stoic diligence of the Mormons whispered out of a pocketful of piñon nuts. The silvery-black gleam of codfish and haddock mirrored ice-sheathed Gloucester schooners plunging home from Georges Bank. That rib roast had recently been part of a trail drive across Wyoming's high plain. The perfume of McIntosh and Northern Spy apples created imagery of sun-dappled brooks frothing down a Vermont hillside.

But many city markets eventually became sites for skyscrapers. Chain stores, with their neon mundanity, could not produce the magical imagery.

During the 1970s, cities again began to realize the value of public markets. During the same years, thousands of farmers and gardeners became aware of the potential profits in roadside stands and pick-your-own berries, sweet corn, melons, apples. Boston rejuvenated Faneuil Hall glories. Washington allocated a farmers market to a Potomac hillside, east of USDA's headquarters. Atlanta sponsored several block-long farmers markets agleam with everything from peppery sausage, Chinese vegetables, bunches of green herbs, tawny mounds of sweet potatoes and yams, bins of tree-ripe peaches, to fifty-pound sacks of raw peanuts. Roanoke, Virginia, developed so delightful a farmers' market near its mid-city that it lures customers into the Blue Ridge from as far away as Richmond.

Farmers who decided to invest in roadside stands or pick-your-own crops learned that they could gross up to $100,000 a year, even in such short-season regions as New York's Catskills and Michigan. The stands that refuse to deal in "shipped in" produce open when their lettuce is as high as a rabbit's nose and the parsnips have achieved their winterlong ripening. Some of these stands also handle locally made cheeses, maple syrup, and homemade pastry. Sugar peas, parsley, strawberries, snap beans, baby carrots, bush berries, tomatoes, beets, thyme and tarragon, sweet corn, squashes, okra, peppers, peaches, pears, honey, basil and apples follow with soldierly precision.

At pick-your-own farms, the owners provide containers. You weigh your pickings and pay on the way out. An afternoon's outing to a farmer retailer provides the therapy of countryside plus a trunkful of home-grown, fresh produce that can be quick frozen or transformed into a week of scrumptious dining.

Newspapers and regional magazines are beginning to run lists of on-the-farm produce stands during the harvest season. Connecticut's Department of Agriculture at Hartford offers a free bulletin listing every farm and orchard in the state that has products for sale. Other states and regions are bound to imitate the example.

Rediscover Your Kitchen! The deluge of advertising by fast-food chains and frozen-dinner processors, inflation, and the increase of "working mothers," have reduced millions of American kitchens to a microwave oven with its ten-minute sessions, a refrigerator for the breakfast sweet roll, a coffee pot, and storage space for the sugary "goodies" munched during television prime time.

There can be as much therapy in home cooking as there is in jogging. A good cook controls the family diet and makes it more delectable than a seventy-dollar meal at the Old Depot. Shopping trips, even to supermarkets, can be serendipities when you are armed with data about calories and read the "contents" labels on canned goods and frozen foods. With modern equipment, preparation of a delightful meal at home doesn't require any more time than "primping up" before driving off to the Old Depot.

We also need more integration in the kitchen. The most publicized chefs at restaurants are male, but home cooking in the United States has long been considered a "chore for the womenfolks." The kitchen was the woman's domain; only the outdoor barbecue was presided over by the man of the family. But changes in our pattern of living are being reflected in our kitchens as well. Working couples, and working parents, are finding that both have roughly the same amount of time at home—time that must be shared with each other, with the children, and with the whole range of housekeeping chores. Men are discovering the delights that come with the preparation of a tasty specialty for family and guests to enjoy. For a variety of reasons, I became the family cook when I was twelve years old. In recent years, as an author working at home and my wife at work as a professional educator, preparation of dinner has been largely my chore. It gives me a change of pace, stimulates ingenuity, and breeds caution on shopping trips.

Youngsters, too, quickly develop cookery skills. The intricacies of making cakes, cookies, sauces, and breads fascinate even prekindergarteners. Children get a special satisfaction from seeing the produce they have picked transformed into applesauce or jam—as they apply every wooden spoon in the kitchen to the task!

Go beyond the food page and experiment with such delectables as dandelion greens, ground cherries, leeks, elderberries, quince, chokecherries, barberry, purslane, herbs, mung beans, and stew meats. Recipes for the use of these excellent "old-timers" are available in the better cookbooks, such as *Joy of Cooking, The American Heart Association Cookbook,* and *Craig Claiborne's Gourmet Diet.*

Form a Co-op! Join, or form, a consumer cooperative. This will enable group purchasing of processed and natural foods at wholesale prices. Membership can be limited to a few families. For generations, Americans working overseas have used the cooperative technique by teaming up to buy caselots of goodies from home and needed supplies via tramp steamer or container ships.

Canned goods, cheeses, locally grown produce, rice, beans, citrus, and nuts are ideal foods for a neighborhood co-op. By dealing with a produce wholesaler, one Pennsylvania co-op averages savings of 50 percent on fresh vegetable costs. The produce is delivered to a church basement, where co-op members pick up their allocated shares at scheduled times. If refrigeration and a member with butcher experience are available, contracts can be negotiated with packers or wholesalers for weekly or monthly deliveries of meats at costs considerably below those at supermarts, and with the probability of better quality.

Fruit and nut orchardists offer lower rates for group purchases. Social clubs, church groups, PTAs take advantage of these offers by using the co-op technique for funding special projects. For example, alumnae of a national sorority in northern Virginia earn a profit for their philanthropic projects each Christmas season by selling bags of shelled pecans. In 1983, they offered the pecan halves at four dollars a pound; mail-order catalogues and retail stores priced the same quality and size of pecans at seven to nine dollars a pound.

With cooperative sharing of bookkeeping, packaging, and checkout tasks, the co-op can use some of the savings on food bills to rent a distribution center, buy refrigeration equipment, and experiment with more types of food. Neighborhood cooperatives sell gasohol at the service stations they run. The New England Food Cooperative Association represents 230 neighborhood groups with a total annual gross of $5 million. Many states operate cooperative extension services in their capital cities. Information about founding and operating cooperatives can be obtained by mail. The Cooperative League of the USA, 1828 L Street N.W., Washington, D.C. 20036 is a good source of data about cooperatives.

Alert the Media! Heckle and re-heckle the editors of local newspapers and your favorite magazines to allocate more news and editorial page space to the crises of the American land, the defects in our system of food distribution, the loss of economic independence by our food producers, and the tragedy of bureaucratic naiveté.

The spectacular increase of federal spending on various agricultural relief projects after the 1930s caused the urban press—and eventually television—to focus their agricultural reporting on Washington. The secretary of agriculture, congressmen, lobbyists became the accepted voices of our food and fiber production problems. Tons of mimeographed speeches and "statements" were cranked out by government publicists to be stuffed in reporters' pockets and become the basis for "interpretive" news stories and editorials about "the farm problem." Urbanites were conditioned to assume that agriculture and the welfare of the land was "a Washington affair." When agitation about environmental pollution became widespread during the 1960s, the press treated it as a separate subject, with little or no connection to the land's well-being. Subsequently, the government established the Environmental Protection Agency as a bureaucracy independent of USDA administration. EPA paid little attention to the land and other natural features of the environment and become involved in political struggles about toxic wastes.

When indignant farmers organized tractor and trailer protest marches to Washington, most of the media focused their reports on the traffic jams and damage to grass plots in downtown Washington. When, during July, 1983, the White House again changed course and approved a plan to sell nine million tons of grain a year to the USSR, little attention was given by editorialists or columnists to the impact this would have on food prices, on future farm prices, on grain supplies for the starving millions of Africa and Asia, or on the status of "Uncle Sam's image" in Canada, South America, and Europe. When, during the same month, television networks aired "specials" about USDA's vast hoard of foods stored in caves and warehouses at exorbitant rental fees, the name of the principal leaseholder of the warehouses—one of our largest middleman conglomerates—was not given. Of the thousands of investigative reporters, columnists, feature writers and anchormen, editorialists, and home economists responsible for reporting about our foods, agriculture, and economic welfare throughout the nation, not more than fifty are doing a competent job—and their task is compounded by the "Sam Slick" technique of lobbyists and advertisers.

American publishers share some of the blame for the neglect of both land awareness and the sources of our "highest living standard on earth." Canada's authors and publishers have long contended that American literature is based on heroes and victories, while Canadian literature focuses on environmental survival. There is truth in the comparison. American literature is replete with biographies of "bad guys" and "good guys," victories in science and engineering, victories in physical fitness and artful use of cosmetics, novels where sex acts are described with cookbook monotony, cartoon books about cats, and get-rich-quick formulas. But books about agriculture, the vanishing land, the follies of our distribution system, bureaucratic indolence, dwindling water reserves, the crises heralded by acid rain—all are considered "a drag that won't sell."

We need more, and better, reporting about the land and its problems as premier news, as prime-time television features, and as literature worthy of shelf space alongside *Grapes of Wrath*, *The Oregon Trail*, *John Brown's Body*, and *Walden*.

The changes cannot be mandated by a government agency or a President's press conference. A return to land awareness can be achieved only by audience demand. Letters—to editors, to publishers, to networks, to film producers—are the most effective tools.

Checkmate the Legislators!   Keep track of the voting records of your legislators on bills influencing land policy, food and fiber production, food labeling, pollution control, and other matters dealing with the land and its harvests. Write them letters stating your convictions about the monopolistic tendencies of a food distribution system that awards 72 percent of the retail price to middlemen and 28 percent to producers; about the poisoning of our atmosphere and waterways by careless use of fuels, insecticides, and factory wastes; about the annual erosion of five billion tons of our topsoils; about the annual loss of millions of acres of tillable land and productive forest to the realtors' greedy development of suburbs and shopping plazas, the processors' decentralized factories, and strip mines; about the international politicking that channels our grain surpluses into Soviet livestock bins and dictators' warehouses instead of to the world's starving millions.

Quantity, rather than quality, makes the impact on today's legislator. The regiments of professional lobbyists in Washington, in state capitals, in county seats have been scientifically organized during the last half century and have the financing and advertising power of the conglomerates behind them. Obviously, the lobbyist has the "inside track." Letters from non-influential taxpayers have a tendency to pile up on secretaries' desks for consideration based on the size of the stack.

But as public awareness of our vanishing land and its potential perils develops, stacks of protesting letters will multiply, and generate political action to undertake major changes in our free-enterprise system.

"The real and permanent prosperity of a country begins when the agriculture has evolved so far as to be self-sustaining and to leave the soil in constantly better condition for the growing of plants," Cornell's great botanist/philospher, Liberty Hyde Bailey, wrote in 1897. Erosion, imminent drought, political chicanery, economic serfdom for the majority of agriculturists—all these things testify that real and permanent prosperity will be more difficult to achieve than it was a century ago, even with our vast resources of scientific research and technologic skills. The homey projects outlined in the pages of this chapter can be first steps toward the self-sustaining prosperity envisioned by Bailey. They dramatize how we depend on the well-being of the countryside, of our topsoils, water, and atmosphere.

We must also regain appreciation for the fact that foods and fibers are not the only rewards of an American future in green. The beauty and serenity in a green countryside have such strong influence on mankind that they must be considered necessary for our psychological survival. As the caretaker of green pastures, shimmering cropfields, the earth song of baritone brooks, contralto birds, and the soprano of wind in treetops, the agriculturist is also a guarantor of our sanity and delight.

CHAPTER SIXTEEN

Futures in Green

A Creationist believes that the Garden of Eden was a biologic Paradise, sullied only by a snake peddling apples. A believer in Evolution knows that human dependence on nature has been intimate for millions of years. We instinctively associate the countryside with beauty and serenity and find therapy by vacationing there or even driving through. For both Creationist and Evolutionist, green pastures, rustling fields of grain, hillside orchards, and white farmhouses with red barns shaded by gnarled trees instill a peace of mind in the viewer that cannot be achieved on our Fifth Avenues, Michigan Boulevards, or Rodeo Drives.

The therapeutic values of countryside have been ignored by the economists, politicians, and lobbyists who have argued and plotted about the "farm problem" during the past 120 years. Yet that therapy is as important to our sense of well-being and the perpetuation of democracy as freedom of speech and worship. The verities of the American way were sired and weaned in the countryside. Our mores, our democratic goals, our individualism, our sense of neighborliness—all have rural roots. "Green pastures" and "country folk" are direly essential to our future.

The "farm country" is still out there for the sampling in every state, particularly along the highways that the map-makers indicate with tiny blue lines. My wife and I became devotees of "the little blue roads" a long time ago and used them again on the serendipities that yielded much of the background information for this book. Usually the little blue lines in the East follow gradients hoofed out by herds of deer, elk, and bison before 1800 or by cows, sheep, and foraging pigs since then. They are leisure roads, winding up hillsides through rhododendron forests, ambling along the bank of a brook, plodding between a horizonful of corn and a hillside of fruit trees. West of the Appalachians, the roads belie their nineteenth-century birth by straightaways and right-angle turns that follow the platting of township surveyors.

The cupola dome of the courthouse still dominates the skyline of county seats. The white farmhouse and red barns still flaunt Greek Revival and Penn Dutch pride. A lunch stop at a Main Street cafeteria can usually evolve a half-hour "rundown" on crop conditions and "those yahoos in Washington" with farmers at an adjoining table. Only the little blue roads lead to the awesome beauty of redbud in blossom along the rattlesnake fences that surround Abraham Lincoln's birthplace at Hodgenville, Kentucky; the starkness of cliffs, river, and trees framing Missouri's Mark Twain Memorial at Florida; and the dazzle of scarlet cliffs guarding the eastern approach to the emerald valley of Wyoming's South Pass. The little blue roads joyously reveal the heartlands of our folkways, of our concepts of democracy, of our peace of mind, as well as the sources of our highest living standard on earth.

But the heartlands are vanishing. Only 2 percent of our population grow the vast harvests we deem essential to our standard of living. Fewer than one billion acres of land now yield these supplies and simultaneously serve as our source of serenity and democratic ideals. Each year thousands of farmers are forced into bankruptcy by economic pressures and millions of acres of countryside are technologized by industry.

Young McCormick did not visualize such catastrophe for the

American land and its proud "ownership in fee simple" when he hammered out his wheat thresher gadget on the family's blacksmith forge. Amos Eaton was not plotting vanishing land and blind worship of the machine when he convinced New York's legislature of the prosperity that could be developed by the Erie Canal. Thomas Edison foresaw no grim future for our "green mansions" and their verities when he tinkered with glass tubes and carbonized string until electricity would make them glow with sunlight brilliance.

Humane cooperation between technology and the land is essential to our futures in green. Our machine worship has become so hypnotic that even the meaning of "technology" has been distorted. The word has its roots in the Greek word *techne*, meaning "art" or "skill." The primary meaning of "technology" is the sum of ways in which a social group provides itself with the material objects of its civilization. Ever since Creation—or, depending on your convictions, the evolution of *Homo sapiens*— the botanic and zoologic harvests obtained from the intricate atomic machinery of dirt-sunlight-water-seeds have been the material objects of human survival. Breathable air and potable water come from the same machinery of Nature. Green growth was our first technology. It continues to be our most essential technology. But its perpetuation cannot be guaranteed by government edicts or the supermarkets or the conglomerates or the regiments of lobbyists in Washington and the state capitals.

Perpetuation can be achieved by a "Technogate" confrontation that will convince professional scientists and industrial leaders to conform to humanitarian and democratic principles in their use of the technology that involves land.

Five drastic changes will be essential to humane cooperation between technology and the land.

Collective Bargaining Agreements.   Three crises looming on the American horizon indicate that the time is at hand to undertake "think-tank" arbitration by and for labor, agriculture, and industry. The crises are: the urgency for massive repairs in our transcontinental system of highways; the impending replacement of workers by robots; and the imminence of irradiated foods that do not require canning or refrigeration.

Dangerous deterioration of our four million miles of highways, streets, and throughways will, during the next decade, force repeated increases in gasoline taxes plus long, bumpy detours on highways. Pavement that is twenty-five to thirty years old has flaked and bulged. Bridge cables and steel are eroding; some bridges have collapsed. Guesses about the repair costs range from $625 million to $3 trillion (three times as much as the national debt). The highway crisis will affect the trucking industry's deliveries of foodstuffs. On the other hand, what's left of our network of railways is in such decrepit condition that it will cost billions of dollars and a decade of repair work to restore them to the efficiency of the Fast Mail, Santa Fe Chief, and Twentieth Century Limited years.

Meanwhile, industry "modernizes" by replacing skilled workers with robots and by stressing computer and electrical engineering degrees for new workers. The prospect looms for loss of jobs by millions of middle-aged employees. Organized labor had multi-reasons for discussing new techniques and opportunities in food and fiber production and distribution.

The crisis confronting canners and frozen-food processors comes from a quarter century of European experiments in irradiating foods with gamma rays. Rays of cobalt 60 or cesium 137 quickly alter the metabolism of microorganisms that cause food spoilage, thereby preventing the microorganisms from multiplying. Irradiated fruit, vegetables, poultry, meat, fish, even rice pudding have long shelf-life without canning or refrigeration. The irradiated food does not become radioactive, and the cost is only a few pennies a pound.

The Soviet Union now encourages commercial sale of irradiated potatoes, onions, fresh fruits and vegetables, dried fruits, poultry, and food concentrates. Shops in the Netherlands offer irradiated asparagus, strawberries, mushrooms, shrimp, frog legs, snails, bread, and fish filets. South Africans irradiate their delicious papaya, mango, and avocado.

Eventually, irradiated foods will severely reduce the production of canned goods and frozen foods. Also, it is possible that equipment will be developed to irradiate foods at fieldside. These developments will, in turn, influence food warehousing as well as the display areas of supermarkets.

The most reluctant recruit to any cooperative program of agribusiness research may be the agriculturist! The dream of economic, as well as social, independence persists on most farms and ranches—the agriculturist has always been America's staunchest individualist. The environment demands it. Weather, livestock, ripening harvests will not abide a strike or a slowdown. Neither livestock nor crops respect the five-day week. Consequently, repeated efforts to persuade agriculturists into labor unions have had little success. Dour suspicion toward big business and "the damned bankers" initiated the Granger and Greenback movements and launched the farmers' cooperatives. Professional farmers' groups, however, aren't able to agree with one another, as attested by the rivalries of the National Grange, the Farm Bureau Federation, the Farmers' Union, and similar groups.

But the agriculturist of the 1980s is not the homesteader of the nineteenth century or the monarch of a self-sufficient family farm in the 1920s. University training, acute dependence on machinery manufacturers and fuel peddlers, the price manipulations of conglomerates and "futures" gamblers have all forced him to acute social and economic awareness. Expensive machinery, petroleum fuels, and dependence on the middleman's processed livestock feeds have impoverished him. Harvest prices fixed by conglomerates and the futures markets forced him into exploitation of his land—or bankruptcy.

The agriculturist, like the labor leader and the industrialist, should welcome development of the agribusiness research centers advocated by Dr. John Davis, with each regional center's agenda determined by "a policy board of farmers, deliverymen, processors and consumers." Lower costs for agricultural machinery, use of farm-grown motor fuels and their protein-rich slops, and guarantees of forty cents of the retail dollar for the producer

could assure the farmer of a good living and end the politically
poisoned handout of crop subsidies.

Land Centers. Crippled by the greatest public
debt ever accumulated, and simultaneously committed to the
purchase of super-expensive atomic weaponry that, authorities
admit, must be replaced every decade, the federal government
has remained indifferent to programs of land research essential
to our green future.

Perhaps this is for the best! The outpouring of tax refunds for
crop subsidies, export programs, soil conservation, marketing
agreements during the last half century has failed to cure the
socio-economic illness of either the land or its food producers.
Bureaucracy has the awkward habit of tripping over its own feet.

The land is everybody's responsibility for the obvious reason
that it determines everyone's future—or non-future. The programs necessary to assure the preservation of topsoils, a more
democratic system of food distribution, orderly decentralization,
better use of our water reserves, a cleaner atmosphere, the development of new crops through genetic engineering should all
be financed by non-government funds, and they should be administered by personnel who have proven skills in business management, agricultural science, and sociology.

History attests that public change can be achieved without
federal handouts and their inevitable sequel of bureaus, inspectors, congressional committees, "porkbarreling." De Witt Clinton made New York City our biggest metropolis by persuading
New York voters to finance the Erie Canal. Eli Whitney's invention of the cotton gin transformed the South's agriculture and
perpetuated slavery for another seventy years. Private investors
built hundreds of railroads between the Atlantic and the Missouri's valley before the federal government initiated one of the
most disgraceful "plunderbunds" in our history with its land
grants to the Union Pacific and Central Pacific railroads' owners.
Thomas Edison invented the phonograph and electric light bulb,
Henry Ford devised the flivver, the Wright brothers worked out

the airplane—and none of them received a federal grant. Andrew Carnegie pioneered our wondrous system of public libraries, sans federal aid or the monotonies of committee hearings on Capitol Hill. Sweet corn, apple pie, the hot dog, hamburgers, the pizza— all achieved success without a federal grant or act of Congress.

Scores of associations are now working to protect wildlife, recreational areas, civil rights, and health. Unfortunately, most of them use from 25 percent to as much as 85 percent of membership fees and contributions for office space, executive salaries, and elaborate solicitation campaigns. And most of them are "chasing the same rainbow." In contrast, public, non-governmental support of a thorough and democratic policy of land preservation and harvest distribution would ensure protection for wildlife, birds, recreational areas, water supplies, and clean air.

Cooperation among the scores of wildlife, environmental, and social-betterment organizations in fund raising and research programs, similar to the United Way technique, could provide the skills and funds for regional land centers where research and promotional programs of environmental protection, land preservation, agricultural equality, and more democratic distribution could be launched.

Since our weather, soils, rainfall, and crops vary from area to area, the development of *regional* land centers is desirable. Administered by men and women who are trained specialists in business administration, labor relations, and scientific research— rather than political appointees—these centers would be regional experiment sites for environmental, agricultural, and processing techniques. They would also serve as the "think-tanks" for producer-labor-industry arbitration and could offer short-term courses to update teachers and professors on our land and distribution problems. Public support of, and participation in, these centers could reduce the federal government's budget by at least $50 billion per year.

A Department of the Land.   Drastic reorganization of the federal agencies and departments that deal with the land is long overdue. Only four years after we bullied California and the Southwest away from Mexico by means of the Bear Flag Revolt and the War with Mexico, the Department of the Interior was founded. All of the government's "public lands" were placed under the jurisdiction of this agency. One hundred thirty-three years later, 516 million acres of federal land are still under the jurisdiction of Interior.

The Department of Agriculture, founded in 1863, was intended to provide free crop seeds, cuttings of imported plants, and suggestions for crop and livestock improvements to agriculturists. These projects gradually veered the department's efforts to concentrating on promoting the diversified farm, which not only angered livestock producers and lumbermen but gave rise to the urbanite's notion that the farm problem is "something for the Feds to fuss about." After long quibbling and infighting with Interior, the United States Forest Service was led over to the USDA corral. Subsequently, Congress decided that supervision of food stamps and the school lunch should also be a USDA chore. Although our first "pure food" laws and their inspection services were evolved by USDA personnel, Congress eventually ruled that the Food and Drug Administration should be transferred to the supervision of the new Department of Health, Education and Welfare.

When university scientists and protesting young folks began the agitation for clean air and a healthy environment during the 1960s, public response was so vociferous that Congress and the White House agreed there should be an agency devoted to the booby-trapped chore of unfouling our atmosphere and waterways. The result was the Environmental Protection Agency with 14,000 employees, an annual budget of $6 billion, and a sorry record of achievement.

Land is land is land! Interior's public lands and the national parks are land. The farms, ranches, and forests advised and subsidized by USDA are land. Foods and most drugs are dependent on the land. Environmental protection is related more to the land than it is to cities and suburbs, since human health is direly dependent on the land's health.

Inevitably, there should be a consolidation of all of the federal government's involvement in the land. A logical solution would be to abolish USDA and create a Department of the Land. Its domain would include the public lands and parks now administered by Interior, the functions of USDA that are appropriate for a national program of land and harvest distribution reform, the Food and Drug Administration, any remnants of the Environmental Protection Agency that are worth saving, plus all other bureaucratic nooks and crannies dealing with topsoil, water, clean air, sunlight, and the processing of foods and natural fibers. (If the Department of Health and Human Services holds together for another decade, the onerous chores of food stamps and school lunches should be allocated to it.)

The usefulness of USDA's system of county agents also needs careful analysis. The county agent originated during the dawn years of agriculture's transformation from horse and mule power to engine power. In 1912, the education of the average American farmer ended in the fifth grade of elementary school. The county agent helped the farmer understand the flivver, pickup truck, milking machine, tractor, and silo; his feminine co-worker, the home demonstration agent, wrought similar magic by familiarizing farm women with sewing machines, propane gas stoves, electric lights, pressure cookers, and book clubs.

But, since 1912, technology has antiquated the folk image of "the Man with a Hoe." The agriculturist of today and tomorrow has become as sophisticated as any urbanite. In an environment of television, computers, "Flying Farmers," intricate bookkeeping, and scientific skills, it is questionable whether the county agent and the home demonstration agent can continue to be of much service to the agriculturist and his family. (Coincidentally, over the decades, the county and home demonstration agents have failed to expand their services to urbanites; most city folk don't even know who they are, or why. A thorough investigation of the county agent system and its future usefulness is necessary.)

Also, the USDA's farm subsidy system is as moldy as its surplus cheese. Four decades of price supports for grains, dairy products, peanuts, and tobacco at an average cost to taxpayers of ten billion dollars a year have failed to reduce crop surpluses or bring the majority of producers economically adequate prices for their goods. The solution lies in the development of a more democratic system of distribution. The vested interests of lobbyists prevent development of such a system by Washington. Democratic distribution must be a primary problem for the "think-tank" discussions at the sorely needed regional land centers.

The practice of assigning agricultural attachés to our embassies around the world is probably a wasteful expenditure. Most of the attachés' work is done by aides who are natives of the country where the embassy is located, who speak three or four languages fluently, and who have astute insight into the local folkways, the power base, and the modus operandi of their country's agriculture. As a result, most of our agricultural attachés spend their time in social activities, after casually approving the reports prepared by their native aides. The obligatory duties of the attaché will become even fewer if the oligarchic control of overseas grain trade is corrected. In any event, it would be far more businesslike to do away with the agricultural attaché posts and to give more scope and credit to the native aides who are doing most of the job anyway. The chore that really needs doing is to learn far more about the admirable techniques of soil and water conservation in Europe and Asia, more about their forestry practices, more about the urban appreciations of soil and nature overseas— then relay this information home in cogent terms. The native aides are in an excellent position to undertake this job.

With development of regional land centers, the usefulness of the federal government's sprawl of agricultural research projects in and near the District of Columbia would end. This realignment of essential research and development would not only trim the operating budget of the Department of the Land but would further diminish the power of the thousands of lobbyists and pressure groups operating in the District. (After all, lobbyists and pressure groups focus on Washington because since 1900 we have literally become the Centralized States of America, rather than the "united States of America" envisioned by the compilers of the Constitution.)

The duties of a Department of the Land would, thereafter, be restricted to (1) policing the health standards of foods and drugs, (2) enforcing the distribution techniques and prices approved through arbitration at the land centers, (3) administering public lands, seashores, and parks, (4) enforcing protective measures for the environment that have been determined regionally through arbitration at the land centers, and (5) mediating any disagreement on techniques between land centers.

Legal Protection for Our Good Agricultural Land. Despite the unprecedented opportunity to actually own a homeplace, and the prayerbook's admonition to "Give thanks for the increase of the ground and the gathering in of the fruits thereof," destruction of both the ground and its fruits has been the greatest evil of the so-called civilizing of America since 1600. The awesome span of grasses and virgin forest between the Atlantic and the Pacific encouraged the folklore that our farmland and timberland were endless. Warnings to preserve the topsoil's vigor by means of composts and manures and to control erosion were largely ignored. When cropfields wore out, families loaded cherished possessions into a cart and moved to a new homestead; there was always a lot more out west. Repeated plantings of tobacco and cotton impoverished the soils of the South. Hillside plantings, without terracing, eroded New England's topsoils. Vast regions of the Alleghenies' virgin forests were burned off to make room for plantings of vegetables and grain.

The development of automobiles, airplanes, electric power lines launched a new assault on the land's bounties. Highways, airports, strip mines, suburbs, decentralized factories have covered more than 60 million acres of land with layers of cement, steel, macadam, and other materials that will destroy the botanic effectiveness of the usurped land for centuries. Most of these "civilizing" efforts were undertaken without consideration for the potential of the land as a producer of foodstuffs, timber, and bucolic therapy.

We need planning commissions of geologists, botanists, farmers, and realtors in every rural county to identify land that has the greatest potential for food and fiber production. Milk can be graded. Cheese can be graded. Beef can be graded. And land can be graded. Grade A and Grade B lands would be unconditionally reserved for farm and ranch use. Grade C lands would be "developed," provided their occupants did not excessively pollute the atmosphere and water.

Homeowners or renters in the developed lands should be provided with garden space. The quality of soil on garden plots would be routinely improved with compost pits, some sweat, and the discovery of green thumbing.

In Great Britain, France, and Germany, farms and suburbias have become cooperative neighbors. Why not in the United States? The initial steps to preserve our most useful agricultural lands must be taken by citizens' groups, by schools, and by our communication media.

An International Organization to Have Jurisdiction over Grain and other Food Exports and Imports. Although grain exports from the United States rose from 35 to 100 million metric tons per year between 1960 and 1980, and shiploads of grain have become our most important defense against foreign-trade deficits, no international plan has been adopted to stabilize world grain prices or to develop reserve supplies of grain to meet such emergencies as the starving millions in East Africa, the refugees from aggression in Afghanistan and Indonesia, or disaster victims throughout the world. American, French, Swiss, and Brazilian conglomerates continue to control most of the world's grain trade. Wheat continues to be used by dictator countries to wrest profits and political power by proselyting the appetites of their populations from traditional rice, lentils, and rye to the "white man's" squishy white bread. Most of the grain shipped to the Soviet Union is used to fatten

cattle and pigs. The 800 million truly needy receive approximately 10 percent of the grains we export. Meanwhile, our bumper
harvests overflow bins and warehouses to rot or become rat food,
while on-farm prices drop below production costs.

Again, during December, 1982, prospects of a food trade war
between the United States and the ten nations of the European
Community cast a shadow over an international conference about
surplus food supplies. Accusations of more "excessive government subsidies" by both the Americans and the Europeans led
to an impasse in negotiations. Bumper grain harvests in Europe
threatened to reduce our grain exports. Threats were made by
American representatives to "dump" some of our huge government stores of cheese, butter, and other dairy products in Europe, with disregard for the Europeans' taste buds. The political
struggle continued in 1983 when USDA aborted its PIK program
with "bargain sales" of wheat to Egypt and cotton to the USSR.
Taxpayers would, of course, pay the costs.

The most logical agency for stabilization of both production
and trade, as well as for distribution of surplus foods to those
who actually need it, is the Food and Agriculture Organization
(FAO) of the United Nations. But when FAO was chartered, the
cartels' influence succeeded in inserting the condition that FAO
could "give advice on agricultural production" but could not
handle or trade in commodities. That was in 1945. Subsequently,
FAO's personnel have gained far keener insight into the world's
food and fiber production, the areas of acute food shortages, the
political acumen governing shipments of processed and unpro-
cessed foods than any other diplomatic or social organization.
FAO could and should be assigned to put international food's
house in order—administer exports and imports, stabilize prices,
and develop a "food bank" for the needy.

Skittering through Adirondack snowdrifts one December a
generation ago, Dr. Frank Cyr and I sought family opinions about
the worthiness of the new central schools. We discovered that
those who favored central schools invited us to their kitchens for
"coffee, some fresh brownies, and a chat." Opponents of the

schools ushered us to horsehair sofas in their front parlors, sans coffee or brownies.

There will be much horsehair sofa haranguing before the preceding suggestions can be enacted; the normal timespan between introduction of an idea and its public acceptance is forty years. Federal jobholders, lobbyists, scientists hungry for publicity, and "hard-hat" devotees of "In Bucks We Trust" will be the haranguers.

A Technogate and the cooperative planning for our futures in green could assure collective bargaining agreements, land centers, the zoning of farmlands, a Department of the Land, and international cooperation in the food export trade before the year 2000. When the American land wears out, or erodes into the oceans, there isn't any more. Our diet will deteriorate. Our water will become poisonous. Our national pride will shatter in desert winds. We shall lose our earth song.

A few years before the U.S. Office of Agriculture was founded in 1863, an escapee from school teaching wrote a poem. He said, in part:

> To me every hour of the light and dark is a
>   miracle,
> Every cubic inch of space is a miracle,
> Every square yard of the surface of the earth is
>   spread with the same,
> Every foot of the interior swarms with the same.
> Every spear of grass—the frames, limbs, organs of
> Men and women
> And all that concerns them,
> All of these to me are unspeakably perfect
>   miracles.

The writer's name was Walt Whitman. He wrote for the future. He wrote for today. Look to those miracles. Consider them objectively. Learn them, talk about them, teach them. This is our high road to futures in green.

ACKNOWLEDGMENTS

A book is the cumulative product of thousands of conversations and readings, plus the brooding time essential for balancing their logic, and the mental or physical travel needed to assess contemporary environments.

The preparation time for this book was forty-five years, because it began subconsciously when I joined the staff of *Farm Journal* in 1938. The physical travel exceeds 200,000 miles; the mental travel is in the millions.

An honest by-line on this work's title page would read: By Jenkins McMillen Miller Cyr Stefferud Davis Bailey Ranney Hinshaw Zillman Compton Larson Lundborg Scruggs Hoag Neill Park Arnaud Econopouly Ammerman Koutouzis Kirkpatrick Hoagland Hardenbergh Jones Sells Wentworth Anson Terkel Noggle, with interpretation by Howard, and cohesiveness by LaFarge. Even this gesture would slight the hundreds of agriculturists, processors, educators, journalists, historians, craftsmen, and tradesmen who have contributed to my notebooks and files and, worst of all, would fail to acknowledge my dependence on the multi-qualities and contributions of the best companion, Elizabeth Zimmermann Howard.

During October, 1938, Arthur H. Jenkins hired me as an Assistant Editor of *Farm Journal*. The most incisive, but fairest, editor I have ever experienced, AHJ began my "agrication" by ordering me to spend two weeks wandering through Amish farm country, without any money for food or lodging. He then pushed me on to Chicago to cover the International Livestock Exposition *alone* on a four-day deadline. (I had to ask a hand at the King Ranch display, "What is a Santa Gertrudis?")

The "agrication" intensified when Wheeler McMillen became the magazine's editor-in-chief in 1939 and I moved over to roving editor with a transcontinental "beat"; thus began rich relationships with scores of rural America's elite. I am particularly indebted to the four decades of learning gained through friendships with the truly great educator Frank W. Cyr; the world trade and cooperative specialist Raymond W. Miller; the exceptional editor/naturalist Alfred Stefferud; and one of the keenest publicists who ever trod the labyrinths of USDA, W. Gifford Hoag.

Their deductive logic lured me into a curiosity about rural America and its history that was to influence all of my writing. Of the numerous jobs held after *Farm Journal* years, I quickly wearied of the ones that did not permit luxuriating in rural lore and sociology. Thus, I am deeply grateful to the late Wesley Hardenbergh, the late Colonel Edward Wentworth, and Alvin Kreig, who, during my stint as roving editor for American Meat Institute, encouraged me to undertake *This Is the West, This Is the South, The Great Iron Trail, The Horse in America*, and other books.

Correspondence about *The Horse in America* initiated friendship with Blanchette and Leopold Arnaud that led to engrossing seminars on agriculture and regional cuisines. Leopold was the Dean of Arts and Architecture at Columbia University and, later, cultural attaché at our embassy in Brazil. Blanchette and Leo were walking encyclopedias on food origins and mores, as well as the crafts and environments that inspired regional cuisines. They became our mentors for visits to the birthplaces of diversified agriculture, regional cheeses, cured meats, and winemaking; to the homelands of the Conquistadores (Extremadura, Spain), of the Pennsylvania Dutch (the Rhine valley), of denim (Nîmes, France), of the cowboy (the Olympian plains of Thessaly), as well as the Venetian "madame" who invented the display window by posing her most comely prostitutes on the balcony of her establishment.

For advice and data given during the preparation of this manuscript, I also owe thanks to:

Dr. John H. Davis, now a Washington resident, who gave me free rein on the taped interviews in chapters thirteen and sixteen;

Dr. G. Ray Noggle, former chairman of botany at North Carolina State University and co-author of *Introductory Plant Physiology*, who became my guide to the challenges of genetic engineering;

Paul Bailey, the Far West author, who has spun yarns about his Utah youth during the quarter century of our friendship, and who provided the title "Earth Song" for the foreword to the book;

Dr. Paul C. Mangelsdorf, long the paleobotanist of the Harvard Botanical Museum and author of *Corn: Its Origin, Evolution and Improvement*, for data on the American Indian's invention of sweet corn and its discovery by New Englanders and New Yorkers during, or immediately after, the 1775–83 War of Independence;

Nicholas Econopouly, William (Chip) Ammerman, and Jimmy Koutouzis for volunteering as guides and scouts to agricultural and cuisine birthplaces in Greece and the Near East;

David and Sally Compton of Elburn, Illinois, who patiently served as photo subjects for my essay about farms in the *World Book Encyclopedia*, and who have since answered hundreds of questions about the everyday realities of farm life on the prairie;

My daughter, Betsy Williams, of Andover, Massachusetts, for the loan of her research on colonial gardens and the multi-uses of herbs throughout recorded history;

Paul Zillman, a Missouri farm boy and president of Livestock Conservation, Inc., who provided cogent notions about agriculture and food during our rambles through Portugal, Spain, France, Germany, Greece, England, Canada, and the South;

Charles Scruggs, editor of *Progressive Farmer*; Phil Alampi, New Jersey's Commissioner of Agriculture; Dr. Eleanore Larson, an Illinois native; Mrs. Dolores Neill, an Iowa farm girl; former USDA Secretary Ezra Taft Benson—for data all of them graciously provided about past and future;

George W. Ingle of the Chemical Manufacturers Association and various officials of the Food and Drug Administration for the basic data included in this book's "A Food Labels Dictionary";

Roy Park for asking the editors of his chain of newspapers to send me their views about current and future problems in our food supplies;

Wheeler McMillen, now 91, for numerous discussions and for the wealth of data in his 1982 history of agriculture, *Feeding Multitudes*;

Executives of the National Pork Producers Council, the American Farm Bureau Federation, the National Council of Farmer Cooperatives, the National Council for Therapy and Rehabilitation through Horticulture, USDA Secretary Block, Safeway, Inc., and the Food Marketing Institute for answering queries and providing essential data;

Marc Jaffe, editor-in-chief of Villard Books and executive vice president of Random House, for his faith and patience;

Ann LaFarge for resurrecting my faith in the project and so graciously editing the manuscript that she entered my personal Hall of Fame as "one of the five best editors I have ever known."

RECOMMENDED READING

Periodicals

Gardens for All News, the pert and down-to-earth monthly of the National Association for Gardening, Burlington, Vermont.

Horticulture, the venerable monthly of the Massachusetts Horticultural Society that was recently rehabilitated by Horticulture Associates, Boston.

Organic Gardening, the most popular voice of the organic gardening movement, published by Rodale Press at Emmaus, Pennsylvania.

Books

Adams, Ramon, *Western Words: A Dictionary of the Range, Cow Camp and Trail* (Norman: University of Oklahoma Press, 1944. 182 pp.)

Bailey, Joseph Cannon, *Seaman A. Knapp, Schoolmaster of American Agriculture* (New York: Columbia University Press, 1945. 307 pp.)

Bailey, Paul, *Polygamy Was Better Than Monotony* (Los Angeles: Westernlore Press, 1971. 204 pp.)

Barry, Louise, *The Beginning of the West, 1540–1854* (Topeka: Kansas Historical Society, 1972. 727 pp.)

Bartlett, Richard A., *The Gilded Age: America, 1865–1900* (Reading: Addison-Wesley, 1969. 191 pp.)

Bartram, William, *Travels* (Salt Lake City: Peregrine Smith, Inc., 1980. 332 pp.)

Benet, Stephen Vincent, *Selected Works of Stephen Vincent Benet* (New York: Farrar & Rinehart, Inc., 1942. Poetry, 487 pp. Prose, 483 pp.)

Brody, Jane, *Jane Brody's Nutrition Book* (New York: W. W. Norton & Co., 1981. 552 pp.)

Brown, Lester R., *Building a Sustainable Society* (New York: W. W. Norton & Co., 1981. 433 pp.)

Clinkscales, J. G., *On the Old Plantation* (Spartanburg, S.C.: Band & White, 1916. 142 pp.)

Cochran, Thomas C., and Miller, William, *The Age of Enterprise* (New York: The Macmillan Co., 1942. 396 pp.)

Collier, John, *Indians of the Americas* (New York: Mentor Books of New American Library, 1948. 191 pp.)

Cross, Jennifer, *The Supermarket Trap* (Bloomington: Indiana University Press, 1976. 306 pp.)

Cyr, Frank W.; Brunner, Edmund De S.; and Wayland, Sloan R., editors, *Farmers of the Future, a Report of the Columbia University Seminar on Rural Life* (New York: Bureau of Publications, Teachers College, 1953. 85 pp.)

Davis, John H., and Hinshaw, Kenneth, *Farmer in a Business Suit* (New York: Simon & Schuster, 1957. 241 pp.)

Galbraith, John Kenneth, *A Life in Our Times* (Boston: Houghton Mifflin Co., 1981. 562 pp.)

Harris, Ben Charles, *Eat the Weeds* (Barre, Mass: Barre Publishers, 1971. 223 pp.)

Hart, E. Richard, editor, *The Future of Agriculture in the Rocky Mountains, the Report of a 1979 Conference Held at Sun Valley, Idaho* (Salt Lake City: Westwater Press, Inc., 1980. 150 pp.)

Haughton, Claire S., *Green Immigrants* (New York: Harcourt Brace Jovanovich, 1978. 450 pp.)

Hightower, Jim, *Hard Tomatoes Hard Times* (Cambridge: Schenckman Publishing Co., 1973. 268 pp.)

Hoag, W. Gifford, *The Farm Credit System* (Danville, Ill.: Interstate Publishers, 1976. 292 pp.)

Howard, Robert West, *The Horse in America* (Chicago: Follett Publishing Co., 1965. 299 pp.)

Kieran, John, *A Natural History of New York City* (Garden City, N.Y.: The Natural History Press, 1971. 308 pp.)

Lappe, Frances Moore, *Diet for a Small Planet* (New York: Ballantine Books, 1982. 496 pp.)

Liebman, Joshua Loth, *Peace of Mind* (New York: Simon & Schuster, 1946. 203 pp.)

Lingeman, Richard, *Small Town America: A Narrative History* (Boston: Houghton Mifflin Co., 1981. 547 pp.)

Lundborg, Louis B. *Future Without Shock* (New York: W. W. Norton & Co., 1974. 155 pp.)

McKelvey, Blake, *The Urbanization of America, 1860–1915* (New Brunswick, N.J.: Rutgers University Press, 1963. 370 pp.)

McMillen, Wheeler, *Feeding Multitudes* (Danville, Ill.: Interstate Publishers, 1982. 491 pp.)

Miller, Raymond W., *Monsignor Ligutti: The Pope's County Agent* (Washington: University Press of America, Inc., 1981. 230 pp.)

Moore, Arthur, *The Farmer and the Rest of Us* (Boston: Little, Brown & Co., 1945. 226 pp.)

Morgan, Dan, *Merchants of Grain* (New York: The Viking Press, 1979. 387 pp.)

Mumford, Louis, *The Highway and the City* (New York: Harcourt Brace & World, 1963. 246 pp.)

Noggle, G. Ray, and Fritz, George C., *Introductory Plant Physiology* (Englewood Cliffs, N.J.: Prentice-Hall, Inc., 1983. 688 pp.)

Reader's Digest, *Eat Better, Live Better: A Commonsense Guide to Nutrition and Good Health* (Pleasantville, N.Y.: Reader's Digest Association, Inc., 1982. 416 pp.)

Stary, Frantisek, and Jirasek, Vaclav, *Herbs: A Concise Guide in Colour* (London: The Hamlyn Publishing Group, Ltd., 1975. 239 pp.)

Tannahill, Reay, *Food in History* (New York: Stein & Day, 1973. 448 pp.)

Thompson, James Westfall, *A History of Livestock Raising in the United States, 1607–1860* (Washington: USDA Agricultural History Series No. 5, 1942. 182 pp.)

United States Department of Agriculture, *Food from Farm to Table, the 1982 Yearbook of Agriculture* (Washington: U.S. Government Printing Office, 1982. 373 pp.)

————, *Research for Small Farms: Proceedings of a Special Symposium* (Washington: Agricultural Research Service Publication 1422, U.S. Government Printing Office, July, 1982. 301 pp.)

Wechsberg, Joseph, *The Best Things in Life* (Boston: Little, Brown & Co., 1960. 224 pp.)

White, E. B. *Poems and Sketches of E. B. White* (New York: Harper & Row, 1981. 217 pp.)

Wieting, C. Maurice, *The Progess of Cooperatives* (New York: Harper & Brothers, 1952. 210 pp.)

Wright, Louis B. *The Cultural Life of the American Colonies* (New York: Harper & Row, 1957. 220 pp.)

A FOOD LABELS
DICTIONARY

Surveys made during 1983–84 indicated that 8,267
foreign substances were being added to America's processed foods
and that sufficient research for determining their hazards to consumer health had been made on "approximately 1,600 of them.
These additives fall into one or more of five categories: quality
controls, stabilizers, enhancers, sweeteners, and forms of salt. Each
is subject to review of its safety for the intended use.

The *quality controls*, such as lactic acid and potassium bromide,
prevent spoilage or replace vitamins and minerals lost in the processing.

Stabilizers help foods to preserve their processed state during the
weeks or months in warehouses and on store shelves. Thus diglycerides are among the emulsifiers preventing peanut butter or mayonnaise from separating into oily dry layers in the jar. Humectants,
such as sorbitol, maintain the moisture level in brown sugar, shredded coconut, and similar packaged goods. Arabinogalactan is one of
the thickeners used to create smoothness and to prevent ice crystals
from forming in ice creams and sherbets.

Enhancers heighten flavor and add color to a product. Citrus Red No. 2 is one of the dyes used to give strawberry ice cream its traditionally pink color. Disodium guanylate and disodium inosinate are both flavor enhancers. Oleoresins and carrot oil are among the coloring agents of natural origin.

The *sweeteners* added to our processed foods in various concentrations include fructose, dextrose, glucose, honey, invert sugar, mannitol, saccharin, sucrose, and corn syrup.

The most ancient but one of the most dangerous additives to processed foods, table *salt*, assumes many names on food labels. The key word for salt content is sodium.

Food and Drug Administration regulations require processors to list the additives to each product on the label of the container. Since each additive is a chemical, polysyllabic chemical names are used, many of them with Greek or Latin origins. The regulations, however, do not require processors to state the purpose of the additives, or the percentages of the salt, sugar, and other potentially dangerous additives used.

The following table lists alphabetically the additives—synthetic or natural—most frequently used in our processed foods and the reasons for their use.

ADDITIVE	USE
Acacia	(a food thickener made from stems and branches of the acacia tree; also known as gum arabic)
Acetal	A synthetic flavoring agent, also used as a solvent in perfumes.
Acetaldehyde	A flavoring agent that occurs naturally in some fruits and vegetables.

ADDITIVE	USE
Acetic acid	An ingredient of vinegars; controls deterioration.
Acetone peroxide	A solvent of fats; used as a bleach for flours.
Adipic acid	Controls deterioration; occurs naturally in beets.
Agar-agar	A stabilizer and thickener made from seaweed.
Alfalfa	A coloring agent for colas, flavorings, and liquors; made from the stems and seeds.
Alginate	A gelatin made from seaweed and used as a stabilizer; salty.
Aluminum ammonium sulfate	A neutralizer and purifier.
Aluminum hydroxide	An alkali used as a leavening agent in baked goods.
Aluminum potassium sulfate	A firming agent and carrier for bleaches.
Amaranth	Earlier derived from coal tar but now from petrochemicals; a dye used for coloring foods, cosmetics, drugs, and known as Red No. 2. Other petrochemical dyes used are FD & C Red No. 3, FD & C Red No. 40, FD & C violet, etc. Widely used to color candies, gelatins, ice creams, medical pills and capsules, lipstick, etc.; the toxicity of these food colorings was being restudied in 1983 by FDA.

ADDITIVE	USE
Ambrette	Seeds of the hibiscus plant provide this flavoring agent for baked goods and sweets.
Ammonium alginate	A seaweed derivative used as a thickener and stabilizer.
Ammonium chloride	A dough conditioner; salty.
Ammonium phosphate	Acid ingredient of baking powders.
Ammonium sulfide	Although it will give a patina to bronze, this is used as a synthetic-spice flavoring in baked goods.
Amyl butyrate	Used as a flavoring agent in gelatins, baked goods, chewing gum; occurs naturally in cocoa.
Amyl formate	(SEE Formic acid)
Amyris oil	(SEE Sandalwood oil)
Anethole	Occurs naturally in anise and fennel; widely used as a flavoring agent.
Angelica	This herb, native to Europe and Asia, provides aromatic seeds, leaves, stems, and roots for use as flavorings.
Angostura	A flavoring agent made from the bark of a South American tree.
Anise	A licorice-like flavoring agent made from seeds of the anise plant; also source of the world's most ancient liquor.
Annatto extract	A yellow dye from a tropical tree; used as a coloring agent.

ADDITIVE	USE
Arabinogalactan	A stabilizer obtained from larch wood.
Asafetida	An extract from the roots of various plants native to western Asia, this is used as a flavoring for baked goods, meats, ice creams; also known as "Devil's Dung."
Ascorbic acid	A synthetic source of vitamin C; widely used as a preservative and antioxidant.
Aspergillus	A form of fungi used to soften beef tissues and bakery products.
Baking soda (Sodium bicarbonate)	A by-product of salt mining and multi-useful as a leavener and cleaner.
Balsam of Peru	A flavoring agent extracted from evergreen trees.
Basil	A flavoring agent extracted from the herb, sweet basil.
Bay	The arrow-shaped leaves and extracted oil of the bay tree, a type of laurel native to the Mediterranean and prolific in California.
Bentonite	A clarifying agent obtained from clay.
Benzaldehyde	A family of almond-like flavorings, synthetic and natural.
Benzoate of soda	A soda derivative used as a preservative.
Benzoin	A family of resins, obtained from fruit-tree barks and

ADDITIVE	USE
	tea, used as preservatives and flavoring agents.
Benzyl acetate	Acetic acid, used as a synthetic flavoring agent.
Benzyl alcohol	A flavoring agent extracted from jasmine, hyacinth, raspberry, tea, and other plants.
Bergamot	A natural flavoring extracted from the rind of the bergamot orange.
Borneol	A nut-like or spicy flavoring that can be extracted from thyme, coriander, strawberries, etc.
Bromelin	A meat tenderizer obtained from pineapples.
Butadiene	A by-product of petroleum gases; used in chewing gum.
Butyl alcohol	A flavoring agent that occurs naturally in apples and raspberries.
Butylated Hydroxytoluene (BHT)	An antioxidant. (Its use is forbidden in England because of effects on the nervous system.)
Butyric acid	A derivative of butter and some fruits; widely used as a flavoring.
Caffeine	A by-product of coffee, cola, and maté leaves; used as a flavoring in cola and root beer; a stimulant that can be dangerous.

ADDITIVE	USE
Calamus	A flavoring made from the dried root of the sweet flag plant.
Calcium ascorbate	A preservative and antioxidant made from vitamin C and calcium carbonate.
Calcium carbonate	A neutralizer and firming agent obtained from powdered limestone, marble, or coral.
Calcium chloride	A firming agent used in canned goods and cheese making.
Calcium disodium (EDTA)	A preservative widely used in canned goods.
Calcium hexametaphosphate	Widely used as an emulsifier and texturizer in cheeses, hams, ice creams.
Calcium hydroxide (slaked lime)	An alkali used as a firming agent and egg preservative.
Calcium oxide (quicklime)	An alkali used in baked goods and dairy products.
Calcium phosphate	Used in its various forms (Di-, Mono-, Tri-basic) as a mineral supplement, anticaking agent, jelling ingredient, and acidulant.
Calcium silicate	An anti-caking agent; also used in highway construction.
Calcium sulfate (Plaster of Paris)	A firming agent and conditioner in canned goods and bakery products.
Calendula	A flavoring agent made from marigold blossoms.

ADDITIVE	USE
Capsicum (Cayenne pepper)	A natural spice and flavoring.
Carob bean	(SEE Locust bean gum)
Carotene	A yellow dye extracted from carrots, egg yolks, etc.
Carrageenan	An ancient stabilizer and emulsifier made from the seaweed, Irish moss.
Cascara	Used both as a flavoring and a laxative, it is made from the cured bark of a plant native to our Pacific slope.
Cascarilla bark	A flavoring for beverages and pipe tobacco made from bark of a tree native to the West Indies.
Cassia	A natural flavoring made from bark of an Oriental tree.
Castor oil	A flavoring made from seeds of the castor oil plant; also an anti-sticking agent for candy, and an ingredient of undertakers' embalming fluid.
Catalase	An enzyme made from cow's liver; used in cheesemaking as an antioxidant.
Chlorine	Used as a flour bleach and oxidizer.
Chlortetracycline	An antibiotic used as a dip to preserve poultry carcasses.
Cholic acid	A bile derivative used as an emulsifier.

ADDITIVE	USE
Citric acid	A by-product of sugar refineries and citrus; widely used in curing meats and preventing off-flavors in processed foods.
Citrus Red No. 2	(SEE Amaranth)
Cobalt salts	Derived from the metal, cobalt; used in processing beer.
Cystine	An amino acid derived from urine or horsehair; used as a nutrient supplement.
Decanal	A synthetic flavoring agent with fruity odor.
Dextran	Polysaccharides made by growing bacteria on sugar; used in beer and candies.
Dextrin	A foam stabilizer and thickener made from starch.
Dextrose	Corn syrup; used in hundreds of processed foods.
Diatomaceous earth	Silica made from fossil algae; used in toothpastes and as an absorbent.
Diethylstilbestrol	A synthetic used to fatten livestock—although known to cause cancer.
Diglycerides	Emulsifying and defoaming agents made from fats and oils and used to maintain softness in processed foods.
Disodium guanylate	A flavor intensifier that occurs naturally in mushrooms.

ADDITIVE	USE
Disodium inosinate	A flavor enhancer.
Disodium phosphate	A salty emulsifier and pH control used in pasta products, canned milk, meats.
Erythorbic acid (Isoascorbic acid)	An antioxidant used in meat processing, bakery products, and beverages.
Estragon	A flavoring made from tarragon leaves.
Ethyl acetate	(SEE Acetic acid)
Ethyl butyrate	(SEE Butyric acid)
Ethyl cellulose	A by-product of wood pulp used as a filler in candies and chewing gum.
Ethyl formate	A widely used synthetic flavoring and mold inhibitor; derived from formic acid.
Ethyl lactate	(SEE Lactic acid)
Ethyl vanillin	A synthetic flavoring agent with strong vanilla odor.
Eugenol	A derivative of clove and cinnamon used as a flavoring, defoamer, perfume ingredient, and toothache remedy.
FD & C colors	(SEE Amaranth) A food, drug, and cosmetic colorant.
Fiber, dietary	Complex carbohydrates in food that cannot be broken down by enzymes during digestion. They serve as laxatives, as reducers of cholesterol and blood-sugar levels, and as major aids in weight reduction. (Foods with high

ADDITIVE	USE
	dietary fiber content include: bran, Grapenuts, shredded wheat, grits, raw apples, pears and grapes, raw carrots and celery, cooked parsnips, kidney beans, lentils, peas, and potatoes.)
Formic acid	A corrosive ingredient of fruits and tobacco leaves; a synthetic form is used to flavor baked goods, candies, etc.
Fumaric acid	An essential part of plant and animal tissues, it is used as a leavener, acid, flavor, and antioxidant in processed desserts, baked goods, and candies.
Furcelleran	A seaweed extract used as a stabilizer and thickener.
Furfural	A synthetic used as a flavoring, as well as an ingredient of insecticides and fungicides.
Furfural alcohol	A by-product of corncobs and coffee beans used as a flavoring for bakery products, ice creams, beverages.
Fusel oil	A synthetic flavoring whose major ingredient is toxic amyl alcohol.
Galbanum oil	The oil of an East Indian plant used as a ginger flavoring agent.

ADDITIVE	USE
Gelatin	A thickener and protein made from animal skins and carcasses.
Geraniol	A synthetic with rose odor used as a flavoring agent.
Geranium root oil	A flavoring agent made from geranium leaves and rose petals.
Ghatti gum	The resin of an Asian plant used as a flavoring.
Gluconate	A sugar by-product used as a sequestrant and firming agent.
Gluconic acid	A by-product of corn used as a diet supplement.
Glucose	A form of sugar that occurs naturally in corn, grapes, and blood.
Glutamate	The salt of glutamic acid; used to enhance meat flavors.
Glutamic acid	An amino acid made from vegetable proteins and used as a salt substitute and to enhance meat flavors.
Glycerol	A by-product of soap manufacturing used as a sweetener, humectant, and solvent.
Guar gum	By-product of seeds of a plant cultivated in India and used as a thickener for salad dressings, candies, cream cheese; also a laxative and an appetite suppressant.

ADDITIVE	USE
Gum tragacanth	The resin of plants grown in Asia Minor and used as a thickener and stabilizer.
Heptanal	A distillation of castor oil used in synthetic fruit and nut flavorings.
Heptylparaben	A synthetic preservative.
Hexane	A petroleum by-product used as a solvent.
Hexyl alcohol	A synthetic flavoring and solvent.
Hydrochloric acid	Used as a colorless gas with pungent odor to make corn syrup, sodium glutamate, beer, gelatin.
Hydrogen peroxide	Oxidizer, bleach, preservative for cheeses, milk, butter, and tripe.
Inosinate	A salt prepared from meat or fish; used to intensify flavor.
Inositol	A by-product of corn and a member of the vitamin B complex, it is used as a diet supplement.
Invert sugar	A blend of glucose and fructose. Honey is largely invert sugar. Retains moisture in the product.
Iodides	Various forms of additives containing iodine; these include cuprous iodide, potassium iodate, and potassium iodide.

ADDITIVE	USE
Ionone	A flavoring agent found in an Australian shrub, boronia.
Iron salts	Widely used as a mineral supplement in cereals, flours, pasta, and usually identified as "ferric" or "ferrous" (ferric phosphate, ferrous fumarate, etc.).
Isoamyl alcohol	A synthetic flavoring agent and toxic depressant.
Juniper	The berries and oil of the juniper tree, widely used as a flavoring for beverages, bakery products, ice creams, and an essential ingredient of gin. (It can also be used in fumigating.)
Karaya gum	Resin of a tree grown in India and used as a filler for gumdrops, custards, etc.; also a flavoring agent and laxative ingredient.
Kola nut	A tree seed, containing caffeine, grown in Africa, West Indies, and Brazil; used as a flavoring.
Lactic acid	A by-product of molasses, sour milk, potatoes; used as an acidulant and flavoring agent.
Lanolin	The fat obtained from sheep's wool and used as a chewing gum base, as well as in cosmetics and soaps.

ADDITIVE	USE
Lavandan oil	Obtained from a lavender-like plant, it is used both as a fruit flavoring and a fumigant.
Lecithin	A by-product of eggs, soybeans, corn; used as an oxidant, defoamer, and emulsifier.
Limonene	A synthetic flavoring agent, with spicy odor; widely used in chewing gums, ice creams, beverages.
Linalol	A synthetic flavoring agent, with floral odor; used in foods as well as perfumes.
Linalyl acetate	A synthetic flavoring agent, with floral odor; used in canned goods, candies, bakery products, chewing gums, and perfumes.
Linden flowers	The small, white flower of the linden tree; used as a flavoring agent for processed fruits and vermouth. Makes an excellent tea when dried.
Linoelic acid	One of the essential fatty acids found in many vegetable oils; used in emulsifiers and vitamins.
Locust bean gum	Also called carob bean and St. John's bread, it is an extract from seeds of the carob tree. It has a high protein content and is widely used as a thickener and stabilizer of processed foods.

ADDITIVE	USE
Lupulin	The extract of the venerable hop plant, long an essential of beer brewing.
Lysine	An essential amino acid, isolated from milk or blood and used commercially as a food enricher, especially in breads and cereals.
Magnesium	This metallic element is used in combination with other minerals (i.e., magnesium phosphate, magnesium oxide, magnesium hydroxide) as a mineral supplement, a neutralizer, an anticaking agent, a firming agent.
Malic acid	A by-product of fruit, coffee, rhubarb root, it is used as an alkali-control and flavoring agent.
Mannitol	Usually obtained from seaweed and used as a texturizer and sweetener.
Menthone	A synthetic flavoring used to enhance fruit and mint flavors.
Methionine	An essential amino acid used in dietary foods.
2-Methoxy-4-methylphenol	A highly caustic synthetic used as a flavoring.
Methybenzyl alcohol	A synthetic flavoring agent containing poisonous wood alcohol.
Methyl ethyl cellulose	A by-product of wood pulp; used as a foaming and emulsifying agent.

ADDITIVE	USE
Methyl salicylate	A lethal acid widely used as a flavoring agent.
Monosodium glutamate (MSG)	The salt of glutamic acid, obtained from seaweed, soybeans, sugar beets, and used to intensify flavorings. (Banned from use in baby foods.)
Monosodium phosphate	A by-product of fat used as an emulsifying agent.
Myristic acid	Obtained from animal or vegetable fats and used as a flavoring in desserts.
Nerol	A mixture of terpene alcohol, it is used as a base for perfumes and as a flavoring agent.
Nicotinic acid	Processed from liver, legumes, cereals, it adds the essential nutrient niacin to breakfast cereals, peanut butter, pasta, and enriched flours.
Nitrate (Potassium and Sodium)	Potassium nitrate was long known as "saltpeter." Both nitrates are used as a color fixative in meats and to increase burning properties of tobacco. (Both are suspected of causing cancer.)
Nitrite (Potassium and Sodium)	Also used as a color fixative in meat, and as a bleach and meat tenderizer. (Suspected of causing cancer.)
Nitrogen oxides	Poisonous gases used to bleach flours.

ADDITIVE	USE
Nitrous oxide (laughing gas)	Used as a whipping agent and propellant for whipped toppings—and as a rocket fuel.
Nonanoic acid	A synthetic flavoring agent for desserts.
Nonyl alcohol	A synthetic flavoring agent believed to cause damage to liver and central nervous system.
Octyl propionate	A synthetic fruit flavoring.
Oleic acid	A by-product of animal and vegetable fats, used as a de-foaming agent, lubricant, and flavoring.
Oleoresin	A natural plant oil, or resin, extracted by solvents and used as a flavoring or food dye.
Olibanum oil	A distillation of the biblical plant-resin frankincense; used as a flavoring.
Origanum oil	A distillation of herb flowers and leaves; used to flavor sausages, bakery products, etc.
Ox bile (Osygall)	An emulsifier made from the bile of oxen.
Oxytetracycline	An antibiotic fed to fowl; also used to retard rancidity of the carcasses.
Palmitic acid	A by-product of palm oil or vegetable tallow; used as a butter and cheese flavoring.

ADDITIVE	USE
Pantothenic	Obtained mostly from liver, rice, molasses, it is one of the essentials for metabolism of foods and is used in special diets.
Papain	The protein-digesting enzyme obtained from papaya, and the principal ingredient of meat tenderizers.
Petrolatum	Petroleum jelly; used in candies, baked goods, and as a coating of fruits, vegetables, cheeses.
Phenethyl alcohol	A synthetic flavoring with rose odor.
Phenyl acetate	A toxic flavoring agent made from phenol and acetic chloride.
Phosphate	The salt or ester of phosphoric acid obtained from phosphate rock and widely used in combination with calcium, magnesium, sodium, etc., as a supplement, emulsifier, or texturizer.
Polysorbate 60, 65, or 80	Derived from vegetable oils and acids; used as emulsifiers and foaming agents.
Potassium alginate	A stabilizer made from tartaric acid.
Potassium bromide	A preservative used on fresh fruits and vegetables.
Propionic acid	A flavoring agent obtained from wood pulp; also used as a preservative.

ADDITIVE	USE
Propylene glycol	A petroleum by-product used as a solvent and color control.
Pyridoxine hydrochloride	An enzyme obtained from yeast, liver, and grains, that aids metabolism.
Quinine	An extract from the bark of the cinchona tree, a native of South America; long used to treat malaria and fevers, it is also used as a flavoring agent for some beverages as well as in bitters.
Rennet (Rennin)	An enzyme made from the stomachs of calves and used in cheesemaking and in junket.
Riboflavin	A component of vitamin B, processed from milk, eggs, malts, liver, etc.; used as an enrichment for cereal, peanut butter, pasta, and baked goods.
Rose hips extract	Wild rose hips, rich in ascorbic acid.
Rue	Dried blossoms of a plant grown in Europe and Asia; used as a flavoring agent.
Salicylic acid	A combination of toxic phenol and carbon dioxide, used as a preservative.
Sandalwood oil	Extract of roots and heartwood of a tree grown in the East Indies; used as a flavoring and perfume.

ADDITIVE	USE
Silicon dioxide	Processed from sand or crystalline rocks and used as an anti-caking agent, filler, and defoamer.
Sodium acetate	A salt used as a preservative and alkalizer.
Sodium bicarbonate	Baking soda; an alkali processed from soda ash and carbon dioxide.
Sodium chloride	Table salt. (A major source of high blood pressure.)
Sodium citrate	A salty emulsifier.
Sodium diacetate	A preservative in baked goods.
Sodium hydroxide	A salty alkali used on pretzels, canned peas, and cocoa products.
Sodium nitrate and nitrite	(SEE Nitrates)
Sodium sulfate	A stimulant of saliva, it is used as a chewing gum base.
Sodium sulfite	A salt used as a preservative and bleach.
Sorbic acid	Processed from berries of the mountain ash as well as synthetically, it is used as a yeast and mold inhibitor.
Sorbital	A sugar substitute that occurs naturally in fruits. seaweed, and the berries of the mountain ash.
Sorbose	A fermentation of sorbitol used in vitamin C pills.
Sucrose	Cane or beet sugar.

ADDITIVE	USE
Sulfur dioxide	A poisonous bleach processed from sulphur; also used as a preservative.
Tagetes	Extracts of the petals of the Aztec marigold blended with chemical herbicides and used to add yellow color to chicken skin; also a fruity flavoring.
Talc	Powdered magnesium silicate; used as an anti-caking agent and chewing gum base. (Suspected of causing cancer.)
Tannic acid	A by-product of the bark of hardwood trees; used as a flavoring and refining agent.
Tartaric acid	A by-product of the wine industry, it is an ingredient of baking powders and is used to adjust acidity in candies, jellies, baked goods, and dairy products.
Thiamine hydrochloride	A synthetic B_1 vitamin used as a dietary supplement.
Vanillin	A synthetic vanilla flavoring made from wood pulp.
Vegetable gums	Acacia, carob bean, guar, tragacanth gums are used as stabilizers and thickeners.
Xanthophyll	A yellow coloring agent made from flower petals or egg yolks.

ADDITIVE	USE
Ylang-Ylang oil (Cananga oil)	A yellow oil with floral odor made from Asian tree blossoms and used as a flavoring agent.
Zinc	An essential mineral source added to foods in various compounds, such as zinc acetate, zinc carbonate, zinc chloride, zinc oxide.

INDEX

ABOUT THE AUTHOR

Robert West Howard, a prolific writer and reporter for many news publications, lives in South Carolina. His hobbies include American research, paleontology, and gardening. He is the author of many magazine and encyclopedia articles, and of twenty-five books on various aspects of American history, including, most recently, *Niagara Falls* and *The Dawnseekers*.